Arden,

Paddling to Winter

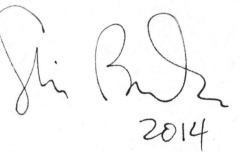

Dream big & go on
lots & lots y adventure.

2014

Paddling to Winter

A Couple's Wilderness Journey from Lake Superior to the Canadian North

By Julie Buckles

Photography by Charly Ray

Raven Productions, Inc.
Ely, Minnesota

Published September 2013 by
Raven Productions, Inc.
P.O. Box 188, Ely, MN 55731
218-365-3375
www.RavenWords.com

Cover and Map Design	Jill O'Neill, Graphically Put
Cover Photo	Bob Gross, Hired Lens Photography

Printed in Minnesota
United States of America
10 9 8 7 6 5 4 3 2 1

Library of Congress Cataloging-in-Publication Data

Buckles, Julie, 1964-
 Paddling to winter : a couple's wilderness journey from lake Superior to the Canadian north / by Julie Buckles ; photography by Charly Ray.
    pages cm
 ISBN 978-0-9835189-2-1 (trade pbk. : alk. paper)
 1. Canoes and canoeing--Saskatchewan--Wollaston Lake. 2. Wilderness survival--Saskatchewan--Wollaston Lake. 3. Winter sports--Saskatchewan--Wollaston Lake. I. Title.
 GV776.15.S37B83 2013
 797.1220971--dc23
                          2013029340

To my parents, who sent me off ready to explore the world; and to Charly, who took my hand and said, "Let's go."

Table of Contents

Introduction

PART I   PADDLING

PART II   WINTER

Introduction

I watched a movie a few years ago called *Lovely and Amazing*. In it Catherine Keener plays a woman who has one story to tell: she gave birth without drugs. She tells her story often to trapped audiences everywhere. Her daughter is ten years old. The point is that she needs to move on, get a life. I empathize with her.

Our trip is fourteen years old as I finish this book. I've been ready for a while to send it off into the world. I have spent the bulk of my thirties planning for, doing, and then writing about The Trip. It is my story, our story. Charly would tell a different story—just as true as this one attempts to be. His would talk more about geography, maps, and ecology because that is where his passion lies, though he says he loves my version.

I began our canoe journey intentionally planning to not write about it. As a journalist, I had spent years writing a lead in my head before I'd even finished an interview. I wanted to experience the landscape on its own terms, without my journalistic lens. I stuck to my original intent—returned home, resumed my former life, moved on. But then, 2001 happened. I experienced a miscarriage and a bizarre condition called a molar pregnancy; and then the Twin Towers fell. I felt like I was walking under water. The Trip became my lifeline. I wanted to write about it. I wanted to remember the woman—now terrified to get on an airplane—who had paddled so far through the North American wilderness.

I looked at the slides from our trip for the first time in a long while. I was awed by how young, how healthy, how happy we looked. It truly was a lovely and amazing journey. An expedition is a lot like childbirth—filled with euphoria and pain and then, when it's over, diminished memories of long portages, boring days, and biting blackflies. Ready to do it again.

I've attempted to remain truthful to the time, to who we were then instead of who we are now, and to not make us any wiser than we were. I wrote this book to rediscover myself, and as I finish I think I've found the woman who said "Yes" without hesitation to eighteen months in the wilderness. For that I am grateful.

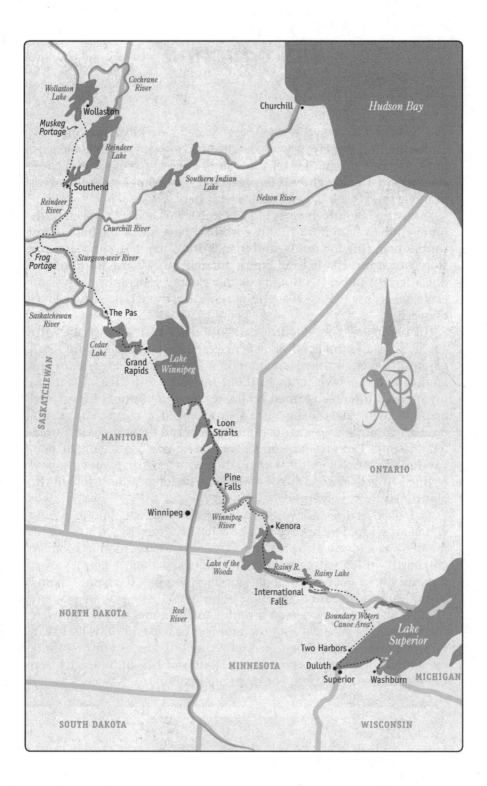

Part I
Paddling

The Washington Canoe Club on the Potomac River, site of Charly's and my first paddle together

1

First Date

C harly liked to say that The Trip began with a paddle stroke on the Potomac River near Georgetown in Washington, D.C. I'd say it began even earlier. Charly rolled into my life in much the same way that he pushed his bike into the fourth-floor conference room each week—quietly, quickly, forcefully. Looking like a highly toned athlete with shoulder-length hair and smelling of the good kind of sweat—a healthy, manly, worked-hard-for kind of sweat—he arrived with one gloved hand on the handlebar, wearing ripped biking shorts and a tattered T-shirt. His beard gave him the look of someone older and wiser than twenty-four, but his smile was that of a boy.

Fifteen of us met weekly in a conference room overlooking Dupont Circle to talk about democracy, a fair economy, and social justice. My friend Dawn led these Good Society discussions, which were part of a larger project at the Institute for Policy Studies (IPS) where we both worked. Charly worked across town as a wetland specialist for the Environmental Protection Agency. He came because his housemate worked at IPS and because he had a passion for politics. The Good Society group talked about new ways to live—ways not driven by money, power, and work. Between debates and discussions, Charly and I eyed each other but rarely spoke to one another directly. He was intense, passionate, and highly intelligent, spouting names I'd never heard of: Helen and Scott Nearing, Edward Abbey, and Gary Snyder. I had correctly cast him as a tree-hugging nature boy. "His type never goes for me," I told Dawn.

Later he confessed that I had scared him. I was sassy, outspoken, and in love with urban living. I wore black cowboy boots and men's white T-shirts, resided in the hip Adams Morgan neighborhood, and rode a three-speed bicycle to work. Originally from a farm in Wisconsin, I had lived in London, traveled to Europe twice, and landed my dream job as director of membership and publications at IPS, working next to left-leaning activists, filmmakers, and authors.

The Good Society discussions started in the fall of 1992 and ended temporarily in December. Charly asked me to lunch a week before Christmas "to learn more about Wisconsin." His plan was to transfer to Chicago, eventually move to northern Wisconsin where the air was clean and the land was cheap, and live out his homesteading fantasies. He said he needed survival tips. We walked to Pita Hut, a favorite lunch spot serving Middle Eastern food, where Charly sneezed, coughed, and blew his nose into a well-used cloth hanky. He had a cold, he told me. I have no tolerance for sick people. I was raised by a critical-care nurse and a dairy farmer of hearty Norwegian stock, and as a kid I needed to provide proof of being near death to garner any attention. Charly and I ordered pita sandwiches, Dutch treat, and carried our trays to a table near the window.

"So in rural Wisconsin, how does a city slicker fit in?" he asked.

"You need a skill," I told him. "If you have something useful to contribute, people will come to you." My impression was that he was far more serious than I had originally thought. Apparently he really did just want to talk about Wisconsin, so I told him what I knew about rural life, tried not to breathe in any of his germs, and wished him good luck, expecting I'd never see him again.

When our Good Society group reconvened in the spring, I walked into the same fourth-floor conference room and there sat Charly with his back to me, his bike leaning against the wall. Surprised, I walked over and said something that shocked the hell out of him—and me: "I'm really happy to see you."

"You are?" he asked.

"I am," I said, as if just deciding. "I thought you were transferring to Chicago."

"I didn't get the transfer. I'm planning to head to northern Wisconsin later this year."

The next week, Dawn invited us for dinner with a small group of friends—a deliberate setup. As we sprawled on the floor of her basement apartment, digesting pasta and sipping wine, the conversation turned to *Generation X: Tales for an Accelerated Culture,* a book Dawn had just read. "We need to tell our stories," she said. "Does anyone have a story?"

Charly didn't hesitate. He told us about the time he and his buddies ran into a musk ox while they were on a seven-week paddling trip in the

Northwest Territories. He and his paddling partners, Chris and Jim, were taking a rare day off to hike and explore an island on Yathkyed Lake. "There are no roads between Yathkyed and the North Pole," he explained. They had paddled about six hundred miles and had not seen any other people the entire trip.

Walking around the island on Yathkyed Lake, they spotted "this thundering thing that looked like it was the size of a giant woolly mammoth," he laughed. "When we looked them up later in our field guide, we found out that they're actually four to five feet high at the shoulder. But from where we stood, it looked like a seven-foot-tall rolling lint ball."

Charly hadn't realized that musk oxen lived in that region. "It was like seeing a wild monkey in Chicago," he laughed. The three twenty-year-olds watched through binoculars as the ice-age relic galloped across the rolling tundra, disappeared behind a hill, and then reappeared, getting closer and closer.

"Chris said, 'I think it's following our trail.' And sure enough, it followed our route like a bloodhound on a scent," Charly told us. Obviously not out for a casual run, the musk ox was fast closing in on them. They looked around for options, but the landscape was treeless—flat rocks and rolling hills stretched for miles in every direction.

The musk ox charged over the nearest hill and vanished into a dip below them. For a moment they hoped that it had lost interest. Then came a clattering of hooves. Suddenly reappearing just a few yards away, the musk ox ran straight past them for about twenty yards and then wheeled around to face them, snorting and pawing the ground close enough that the three suburban boys could get a good look at its sharp horns. They had a few moments to ponder their uncertain future.

"Chris read later that when the musk ox bulls are in their rut, they are very dangerous, especially if they sense a threat to their territory. I'm guessing he was in rut."

All three hikers jumped into the only shelter around—a crack in the ground. "Problem was, the crack was only five feet deep and just long enough for the three of us to stand in, and we were all at least six feet tall. Our heads were sticking up like golf balls waiting for this thing to knock them down the fairway."

The musk ox pawed the ground, ripping up a willow bush and tossing it into the air along with chunks of dirt. "I decided our only hope was to take the offensive, so I jumped out of the crack, waving my arms and howling like a wolf. Then Chris and Jim joined me, howling and waving their arms." It worked. The musk ox snorted, scratched the earth, and turned around and ran off.

Wow! None of the rest of us had stories like that. We peppered him with questions: Where? How? When? Charly pulled an atlas from Dawn's crowded bookshelf and turned to the northern part of Canada.

He had completed three Canadian canoe expeditions—one two hundred miles, one seven hundred miles, and one eight hundred miles. He showed us the routes he had followed. I'd never heard of anyone other than polar explorers going on such long, remote expeditions. Even though I'd grown up romping around a dairy farm, I'd never paddled a canoe or been backcountry camping. But what I loved most about his story was that he had told it with such humor, humbleness, and excitement.

The next day Charly invited me for an evening paddle on the Potomac River. After years of drinks in bars, parties, and movies for first dates, I was intrigued. Paddling appealed to me from the start: technically simple with no fancy terms to learn or equipment to acquire. I had grown up baling hay and milking cows, and I enjoyed that kind of mindless task. As we cruised along the river, Charly pointed out wildlife, including a yellow-crowned night heron. "They make short cries like *woc, woc* as they fly over," he told me. On cue, one flew overhead crying *woc, woc, woc*. I was smitten.

After that night, I asked Charly to the movies, to book readings, and for beers after softball games. He asked me to his group house to brew beer. The first thing I noticed on his wall was a map of North America with a highlighted line drawn from Lake Superior to the Arctic Ocean. "What's the line for?" I asked.

"It's my dream canoe trip," he replied.

He might have told me he wanted to fly to the moon—it seemed about as likely. "How many miles is that?"

"About three thousand. I've always driven to here," he said, pointing to Wollaston Lake in northern Saskatchewan. "I want to paddle the whole way next time—no cars, no roads."

Little did I know then how his dream would become my own.

2

We're Off!

T hree more minutes," Charly shouted, tossing stacks of papers, files, and documents into cardboard boxes.

With plans to paddle our canoe three thousand miles starting from our back door at the Sioux River Beach on Lake Superior in Wisconsin, Charly and I were almost ready to start our honeymoon—The Trip that I'd found unimaginable six years earlier. We intended to paddle seventeen hundred miles to northern Saskatchewan, stay there for the winter, then snowshoe two hundred miles farther north in the spring, and paddle another eleven hundred miles to Gjoa Haven on the Northwest Passage of the Arctic Ocean. We would be gone eighteen months.

From the second-story window I glanced across the highway at Lake Superior. We couldn't have mail ordered a finer May day to begin: bug-free, sunny, and calm. Charly was the architect of this trip, designing the route; I was the general contractor, moving everything along. We had to leave sometime, and I had chosen noon on May Day, 1999. Charly would have preferred to stick to his noncommittal departure date of sometime between April 15 and May 15, but I needed a deadline. The old alarm clock read 11:57.

We had prepared for eighteen months of crisis: cold weather, smashed canoe, burst appendix. I had packed enough tampons to supply the female population of our county for a year. We had taken first aid classes and studied wilderness medicine. I had taken swim lessons. We had consulted with doctors about first aid kits and talked to experts about emergency radios. I knew that, statistically, driving a car to the grocery store would be more likely to cause my demise than paddling a canoe to the far north, but still we prepared for the worst.

Even though it was May, I knelt on the floor wrapping Christmas presents. Christmas is a huge deal in my family, and I would be missing my first one with them, so I wanted to have gifts ready for everyone. I wiped beads of sweat from my upper lip, leaning back on my heels to look at my husband, laughing at those three words—three more minutes. Two years of planning had narrowed to three insane minutes of details that had more to do with our regular life than with our canoe trip.

I laughed because I had lived with Charly for five years and had been married to him for the last eight months. Last minute projects were his specialty. Pack the bags, load the car, start the engine, and Charly would lean ever so casually into the window on the driver's side and say to me, "I was thinking I would rototill the garden before we go."

"Rototill the garden? The rototiller hasn't worked for months."

"Yeah. But I think I have it figured out."

I nearly threw a glass of juice in his face the time he suggested that we finish installing a chimney before leaving for a friend's wedding reception. Instead of tossing my juice, I practiced Midwestern restraint; I stood up and walked toward the door. I felt an airborne *Mother Jones* magazine graze the back of my shoulder—Charly's idea of domestic drama. I opened the screen door, which never did latch properly, and prepared to leave, only to discover the car battery was dead. Charly opened the squeaky door. "Don't leave," he said. He didn't know about the dead battery yet.

"Okay," I replied. We jumped the battery with our 1979 red Ford truck and left together for the reception.

But now was the big goodbye. Three more minutes.

My mom, dad, brother Link, and father-in-law, Herb, had driven north to send us off. They had been helping with last minute chores. Dad wrapped his thick hands around the Hoover Quik-Broom and maneuvered it back and forth and around and behind me. Herb scrambled to stay ahead of Dad, pushing furniture out of his way. Between the on and off of the vacuum cleaner, I could hear Mom and Link downstairs laughing as they loaded three months of trail food into Mom and Dad's van.

I had taken my last indoor shower, packed away my civilian clothes, and now wore the Army surplus shorts that would be a major part of my wardrobe for the next four months. Charly continued the process of shutting down his office, which was located on the second floor of an old abandoned tavern we had transformed into Trip Headquarters. We had baked, dried, and sealed our food in the kitchen; sorted, piled, and packed our gear and clothes in the dining room; rolled and unrolled maps on the bar; and made countless phone calls from the office since disconnecting our home phone six months earlier—a cost-saving measure.

"I'm ready," Charly said with a grin as he stumbled down the stairs carrying a cardboard box for storage.

"I guess no one eats around here," grumbled my father-in-law, who had lost patience with our structureless lifestyle. Herb was a seventy-one-year-old retired banker with wire-rimmed glasses and not much hair. He had colon cancer that was in remission and had been diagnosed with heart disease. In an attempt to avoid surgery on his blocked arteries, he'd chosen to treat his ailments with a diet of whole foods and other alternative remedies. In the process he had lost at least twenty pounds, and if he didn't eat regularly he turned cranky.

"Here, Pop, I'll make you a sandwich," Charly said, dropping the box and reaching for the half-empty jar of organic peanut butter and a loaf of leftover bread.

"I'll see you down there," I whispered to Charly and walked out the door.

At the beach a rainbow of colorful canoes and kayaks lined the wild white stretch of sandy beach. About forty friends stood in small groups on the hot sand, laughing and telling jokes. Dad walked by with a quart of ice cream. "Lunch," he said, handing me a spoon. I dug into the local Tetzner's cherry-nut ice cream, which was turning soft from the sun.

In the world of canoe expeditions, the one we'd planned was not particularly ambitious or risky. Four things made our trip noteworthy: we were leaving from our own backyard; we had grown, harvested, and dried much of the food for the trip; we planned to stay north through the winter; and we'd built our own wood and canvas canoe.

Charly and Herb arrived with Rick, a reporter from the *Ashland Daily Press*, my former employer. Rick stood near the water's edge interviewing Herb, who wore a wetsuit and powder-blue life jacket, looking just as pleased as when he'd been Charly's best man. Herb had taken Charly's mother sailing for their honeymoon. They say the apple doesn't fall far from the tree. Charly was a different variety of apple, but he definitely fell from Herb's branches.

"Haven't you ever wondered what it would be like if you just walked out your front door and kept walking?" Charly asked as Rick scribbled in his notebook. "Well, this is the non-road version of that."

"Not many women would choose this for their honeymoon," Rick shouted over to me.

"Not many women are married to Charly Ray," I laughed.

No more minutes left. I looked at Charly and nodded toward the canoe. He gave me a wink. It was time to go. We looked like two kids on their first day at camp. Charly wore his new One Less Motor T-shirt with a canoe on the front that I had given him and a brown felt hat from my mother. I sported a fresh bobbed haircut and donned a Gap baseball cap and sunglasses. Our legs looked as if they hadn't seen the sun for seven months, which they hadn't. I loaded my Siberian husky, Knock-Knock, into the bow by my feet. She was invited for only the first day.

It was eighty degrees with mile-high blue skies. The leaves of the aspen trees were just beginning to bud their bright greenish-yellow haze. To the east, radically different temperatures between the recently thawed lake and the unseasonably hot air twisted the light into shifting mirages. We'd planned an easy first day—just eight miles to Bayfield, where we would camp at the city campground and meet friends and family for dinner. Friends paddled ahead of us, forming a flotilla that included Herb in a borrowed kayak and Dad and Link in a red tandem kayak.

With every paddle stroke, the stress of the last few weeks lessened. The forward motion carried us further from the chaos and tedium of preparations and closer to adventure and freedom and togetherness. After months of scrutinizing maps, making our canoe, revising menus, packing and repacking food, sorting gear and clothes, we were really doing it.

"People are taking bets on how long you'll last," my friend Phyllis commented.

"The canoe trip or our marriage?" I asked.

"Both," she smiled. "But I know you two will make it."

A slight afternoon breeze blew across the water, and one by one canoes and kayaks turned back to shore. Dad and Link remained, and the four of us paddled to a spit of sand near Pikes Creek to wait for the breeze to die. Knock-Knock sprinted back and forth. Even though we had planned and organized this expedition together, Charly and I had barely spoken in over a week. Each of us had taken charge of our own pieces and hoped the puzzle would all come together. Tired and hungry, Charly and I ate granola and dried venison, then stretched out on the sand. Two miles into our first day, we fell into a long-overdue nap—and didn't care.

"How are you two going to make it to the Arctic if you can't stay awake for more than an hour?" Dad asked. He looked at Link and they doubled over laughing.

The next morning, my father-in-law stood on shore at the city campground, wearing baggy blue jeans and a flannel shirt. He looked sad, proud, and conflicted as we paddled away. He appeared so thin and frail. I was reminded that this man who always seemed so overbearing and strong was also a widower with a weak heart. He held his hand up and gave us a small wave. After a minute of paddling, I turned back to see him growing smaller with every stroke. I looked again and he was gone.

3

I Do

On our fourth morning I sat cross-legged looking out at Lake Superior, eating granola and reading the *Ashland Daily Press* with a picture of Charly, Knock-Knock, and me on the cover. I thought more about Rick's statement that not many women would choose this for their honeymoon and my reply that not many women are married to Charly Ray. I had grown up singing and choreographing dance routines to Helen Reddy singing "I am woman, hear me roar." During my formative years my mother had worn a T-shirt that read "A woman needs a man like a fish needs air." I had studied women's history in college and considered myself a feminist.

"Not many women are married to Charly Ray." What a stupid response. True, this trip was Charly's idea and one he knew how to organize and make happen. And true, without him I wouldn't be doing it. But I knew lots of wild outdoorsy women. My friend Ann had dogsledded with her fiancé five hundred miles to Nome, Alaska, said "I do," and dogsledded five hundred miles back with her husband. My friend Gail had organized a kayaking expedition around Lake Baikal in the Soviet Union. At IPS I'd known a woman who sat at the southern tip of Chile listening to a radio while her sister, Ann Bancroft, led an all-women's expedition across Antarctica. I wished I could change my answer.

I thought about this as I sat on a long stretch of white sand beach next to the mouth of Lost Creek. Red pines towered behind me and no cars or houses were in sight. We were camped outside the small town of Cornucopia, home of the northernmost post office in Wisconsin, with our wooden canoe tipped on its side in the sand. We'd brushed on the final coats of red paint just weeks before and brought her down to the lake to make sure she floated. We'd named her *Le Strubel* for Charly's mother, Carol Strubel, who had died during Charly's sophomore year of college. Her brother, Dick Strubel, and his family had given us a wedding present of cash for a canoe. We took the money, drove to the home of wood and canvas canoe builder Jerry Stelmok in Maine, and built ourselves a boat. An E.M. White Guide canoe—quiet, beautiful, and steeped in history—*Le Strubel* looked stunning: cherry wood gunwales, cedar ribs, and copper nails. I had tapped in those copper nails, sanded the cherry wood, and knew each and every one of the cedar ribs intimately. If something happened to *Le Strubel* on this trip, we would fix her with materials from the forest—something we couldn't do with Kevlar, plastic, or aluminum.

I opened the *Daily Press*, which we had purchased in Cornucopia that morning.

Washburn Couple Embark on 18-month Paddle to the Arctic

In the classic fantasy tale "The Hobbit", one of the characters observes that it is risky just walking out your front door—you could be swept up in adventure and wind up who knows where.

For a Town of Bayview couple, a fantasy became reality Saturday, just a mile from their front door, on the warm sands and cold Lake Superior water near the mouth of the Sioux River.

With a last wave of their paddles, under flawless blue skies, Charly Ray and Julie Buckles bid farewell to family and friends, marking the beginning of an 18-month odyssey that will take them 2,700 miles north to the Arctic Ocean.

"Well, Scoop?" Charly asked, looking over at me. "What's your professional opinion?"

"I like it, particularly the Hobbit reference. Though he quotes me as saying 'I fear timber wolves.'" I laughed. "Do I look like Little Red Riding Hood to you?"

"You do have a red hood," he answered, referring to my anorak. "What did you say you fear?"

"I don't remember. Polar bears. Drowning. The usual. But definitely not timber wolves. How about you? What do you fear?"

"That we won't get to the second half of this trip," he answered. I nodded, knowing he was thinking about his dad.

At nine o'clock in the morning it was already eighty degrees, about forty-five degrees warmer than the water. I should have told Rick that it was Lake Superior that I feared most, probably because I knew her best. She was large, cold, and unpredictable. Since moving to northern Wisconsin I had been fed a steady diet of shipwreck tales, including the wreck of the 729-foot *Edmund Fitzgerald* in 1975, immortalized by a Gordon Lightfoot song.

The legend lives on from the Chippewa on down
Of the big lake they call Gitchee Gumee.
The lake, it is said, never gives up her dead
When the skies of November turn gloomy.

"Should we stay or go?" I asked.

"I don't know about heading out into this," Charly said, looking at the two-foot waves.

"It's not that bad," I replied, rinsing my blue enamelware bowl.

Charly pulled a hanky out of the side pocket of his tan cotton cargo pants and blew his nose. I pushed to go, anxious to at least paddle out of our home county. I won.

Charly loaded the canoe. I held the gunwales while standing in leg-numbing water. We carried twenty days' worth of food, a tarp, a bug net, a canvas tent, a woodstove (just for the Lake Superior leg), clothes for the summer (for each of us: one pair of wool pants, one pair of thin cotton pants, one pair of shorts, a few shirts and underwear), a cook kit, two sleeping bags, two sleeping pads, a repair kit, a first-aid kit, maps, a fishing rod, two life jackets, and a spare set of paddles.

We carried two wetsuits, but because it was eighty degrees we weren't wearing them. Wetsuits wouldn't save us if we spilled into the frigid water, but they would add critical minutes before hypothermia set in. The previous day we had paddled through chunks of ice and past frozen waterfalls on the north face of the sandstone sea cliffs. At thirty-five degrees, the lake would claim the life of a submerged human who took more than a few minutes to get out of the water. Tipping over was no small deal.

The heavily loaded canoe was like an overdue pregnant woman—clumsy and unsteady, but full of anticipation for the days to come. Once the canoe was loaded, we snapped on *Le Strubel's* red sprayskirt, covering the canoe and packs. I worked my way into the front opening of the sprayskirt, then stabilized the canoe with my paddle as the waves rocked it back and forth. Charly boarded and we headed into the waves, not looking back. I dug my paddle in deep, the cold water splashing onto my hands. A friend who was working at a construction site on Roman's Point shouted our names from shore as we paddled by, but I couldn't respond. Charly flicked his paddle as a greeting. We both focused on keeping our overburdened canoe upright and moving forward, staying away from shore to avoid the waves bouncing back from the cliffs.

We rounded Roman's Point, following thirty-foot cliffs with pillars of sandstone carved away by the wind and waves. The morning sun lit up the white birch and aspen trees. On the other side of the point it was like another day. Since there were no waves or wind I peeled back the sprayskirt so it rested around my waist.

Fewer than a dozen paddle strokes later, as we entered Bark Bay, the air fell limp, and flies gathered in front of my feet—not a good sign if for no other reason than limp air intuitively feels wrong on Lake Superior. And something about flies gathering at my feet gave me an *Amityville Horror* kind of feeling. Charly and I plunged into an uneasy silence, paddling faster. We cut across the middle of the bay to save paddling miles, then followed the shoreline up a narrow finger of red sandstone toward Bark Point. The breeze built slowly, fluctuating between puffs of hot muggy air and cold crisp air—an onshore breeze that gave us a bit of confidence. Paddling on gently rolling swells, I looked ahead and saw waves breaking but couldn't make sense of them. I checked for a place to pull out, but there wasn't one—just a long stretch of large rocks on a shelf of red sandstone. The swells continued to break into frothy whiteness a little closer now.

"What is that?" I asked, leaning forward to refasten the sprayskirt.

"It's waves breaking on the shoal off Bark Point," Charly responded. "I'll steer us clear of it, then cut over."

I bowed my head and focused on paddling. One, two, three, four ... all the way to one hundred, and then I switched my paddle from the left side to the right. One, two, three, four ... Counting was something I would revert to in moments of stress for the rest of the summer, something I'd never relied on before. Suddenly a breaking wave knocked the numbers right out of my head. The eerie stillness was over. Swells four feet high came at us and broke over the shoal just off to our left. Charly steered the canoe perpendicular to the waves. I knew that if a wave hit us sideways we would be upside down—and up that fabled creek. Fear took hold. I didn't have time to think or to look around, only to react. I kept my head down and my paddle in the water. One wave. Two waves. Three waves. Four.

Charly turned the canoe to the left to round the point. "We made it through the—" he started to say, then barked, "Draw right!"

Using my paddle I pulled the canoe right with all the strength I had and stared *up* at a wave.

"Paddle like hell!" Charly shouted.

I dug in with my paddle just as the wave lifted us into the air. We teetered on the top of a three-foot crest, pausing for what seemed like minutes. It was long enough for me to look down at the shallow, almost-tranquil turquoise pool below. There were smooth round rocks beneath the surface. I wondered how we would land on the rocks below without smashing our wood and canvas canoe into kindling. It was like being positioned at the top of a roller coaster for those few seconds. I tried to remember where I had stuffed my wetsuit. I felt the fear and adrenaline and excitement all at once. And then the wave released us.

"Brace!" Charly screamed. The canoe crashed down, and the next wave broke right in front of me, smashing gallons of ice water into my chest. I. Couldn't. Breathe. I was reminded of lying on a playground after a ball had hit me in the gut and taken my breath away, feeling like I'd never breathe again. My mouth was as dry as a maple leaf in November. My heart pounded and my right leg shook uncontrollably. Water pooled on the sprayskirt in front of me. I couldn't believe we were still upright. I wanted to cry but there wasn't time. I kept paddling. One, two, three, four. . . Charly took us through another breaking wave and then another and another until finally all that remained were rolling swells.

"How you doing up there?" Charly asked.

"I'm okay now that I can breathe."

"Pretty hairy, huh?"

"That's an understatement."

"You know we would have been okay if we'd tipped," he said.

He claimed that with the onshore breeze *Le Strubel* may have cracked, but we could have made it to shore. I looked at the rocky shoreline and felt the cold spray of water and only nodded, doubtful. We did agree that it could have been the end of the canoe. Would we have continued? I'd like to think so. We certainly were close enough to home to regroup.

As we paddled on, the sense of having closely avoided death got me thinking. How would my life have turned out if I hadn't moved to D.C. when I did, or worked at the Institute, or chosen to take the Good Society class, or if Dawn hadn't invited us all to dinner that night, or if Charly hadn't handed me a copy of *Living the Good Life*, or if I hadn't paddled with him on the Potomac River, or hadn't moved to northern Wisconsin? What would I be doing now?

Eight months after Charly had first shown me the map on his wall in Washington, I left the nation's capital doing something I'd sworn I'd never do: move for a man. Charly worked at a YMCA camp and found us a small cabin on the Manitowish River a few miles away. I moved in during one of the coldest winters in Wisconsin's history. We had no clue what we were doing. I was writing and living in a cabin, but it was not the nonstop romance I had imagined. Car batteries froze solid and cracked, water pipes froze and burst, jobs were scarce, and we had no telephone. We also had to tend to the daily domestic chores of life like laundry, gathering wood, cooking, and cleaning. I remember sitting on the bed in the loft, alone, crying because I was folding laundry instead of making love.

I missed lunches in Dupont Circle. I missed the foreign accents and languages of Washington. I missed the high level of political discourse. I missed my friends. I missed my job. But I never seriously considered going back. I quickly ran through my meager savings and was broke. I worked as a fry cook at a bar nearly an hour away for $4.75 an hour and as a bartender for less than that plus tips. I wrote vitamin descriptions for a vitamin company that hadn't upgraded its computers since computers entered the workforce. I didn't publish any short stories or write the Great American Novel, but I worked as a stringer for the *Milwaukee Journal Sentinel* for $25.00 an article, and I started writing regularly for a local tribal newspaper that had enough of a budget to pay me a few hundred dollars for a feature article.

The next fall we planned a paddling trip, and then another. Short canoe trips became an annual ritual, as necessary as having the oil changed in an old vehicle. On each trip we went to wilder places for longer periods of time, but nothing longer than nine days. We bought a cabin on the Sioux River near Lake Superior and learned to garden for food and chop wood for heat. Charly worked at the Sigurd Olson Environmental Institute as the coordinator of the Lake Superior Binational Forum. I started a monthly tribal newspaper for the Bad River Band of the Lake Superior Tribe of Chippewa Indians and became its editor, and later I took a job as a full-time reporter at the *Ashland Daily Press*.

In the fall of 1997 we took a weekend excursion to the Boundary Waters Canoe Area Wilderness. While hiking between two lakes, Charly began to wonder aloud if his dream canoe trip would ever happen and if it should. It had been nearly ten years since his eight-hundred-mile expedition. His friends had moved on, married, settled, lost interest. Maybe it was time for him to do so too. His dream was like a screenplay destined for the slush pile.

After years of living together, of settling into one another, it hit me that day that I was truly, madly, deeply in love with this man, and that I was willing to commit to a lifetime with him. What came from my mouth next was nearly as surprising to me and to him as when I'd said, "I'm so happy to see you."

"Let's get married and go on The Trip."

"You're serious?" he asked again and again. It took months to convince him that I was.

And so we'd been married atop a ski hill overlooking Lake Superior, only twenty-some miles from where we just nearly went for an unexpected and unwelcome swim. Once I'd convinced him that, indeed, I was serious, Charly had written letters to his three friends with whom he had paddled for eight hundred miles and with whom he had planned to return for another expedition. The letter invited them to join us. Not one of them responded in the affirmative. I asked Charly's buddies—the same ones who'd been with him on the musk ox encounter—why they chose not to go. Chris Lunn, a giant man who makes tipis for a living, told me, "Because it's a long time to be sleeping on the ground." Jim Eberhard, a fishing and elk-hunting guide in Montana, responded,

"Charly has a way of making everything sound easy, and it's not always so easy." Not many women would choose this for their honeymoon, but neither would many men.

We rounded Bark Point and rode waves up and down for six miles to the next landing. My legs still shook, but less and less with each mile. I began to enjoy the rhythm of the rolling swells as they gently pushed us toward shore. Later Charly and I noted that our potentially expedition-ending event had happened only twenty road miles from home. We laughed imagining Rick's follow-up story reporting on the canoeists who smashed and dunked on the fourth day of a months-long expedition.

We landed *Le Strubel* on the hot sands of a public beach and campground in Herbster, another lovely and sparsely populated town on Lake Superior's south shore. I hopped out of the canoe and pulled us forward. We collapsed onto the sand, giddy at being alive.

"I think that's enough for today," I said.

4

Love Boat

The city of Duluth, Minnesota, sits on a steep hill—think San Francisco with snow—where Lake Superior's south shore meets Lake Superior's north shore. On Mother's Day, nine days into our trip, we paddled past the port entrance, the furthest inland seaport in the world. Located at the western tip of Lake Superior, this end of the Great Lakes–Saint Lawrence Seaway shipping route is fifteen hundred miles from salt water. Iron ore, coal, and grain from the northern Midwest all leave from the Duluth-Superior port. Limestone, cement, salt, wood products, steel, and coal come in.

We paddled past stadium-size ocean-traveling ships affectionately called "salties" floating off the harbor, waiting their turn to load cargo. The water lay smooth and the wind stayed calm. Our solar radio reported the accidental US bombing of the Chinese embassy in Belgrade and the weather forecast of a front moving in later that day. On shore in Duluth's waterfront parks, families strolled, grilled, and picnicked. Mothers wore corsages. We glided past people who asked where we were going. "The Arctic Ocean," we shouted and laughed. They nodded, looking confused.

We were anxious to make miles on such an unusually calm day. In three days we needed to get to Lutsen, located seventy miles up the North Shore, to meet our neighbors Mike and Phyllis. They had agreed to transport us from Lake Superior to the Boundary Waters Canoe Area Wilderness. The BWCAW permit system required that we pick a day and place to enter the wilderness area, so we guessed at May eleventh and chose Baker Lake. We had considered the historic Grand Portage even further north, but decided against the extra time on Lake Superior and the nine-mile portage. The voyageurs had carried ninety-pound packs of furs and trade goods over that crazy portage. I had hiked it and didn't feel the need to carry anything over it. With this trip we tipped our hats to the voyageurs, but didn't attempt a re-creation of their arduous journeys.

We were behind schedule because we'd been windbound on the beach in Port Wing for two days. The realization that we needed to make it to Lutsen in three days set off my inner fascist. Charly wanted to pull over to take a rest and I said no. Charly needed to pee, and I told him to do it from the canoe because we weren't stopping. We paddled easily for twelve hours—from seven in the morning to seven in the evening—stopping only twice before the sun dipped beneath the horizon and a northeast breeze picked up. Charly noted the telltale mare's-tail clouds of an approaching front and steered us to a slick rock near Knife River. We assessed the camping potential: dismal. It was growing darker and windier. Although we had already paddled a full day, I really didn't want to be stuck at Knife River if the weather changed. We could see the lights of Two Harbors ten miles away and knew there was a city campground there. The prospect of hot showers tipped the scales for me. I wanted to continue. Charly wasn't so sure.

Ten miles didn't seem far. Ten miles was ten minutes in a car, forty minutes on a bicycle. But in our canoe, tired from a full day of paddling with a heavy load, we might as well have been doing the breaststroke for as fast as we seemed to move. We averaged two miles an hour if we were freshly rested and in calm seas. At best, we would reach Two Harbors by one in the morning. Had I really thought this through, I would have camped at the slick rock at Knife River. I would have slept on gravel, foregone a shower, and been okay with garbage littered along the shore.

We pulled on our wetsuits and added a few layers of clothing, drank the last of the hot cocoa from a thermos, tied everything carefully into the canoe, and snapped on the sprayskirt. Within an hour, thick clouds covered the stars and moon like a wool blanket, turning the night velvet black. Imagine turning off the lights and then crawling into a sleeping bag headfirst. Now add a blindfold, and that's about how dark it was. I couldn't see the bow of the canoe. Waves crashed on the shoreline, hitting the rocks with a tinny echo before bouncing back. Swells moved the canoe up and down. I focused on making each paddle stroke count.

Usually we paddled a few dozen strokes and then switched sides, because switching made for more efficient paddling and less soreness in our shoulder muscles. The person in front set the pace and the person in back followed. The moment of the switch was a moment of vulnerability. Because Charly and I both had our paddles out of the water at the same time, it was a moment when, if a wave hit us hard or if one of us shifted in our seat, *Le Strubel* could tip over—and the water hadn't warmed any since Bark Point. It was just above freezing. Because of this vulnerability, I opted not to switch. My muscles burned, but I kept paddling on my right side. One hundred, two hundred strokes, until Charly couldn't stand it anymore.

"Switch," he'd call out and I'd have to concede.

That night we continued this way, only switching when Charly called out. As the delirium set in, Charly changed from "Switch" to "Tequila!" then "Cucaracha!"

A rock appeared out of nowhere and I nearly melted down. "I can't see anything," I screeched.

"We're fine. You're doing fine," Charly replied, soothing me back into a paddling rhythm.

Toughen up, toughen up, toughen up, one, two, three, four . . . I repeated to myself.

We passed large lit-up lake homes but no public landing spots. I was ready to camp anywhere. It downright pissed me off to paddle past mansions, a warm light coming from the dining room, knowing how cozy those people were in their houses and how miserable and cold we were. My anger was not based on rational thought, just conjecture. I assumed those people, whoever they were, knew we were on Lake Superior fighting late into the night while they nibbled brie and sipped wine by candlelight.

Charly strapped on a headlamp, but that almost made paddling worse. Now I could see the rocks beneath the surface, boulders rising up out of the crystal-clear water, threatening our canoe. The light turned the water an eerie green and created a halo around boulders like highlighting over text. Charly kept *Le Strubel* a quarter of a mile out from shore to get away from the reflective waves. This made the canoe less bouncy but made me more fearful.

I wasn't much of a swimmer, never have been. I grew up jumping into creeks and ponds but never swimming laps. Strange that a non-swimmer would choose to spend eighteen months on water, but I didn't plan on spending any time *in* it. Could I make it a quarter of a mile in near-freezing water? Probably not. Would I be able to right the canoe and rescue myself? Hopefully, but not likely. In the end, I hoped Charly could save me.

Two hours, three hours, four. It was even darker when we reached Park City Hill near Two Harbors. Fatigued to the point of silliness, Charly shouted "Tequila!" with increasing frequency. I grew even more silent, focusing on pushing the paddle through the water.

We rounded the corner, and I was blinded by rows of industrial lights. It was like emerging from a cave into a spotlight. I cringed as a train slammed and screeched to a metallic halt on the hillside nearby, spewing the smell of diesel fuel into the air. I thought of Ayn Rand's *The Fountainhead*, for no particular reason except it was about the world of industry, and I remembered the trains from the novel and how I had imagined scenes like the one before us. We had paddled into an outpost of industrial civilization where ore is loaded onto huge ships to feed far-away smelters and foundries. I strained to distinguish one man-made item from the next. Red and green navigational lights blinked. A white light flashed from a lighthouse.

"I can't figure it out," I said, trying to stabilize the boat in wavy water.

"I'm pretty sure the campground is around that wall, but let's duck in here and check things out," Charly replied.

I couldn't get my bearings enough to even locate shore. Charly's eyes adjusted, and he steered us to a boat launch with a large parking lot and public restrooms. It was nearly midnight. I remember there was a man smoking a cigarette, sitting in a car with the motor running. I had no idea why he was there. My exhausted brain imagined we would hear about a murder later, and I would provide this clue about the man smoking in his car. I also imagined we might be the ones murdered.

I stood next to Charly, trying to make sense of huge machines moving piles from one place to another. With all the lights, I hadn't noticed a ship the length of two football fields. It was so big that I had thought it was a well-lit loading dock. Later I realized the machines were probably loading taconite onto the ship.

We walked over to the lighthouse to scope out conditions on the other side of a low breakwater. The lake looked rougher but navigable. We only needed to get around this last point into the next bay and we'd be at the campground. Saner, smarter people would have stopped where we were, and we should have, but we were so close to that campground and the hot shower. We both wanted to go for it. Neither of us wanted to camp illegally in an industrial area, knowing a shift in weather would likely force us to stay where we were for days.

We paddled out of the lights and back into the ink-black night. Waves hit the right side of the canoe. We had come too far to tip now and I dug in. Around the corner, another well-lit industrial plant killed my night vision. We had paddled for an astounding sixteen hours and covered thirty-seven miles. A little farther and my feet touched the rocky beach at the campground. Charly and I met midway between the stern and bow and hugged. "We made it," I said. It was one in the morning.

Five minutes later—let me repeat that—*five minutes later* the wind picked up to a speed of forty miles an hour. I knew the wind speed because Charly clocked it with his anemometer. Waves started to crash on shore. We carried everything to higher ground, set up camp, and slid into our sleeping bags, asleep before the bags even warmed from our body heat.

"Wake up, Jules! We gotta move," Charly said, shaking me. He was already dressed in his wool pants and tan anorak and was grabbing his felt hat. It was cold enough that I could see my breath. Outside a gale threatened to flatten our tent. I looked out the doorway at the grainy morning light and reluctantly crawled out of the warm sleeping bag, wiping crusted drool from my chin. I helped move the soggy tent, sleeping bags, and canvas packs a few sites farther inland where a large spruce tree could give us a little protection from the wind. Standing in my long underwear, I looked around the campground. We were the only campers. The city hadn't yet opened the place for the summer season. I walked hopefully to the restrooms and showers, but I could see the sign on the door from a few paces away: Closed for the Season. I gave the door a tug anyway. Locked. So much for hot showers. I peed behind the building, steam rising from the spot of impact, and walked back to our blustery camp.

"Closed," I said.

Charly looked up and grinned. "I figured as much."

I pulled on my Army-issue green wool pants, brown sweater, red anorak, and white canvas Tilley hat. "Let's go get breakfast," I suggested.

We walked into town and ordered potato pancakes at Judy's Café—a diner filled with blue-collar workers and old timers. Our waitress, Roma, told us it had snowed around two that morning, an hour after we had landed and minutes after we had fallen asleep.

I called my friend Mary Thompson, who lived in Duluth, to tell her to drive up and visit us. We had worked together at the *Ashland Daily Press* until she moved on to the *Duluth News Tribune.* "The paper wants to do a story about your trip," she said.

Charly and I had always just driven through Two Harbors on our way to the Boundary Waters. Now we had plenty of time to explore. We strolled to the industrial spot where we had landed the night before. It wasn't nearly as frightening in the daylight—just a bunch of ships and loading docks.

A reporter and a photographer waited near our tent when we returned. "We could be sitting in the Caribbean, sipping piña coladas," Charly joked. "But none of that hell for us. We're going to sunny Minnesota." I knew that quote would make the paper.

The next morning a gale-force wind continued to blow. Six-foot waves pounded the beach, and rolling swells the size of freight trains cruised down the lake. No one was going anywhere on that water for a few days. Charly called Mike and Phyllis to tell them to meet us in Two Harbors instead of Lutsen.

Again we walked to Judy's Café for potato pancakes. I plugged my quarters into a newsstand outside the restaurant to buy the *Duluth News Tribune*. The cover headline, above the fold, read "Love Boat." Subhead: "Some couples can't hang wallpaper together. These two are going to the Arctic Circle—in a canoe." There was also a full-color photo of Charly and me hugging next to the canoe, a mesh of canvas and wool. We had bumped the war in Kosovo and protests at the US embassy in Beijing from the front page. The guys in the restaurant read the article while I felt my face warm to a splotchy red.

Five minutes before the winds off Lake Superior whipped up violent waves late Monday night, newlyweds Charly Ray and Julie Buckles vigorously paddled their canoe into a quiet Two Harbors campground. They'd been on open water for 16 straight hours.

"Didn't know I was working for celebrities yesterday," Roma teased. She walked behind the counter and reappeared with a map of North America so we could trace our route for her. "I want to go to Churchill someday to see the polar bears," she said.

As we continued to explore town that day, locals stopped to ask us questions about the trip. Where did we buy our canvas tent and portable woodstove? How did we plan to stay warm? What would we do during storms? In the paint aisle at the hardware store a woman hugged me and with teary eyes said, "You two have a safe trip." A boy at the public library told me he wrote a report about our trip for a class assignment. Most of all, people wanted to know how we could afford to take a year off to travel.

In many ways, Charly and I had been training and saving for this trip since we moved to Wisconsin six years before. We'd lived as cheaply, as simply, and as close to the land as time and our abilities allowed. We drove rusty cars and lived in a cabin. Each fall we cut, split, and stacked maple, oak, and birch for heat through the winter. We harvested wild rice in autumn and boiled maple syrup in spring, eventually packing up 110 pounds of wild rice and 80 pounds of maple sugar for the trip. We didn't have many debts—just the remainder of my student loan. Rental income covered the property taxes and expenses. Savings covered the rest. We scraped together secondhand gear through the years of preparation and asked for the rest as wedding and Christmas presents. We didn't have kids and our jobs were ones we hoped we could return to later. We wouldn't be earning any income for the next eighteen months, but we wouldn't have many expenses either. We were living on an average of five dollars per day in exchange for the luxury of so much time.

It rained into the afternoon and night as a steady stream of cars and trucks drove by to check out our camp and to watch the oceanic waves.

Another photographer and reporter stopped by. So did a self-described gear hound interested in the canvas tent and stove. And there were a sweet couple who invited us to breakfast, then gave us a tour of town; Charly's former boss, who brought his dog; a police officer who wanted to retire in four years and paddle for a summer in the Boundary Waters; and Butch, the campground groundskeeper, who flat out said, "I envy you two."

I started to feel like what my dad calls a blow bag, meaning all talk and no action. Through strangers' eyes the trip had become bigger and scarier than I'd imagined. We were only twelve days in. What if I hated it and didn't want to finish? What if it wasn't as great or exciting as people thought it should be? I had never been paddling for more than nine days. I had no idea how I would do on a five-hundred-plus-day trip. Too much chatter and not enough motion started to make me feel useless. I needed to move.

The next day Mike and Phyllis saved us, providing our first truck portage of the trip. They pulled up with Knock-Knock in the back of the truck, loaded the canoe and our packs, and drove us up and over the Sawtooth range. Instead of paddling our way up the rugged Lake Superior shoreline for two to three more days, we started the Boundary Waters portion of our trip camping at Baker Lake with friends.

5

We Got Rhythm

My hiking boots squished and my fingers wrinkled as I unloaded five packs plus loose gear from the canoe for the umpteenth time that day and portaged them overland through drizzling rain. Charly carried the eighty-pound *Le Strubel* on his shoulders, which was even tougher than it sounds. For every portage, he picked *Le Strubel* up by her center thwart, brought her to his thighs, and used the strength of his legs to help swing the canoe upward and flip it over his head so it would land upside down on his shoulders. At the other end of the portage he performed the same ritual in reverse, often on slippery rocks in knee-deep water, his goal being to never let the canoe touch rocks.

The warm wet spell had brought out biting blackflies. "Insidious little shits," Charly muttered from beneath the canoe. Knock-Knock trotted ahead. We had decided to keep her with us for a while. She had her own issues. For one, like most Siberian huskies, she didn't like water to touch her paws, and so I had to create log bridges or lift her out of the canoe and carry her like a new bride to solid ground.

We were heading down the upper Frost River, a headwaters stream born out of the scoured bedrock highlands in one of the wildest sections of the Boundary Waters. It runs through a series of small lakes that are connected by small streams. Where streams turned to trickles or rapids or waterfalls, we portaged our gear and canoe overland.

Boundary Waters aficionados say that the Frost is one of their favorites. I don't get it. The trees are small, the banks muddy, and the portages frequent and unruly. If we had been packed for a weekend, I might remember it fondly, but we weren't. We were hauling twenty days' worth of food, an eighteen-and-a-half-foot wooden canoe, a summer's worth of gear, and a dog that hated getting her toes wet. Also, we hadn't streamlined our gear yet, so we walked every portage five times: three times hauling fifty-pound packs and *Le Strubel*, and two without loads walking back to the remaining gear. So a reasonable 140-rod portage—one rod equals sixteen and a half feet, or about the length of a canoe—became 700 rods of walking, or nearly two miles. Lake Superior had been about surviving big water. The Boundary Waters was about getting in shape. We needed to find our rhythm, refine our systems, and get organized.

The canoe was now our home, a fact that was slowly seeping into my awareness. Charly sat in the stern and I sat in the bow with Knock-Knock between my feet. In such close quarters we were forced to cooperate and coordinate. One portage was so narrow and winding that Charly couldn't get through with *Le Strubel* on his shoulders. We tackled the project together. Charly carried the bow and I the stern, with the side of the boat on our shoulders. We shifted the canoe from shoulder to shoulder as we weaved our way through the trees and brush.

Our friend Jerry Stelmok, who had taught us how to build our red canoe, had joked that Minnesota should be called the Land of 10,000 Portages instead of 10,000 Lakes. He was not far off. The Boundary Waters is a veritable canoeing paradise—or hell, depending on one's feelings about portaging. A major watershed divide cuts across the eastern side of the Boundary Waters, separating the Great Lakes watershed from the Hudson Bay watershed. In crossing this divide, we changed from traveling upstream to traveling downstream.

The Boundary Waters Canoe Area Wilderness covers one million acres and is connected to two other wilderness areas—Quetico Provincial Park in Ontario and Voyageurs National Park in Minnesota. Combined, the region is called Quetico-Superior country and provides more than two million acres of wilderness, including hundreds of lakes and rivers with minimal motorboat or car access. This is canoe country. Charly and I had been coming here every year for an annual fix of clear glassy lakes surrounded by hills of pine trees, glacially polished granite slabs and cliffs, and no lights or roads.

A party of six passed us on the Frost River, and the canoeists said they planned to take the only campsite available for the next ten miles. This bit of bad news started Charly on a rant about the bureaucracy of the US

Forest Service and its permit system, how they charged too much and expected us all to camp at designated sites with wood-sucking fire grates built too high off the ground. "It's one of the most popular rivers and they only have one campsite?" he continued for the next hour, or so it seemed.

We looked for an illegal campsite all afternoon and finally found the telltale signs of a site where other weary campers had slept for a night—fire-scarred rocks and a round flattened spot where tents had been. Charly set up a white canvas tarp to protect us from rain and wind and a bug tent to protect us from biting flies.

I sorted through the bags looking for food and clothing. We pulled the canoe up onto land, tucked everything beneath it, and then sat cross-legged beneath the tarp, listening to a colony of industrious beavers at work. Temperatures dropped to the forties and occasional drops of rain made their way through the canvas overhead. "A little Chinese water torture to end the day," Charly joked and got up to readjust the tarp. The trick of the tarp, which Charly would master later, was getting the angles right so rain would flow off rather than drip through.

A what-have-I-done feeling drizzled over me as I sat there cold and wet, a mosquito buzzing near my ear. I'm the type of person who, when trying a new recipe, rarely reads the recipe through to the end. For the Fourth of July one year I decided, on a whim, to make a Martha Stewart watermelon-shaped cake, complete with the green rind, pink center, and seeds. I had seen the magazine at a friend's house and thought it would be cute. A few hours before the dinner party, which included Dawn, her husband, and their friends, I started on the cake. I realized midway that I was supposed to have made red-colored sherbet in advance. That night I served a red and green blob more akin to a murdered cactus than the quartered watermelon it was supposed to be.

I swatted at a mosquito. I was having those same Oh-I-needed-to-make-sherbet.-How-do-you-make-sherbet?-And-how-many-hours-do-I-have? blues. I was sore, tired, wet, and wondering why I had decided to leave Bayfield County for a canoeist's life. Sixteen days on the trail and I wanted to go home. I wanted a hot shower, a level and ready-made bed, and a roof over my head. Even Knock-Knock looked drenched and miserable. Every backcountry trip I'd taken before had a quick, clearly defined ending. Because I had been running in fifth gear for the past two years—working, planning a wedding, and organizing for the trip—I hadn't paused to think about the finer implications of canoe travel. From the beginning, Charly had repeatedly warned, "This will not be fun; this will be work," and I had shrugged off his words. But what did I know about traveling for a year and a half? Would I really be able to do it, physically or mentally?

"I have to say, today was a hard day," I said, reaching for a brownie.

"It *was* a hard day," Charly agreed.

I nodded. I cast my eyes downward to a brownie with slightly burned edges.

"I wonder if I want to do this for the next year and a half. I mean, we have a good life. Why did we leave it?" I asked.

Charly looked at me, studying my face for a moment.

"I'm not saying, 'Let's quit.' I'm just speculating," I said.

We sat silent for a moment.

"I wonder if I'm doing it just because it was on my life list of things to do," he said.

Charly wasn't kidding on this point. He had made a list of life goals after high school and had stuck alarmingly close to that list, which had included working as an environmentalist, moving to northern Wisconsin, learning to garden organically and hunt and gather, and living on the budget of Henry David Thoreau (money converted to current value, of course). Just hearing him admit he had doubts made me feel better.

I took my last bite of brownie and licked my fingers.

"Why *are* we doing it?" I asked, not necessarily looking for an answer. "Why subject ourselves to this?" There was no cause at stake, no grand prize, no spot in the history books, not even a job waiting at the end. I already missed my house, friends, family—and even Sioux, our loud and demanding tomcat. We'd been on the trail for only two weeks, and I was ready to write my own version of the "Hello Muddah, Hello Faddah" camp song.

"Why are *you* doing it?" Charly asked.

"Because you made it sound so damn attractive."

"That'll teach you to listen to me," he said with a grin.

As we worked our way across Minnesota we became fast friends with our packs. Josephine, a Superior-Quetico brand pack, was made of sturdy blue Cordura with a red patch on her bottom, and she had a bit of a weight problem. She carried the dinner meals. Neither of us wanted to carry her. Holy Boy, named for a character in a favorite movie, *Map of the Human Heart*, was also a Superior-Quetico pack. He was the second heaviest of the packs, but he felt light next to Josephine. He was responsible for breakfasts.

Bertha had been around. A smaller canvas Duluth pack, once dark olive green but now faded to gray, she had been on every trip I'd taken, and she'd seen Charly through at least one other major expedition—the eight-hundred-mile-long canoe trip that he led through the Canadian Barrens. During that expedition Charly's best friend, Jim, had drawn a large Buddha-like woman on her front. She held the lunches. Phyllis, another faded and tattered Duluth pack, was the matriarch of our gear collection. Her status of elder earned her light duty—carrying our sleeping bags and pads—and we vied to keep her company on the portage because she was easy on the back, but Charly didn't think she would survive the whole trip. Madame Boudreau was a classy ash basket made by a woman of the same name in Maine. She carried all of our bulky, bizarre, and breakable items like the sextant—a navigational instrument incorporating a telescope and an angular scale that is used to work out latitude and longitude. She was a joy to carry but more fragile, so we treated her with the most care.

We carried these five friends, along with the rest of our gear, for miles each day over dozens of portages. With time our bodies grew stronger, the packs lighter, and our travel mode more efficient. We reduced the number of trips needed for each portage from three to two and loaded and unloaded the canoe with growing ease. Knock-Knock even adjusted to canoe life, hopping in and out of the front of the canoe like a pro.

We followed the Frost River until it cascaded through a shallow gorge into Little Saganaga Lake. I carried the first load over a mellow forty-rod portage to an island-studded lake with large bays and a breathtaking shoreline. "It's beautiful," I informed Charly as I passed him on the trail. Charly trolled for fish on our way to find a campsite in the early evening light, landing the canoe near a grove of cedars. In a grand gesture of love and goodwill, my new husband offered to haul all the packs up the hill.

We camped on a smooth granite knob that pointed into the setting sun and watched the sky turn gold, then pink, then vibrant purple. I thought about the light. I'd never given much thought to sunsets—they come and they go. But now that we needed the light, I became increasingly appreciative. Every ray counted for making more miles, cooking dinner, getting chores done, and writing or sketching. There was not enough light for what we wanted to do each day. That night, outside began to seep inward. I loved knowing the cycles of the moon, listening for the wildlife sounds, and watching for the constellations in the sky.

The next day I was dipping my fingers into a tuna fish packet—a special lunch treat—when a family of six walked past on the portage. "Where are you headed for?" one asked.

I could have told them about our long-term destination, Gjoa Haven, or even our short-term destination, Wollaston Lake, but instead I told them the more immediate plan of Knife Lake, about four miles and a few portages away.

"You planning to portage in the dark?" asked the grandpa of the group, who was carrying the canoe. Charly and I chuckled, though we didn't get the joke.

"What time do you think it is?" I asked Charly once they had left. "It can't be any later than two o'clock."

He dug for my watch buried at the bottom of his daypack.

"Six thirty."

Six thirty! No wonder I was so hungry. The sun was so bright and was so rapidly changing its position in the sky that I'd lost all sense of time. "I'm taking charge of the time," I said, grabbing the watch from Charly's hand. I strung it on a leather lace next to the orange storm whistle I carried around my neck.

Grandpa's prediction was correct. We made our last portage at dusk. The trail ran through a cedar forest alongside water tumbling over boulders for some fifty vertical feet to Knife Lake. Clouds created a halo around a crescent moon, and the sound of loons echoed in the steeply rising pine-covered hills. Rain began to fall as we ate granola and drank Tang by candlelight.

Spring exploded before our eyes. Sunrise began at four thirty, ducks and loons laid eggs, buds turned to leaves, and Juneberry bushes produced fragrant blossoms. Mayflies and mushrooms appeared, and twenty loons congregated in the middle of one lake as if gossiping about the return trip from Florida. They might have been in the United States or they might have been in Canada, but loons have little regard for such matters. An elegant combination of black and white patterns—black stripes on white neck, white dots on black back—they dipped and dove and spread their wings. Loons are large birds with webbed feet. My biologist friend calls them "barely functional flyers" because they need so much space to take off from the water and considerable concentration to stay aloft. They've been known to get stuck in the north as the lakes freeze around them because they need such a long runway to get airborne. They do better under water, swimming fast enough to catch fish.

Sigurd Olson, a prolific and well-known author who wrote passionately about canoe country, said about loons, "My memory is full of their calling; in the morning when the white horses of the mists are galloping out of the bays, at midday when their long, lazy bugling is part of the calm, and at dusk when their music joins with that of the hermit thrushes and the wilderness is going to sleep."

Their calls echo across the lakes day and night. Biologists have recorded, identified, and named loon vocalizations, which include the hoot, tremolo, contact call, yodel, and flight tremolo. We woke and fell asleep to, paddled and portaged to the loon calls. One rainy afternoon Charly, Knock-Knock, and I sat beneath a tarp on Birch Lake waiting for the rain to stop. Charly fried fish and wild rice cakes for lunch. Knock-Knock sat in an upright position looking out at the rain and the loons, dozing off occasionally. Two loons swam one way and then another, bobbed their heads under water looking for fish, then lifted their wings to air their feathers while letting out their famous quivering warbles. They reminded me of my favorite description of loon vocalizations from a 1917 edition of *Birds of America*: "The cry of the loon has been variously described as mournful, mirthful, sinister, defiant, uncanny, demoniacal, and so on. At any rate, it is undeniably distinctive and characteristic, and is almost certain to challenge the dullest ear and most inert imagination, while in those who know instinctively the voices of Nature, especially when she is frankly and unrestrainedly natural, it produces a thrill and elicits a response which only the elect understand."

Where the Basswood River flows out of Basswood Lake, we portaged around the falls and paddled into a strong eddy at the bottom of the falls. An eddy is a slow-moving whirlpool located behind obstacles in a river, and there the current runs upstream. Paddlers use them as resting spots when running whitewater. Getting out of this eddy proved difficult. We missed our first opportunity and rode the eddy around in a circle, our canoe unsteady with so much weight and a shifting forty-pound dog.

"I don't think that's runnable," I said, gingerly standing up in the canoe to look ahead at a set of roiling waves, including a few white haystacks—obvious spots where the current smashes into boulders and sprays skyward. Due to my lack of experience, I regarded whitewater with fear and loathing. Because of too much experience, Charly felt the same. So we struggled with rapids. Charly took on the voice of a football coach. I became a defensive girl, wanting to quit the team because Coach Canoe talked mean to me. "I vote no."

"It's a simple Class II rapids. Look," Charly said, pointing to a smooth line of glassy water. "We just follow that. Besides, we need the experience. There's no real threat below, so even if we wipe out we just land on shore and dry everything out."

I was skeptical but I trusted Charly. He was such a safety freak that if he said it was safe, it was safe. I left Knock-Knock on shore so she wouldn't be a disturbance. She could run alongside on land, and we would pick her up at the bottom of the rapids. We tied everything in snugly and started smoothly down the lip of the rapids. The current began to pull us hard to the right.

"Draw left!" Charly yelled.

Here I must say something about Charly's tone of voice. The particular tone he used is not his alone. He inherited it from his father, who inherited it from his father, and I can only imagine how many more generations before him. Charly's grandpa, Charles, is said to have stopped a runaway horse mid-gallop with his voice alone. It is a demoralizing, authoritative voice...that I hate.

My mind froze. I drew right.

The water swung us sideways into haystacks and then spun us backwards. Charly let out a hysterical cry that could have meant, "We're going to die!" or "Oh, gosh, the goofy things you do." Water came over the sides of the canoe, filling the bottom of the boat. I watched Knock-Knock run frantically back and forth on shore, getting smaller and smaller as I rode backwards through the rapids.

Somehow, we floated to the end in an upright position. "Do you understand what went wrong?" Charly asked in his schoolmaster instructional tone of voice.

"I don't understand why we didn't tip," I replied, and Charly let out a genuine laugh.

We steered to shore to pick up Knock-Knock, who was still frantic, and to bail out the canoe. The air had warmed to fifty degrees and smelled of sweet and spicy aspen buds, not yet bloomed. We hadn't seen another human all day.

"Sorry," I muttered.

"It's all a learning experience. I knew we were okay even if we tipped. We'd have just been wet for a day."

"You yell and my mind freezes."

"I'll try to keep the yelling to a minimum."

We continued to run rapids for the rest of the day. I improved with each run as I began to anticipate what needed to be done. I would draw right or left before Charly told me to do so. I would back paddle and forward paddle when I needed to. Learning to read a river is like learning a new language, and that day I mastered the alphabet and even started putting letters together. As my confidence increased, Charly relaxed. This was progress. Charly and I pulled together as a team, running easily and smoothly over the last set of rapids for the day.

The Voyageur's Highway was once the most traveled canoe route in North America, and we were on it. One year I'd given Charly a historic map of British North America, circa 1834. Its most detailed section is the Voyageur's Highway. The city of Winnipeg did not warrant a mark, but the trade route was laid out in detail. It was the route of commerce from the early 1600s to the late 1800s. For more than two hundred years beaver pelts were the currency of choice. Furs fueled the economy and exploration.

The voyageurs, who had traveled and traded along the route, and the native people, who have lived there for countless generations, left evidence that could be found everywhere along the Voyageur's Highway. On Crooked Lake we floated next to an entire gallery of rock art. Using pigment that looked like red earth, people had drawn shapes of moose or caribou and another that resembled a dodo bird. There was a devilish-looking animal, a fish in a net, and something that looked to me like a Viking ship. We camped below the pictographs and the next morning got up early, ate granola, filled the thermos with hot chocolate, tied up Knock-Knock, and paddled the empty canoe upriver to get a better look. It was calm and overcast, and fog rose from the river. Charly and I both sketched the pictographs; then he fished and I sketched some more, bobbing in the canoe. A waterfall splashed into the river and we stopped to inspect it.

"Let's follow it," Charly said. We tromped along, looking for the headwaters of the stream. "This is something I've always wanted to do, but usually I'm moving too fast to take the time," he said. We followed the stream up a hill until it disappeared beneath the ground.

The next day we crossed an exposed stretch of water on Lac la Croix. In the frigid early summer, capsizing the canoe could be fatal. A strong headwind had the lake whipped up with whitecaps. We had snapped on the sprayskirt, so Knock-Knock rode in the dark by my feet. The sky looked mean—gray and ready to spit. Cold waves climbed over the side of the canoe and through the skirt, hitting my knees and Knock-Knock's head. She panicked. I panicked. I set my paddle down—a canoeing sin—and reached beneath to calm her.

"Get that dog down! Get your paddle back in the water!" Charly yelled. I struggled to make Knock-Knock sit back down.

She clawed at my legs, attempting to ascend onto my lap, then onto my shoulders, and shoot for the high spot in the middle of the canoe. "I'm trying!" I screamed back, the wind grabbing my words.

"If we tip, we're dead. I mean it! Snap that dog's neck if you need to."

Kill Knock-Knock? I married this guy? Knock-Knock weighed thirty-five pounds and was mostly hair. Our dogsledding friends had given her to us because they thought she would do better one-on-one than as part of the dog team. She was known to freeze when the team ran too fast, and she buckled her legs on the downhill, skidding on her butt. She had an eggshell-colored face with a gray mask, and a nose and eyes of coal. She and I had become constant companions. She pulled me on cross-country skis in winter and followed me everywhere the rest of the time. *Snap her neck?* So this is what watching *Apocalypse Now* twenty-some times will do to a person?

I tried to hold Knock-Knock still between my legs, but holding a panicked Siberian husky is like restraining a toddler who wants to run. She wiggled and wormed while I tried to calm her with my voice. "Don't worry. No one in the front of the boat is going to die today," I whispered to her. I unsnapped the sprayskirt so she could look around at the lake. I squeezed my legs so she couldn't move. A wave lapped up over the boat, smacking her in the head. I paddled hard into the wind, watching the shore get closer. As we pulled near shore, Charly immediately sensed the chill from the front of the canoe.

"I'm sorry," he said as we unsnapped the spray skirt, climbed out of the canoe, and pulled it to shore.

I didn't speak. I couldn't. I was too angry. Knock-Knock trotted toward a rock, sniffed a gull's nest, and then ate the eggs.

"I'm sorry," he repeated, looking at my back.

I turned toward him. "There's no reason to use scare tactics out there. Do you really think that helps?" I asked.

"I know. I know. I freak in crisis situations. It's a character flaw."

"Try to get it under control," I said.

We stood in silence; the only sounds were waves hitting the rocks and Knock-Knock licking her lips. There was no other choice but to forgive him. Traveling as a couple in a canoe forced resolution to squabbles that could potentially play out for weeks, if not months. The round-the-clock closeness inspired a quick kiss-and-make-up philosophy, but more than that, we needed one another to power the canoe, to set up camp, to be entertainment. I had no one else to talk to. And most importantly, there was nowhere to go. If I had wanted to walk away, I couldn't have, so the better solution was to suck it up and have some fun.

"You told me to snap her neck."

"I'm an asshole," he said, opening his arms in surrender.

Charly looked truly humiliated. I leaned over and gave him a hug.

By noon we decided to take an afternoon break and allow the wind to die before we made a two-mile crossing. We had been in the Boundary Waters for twenty days and were making good time. We could afford to take an afternoon off. Plus, we needed to dry our damp clothing and gear before it got moldy. It looked as if a tornado had hit our small town of two by the time we pulled everything out of our packs. Gear and clothes were strewn from one end of the beach to the next—pans, bowls, and plates at one end and sleeping bags piled in a heap at the other. We rigged a clothesline between a birch tree and a pine tree to hang our soggy clothes.

A foot-high pile of leaves and twigs covered the beach, and bugs crawled beneath and above, making the beach look very much alive. Charly sketched the bug life on shore: ladybugs dressed in red with black polka dots and an unidentified bug with orange legs and a black body. The air smelled of spring, of cherry blossoms, and of old and new leaves. The songbirds chattered and loons called. I sat on shore watching the white-capped waves groove on by.

Charly stripped naked and "swam" for a few screaming seconds in the cold water, then laid in the sun beneath the bug tent. I heated a solar shower in our black bag and bathed in the sunshine. Knock-Knock curled into a ball and slept for most of the afternoon.

"We need to make bread," Charly said, propping up on his elbows.

"Go ahead," I responded, grinning, knowing what he was up to. He meant that I needed to make bread. A few lazy moments passed.

"We need to make bread."

"Go ahead," I repeated.

"I am. Right now. I'm working on it."

I baked cranberry-walnut bread in the Dutch oven, and then because I already had a fire going, baked a pizza: whole-wheat crust, rehydrated spaghetti sauce, mozzarella cheese, sausage bits, rehydrated pineapple, and onions. We had packed pantry-style, bringing bags of ingredients rather than packing up individual meals, and it paid off. It allowed for creativity and flexibility, and it prevented us from getting bored with the same meals.

As usual, the lake calmed itself in the early evening and by eight o'clock glassed over. "Time to go," I said. The lack of wind only encouraged a barrage of mosquitoes and blackflies. We quickly loaded *Le Strubel* and paddled into a molten-orange sunset. Behind us the sky brushed indigo around a three-quarters-full moon. We paused to float just a moment. Loons let loose tremolos in the distance, peepers peeped, and we heard the hum of motors. One loon popped up close enough for me to touch with my paddle. Another loon popped up and the two made meow-like sounds until one of them hollered and the couple moved on. We were headed for the Lac la Croix Indian Reserve in Ontario, marked only as "Indian Village" on the map. As the sky darkened, Charly navigated using a red light on a tower in the distance. We camped on an island across from the village—nothing fancy, just a flat spot in the woods, but it did offer a unique wake-up call: the scream of merlins feeding their young in the top of a jack pine.

An old woman stood on the dock as we paddled toward the village in the early sunlight. "More dogs than people here," she told us.

We were the first breakfast customers at the Let's Eat diner. I walked to the bathroom and was surprised by the image of myself in the mirror. It had been nearly a month since I'd seen my own reflection. I was blond, really blond. My hair had always teetered between brunette and dusty blond, but was never this white. And I was tanned—weathered really. I looked like the Scandinavian woman that I was. I splashed water on my face, brushed my hair with my fingers, and walked back out.

We had each ordered the special—two eggs, bacon, and hash browns. It was great to be waited on and to eat fried eggs. Locals filtered through the restaurant, curious about our route. "Canoeists!" exclaimed one jovial gentleman. The consensus formulating was that the water was high; we should take out before the bridge near Snake Falls. A few customers were enthused to tell us about one canoeist who smashed against the rocks.

After a morning of "Be careful," we heeded the advice and took out at the bridge before Snake Falls and so began a 150-rod portage instead of a 50-rod portage. "These are barely Class I rapids," Charly said as we portaged along a trail next to the ripples in the water, trying to convince me to put the canoe back in the water. I refused.

"That's how all expeditions go wrong; they don't listen to the locals.

Remember Hubbard," I said. In preparation for The Trip, I had read books by people who had bumbled their way through the wilderness and managed to live. My favorite was *Lure of the Labrador Wild*, the story of an ill-fated 1903 expedition, known as the Hubbard expedition, into the unexplored Labrador wilderness. Leonidas Hubbard Jr. and his two pals disregarded directions from locals and turned right instead of left. They spent a summer and fall living off fish and wild peas while thrashing though the wilderness. Hubbard died of starvation, but the other two stumbled around until they were eventually found shoeless in the snow.

"You know, this is the locals' idea of a good time," he joked. "Telling the canoeists to get out before the bridge."

We portaged the full 150 rods and put the canoe back in, a mellow current pulling us down sunny Namakan River, part of the traditional voyageur route. We ran Class II and Class III rapids for most of the day without incident, reaching a set at the end of the day.

"It's easy," Charly said. "We just ride the chute on the right."

I hesitated.

"Seriously, you can do it. We can do it. We've done much bigger rapids already."

"Alright, let's do it, but no yelling."

We started out by moving forward, paddles in the water, slowing the action. I paddled backwards to just under-match the power of the rapids. I had learned by now to keep my paddle in the water to stabilize the canoe and allow for quick reactions. I also wanted to slow the canoe as we headed into the whitewater. Charly maneuvered us to the right side and we rode a long slippery slope. I pulled us right and then left, and we landed in a large eddy at the bottom.

"Classic expedition whitewater," Charly said.

"Hey, hey!" I shouted. "That was fun."

"See, not so bad, eh?"

For the day's finale, we portaged around the High Falls and camped with the waterfalls in full view. An island of pine trees split the falls into two with a good thirty-foot drop on both sides. Charly cast his line in the pink glow of the sunset, fishing for walleye. He caught three and fried them for dinner. We spooned beneath our sleeping bags, watching the nearly full moon shimmer silver off the slick lip of the falls.

"I wish you could have met my mom," Charly said, his arms wrapped around me.

"Where did that come from?" I asked, looking over my shoulder.

"I don't know, just thinking about her and you."

"You think she would have liked me?" I asked.

"Once she got past the fact that you weren't the suburban type."

In my mind Carol Strubel Ray was the missing piece to the Ray family jigsaw puzzle. She had died of lung cancer in her fifties when Charly was a sophomore in college, the year before his last expedition. I'd seen pictures of her—beautiful, with a radiating smile. She was an artist, a homemaker, and a budding interior decorator just about to find herself when she was diagnosed. I deduced that Charly got his poetic side, goofy sense of humor, and smile from her. Carol started a journal when she found out she had cancer. She wrote mostly of daily comings and goings and doctor appointments. But during her last Christmas, when Charly was home on break, she wrote, "Charly is the same— shooting for the moon. . . so wholesome and caring . . . I wonder if [he] isn't too serious." That line, echoing my own thoughts at times, welded a connection between my mother-in-law and me.

"I wish I could have met her," I replied, drifting into sleep.

"So do I," Charly replied. "So do I."

6

Family Vacation

When Charly and I first decided to marry, we stayed mum about our decision for weeks. We wanted time to let the decision settle in. Finally I couldn't stand it any longer; I needed to tell someone, to make it real. It was June when I called my parents, and with each of them on the line, I told them that I had big news. Charly paced in the kitchen, a dish towel in one hand, a wet bowl in the other. "We're getting married!" I shouted. The news was met with silence. Stunned silence. It was like they each had ice cubes stuck in their throats.

"Well, aren't you going to say something?" I asked.

"I thought you were calling to tell us you'd bought a horse," Dad replied.

We saved the news of the "honeymoon" for a later date. We invited Mom and Dad for an October weekend in the Boundary Waters. They had never been there and we had promised to take them. Sitting around a campfire with loons warbling and otters splashing, Charly laid out our larger, grander plan: Lake Superior; Voyageur's Highway; eighteen months, by canoe, up north, over winter, by snowshoe and then canoe again; all the way to the Arctic Sea. And with each word, my mother's silence grew louder. It intensified and expanded and deepened until I couldn't hear anything else but the silence.

Dad reacted with giddiness. He had questions—lots of questions—and became manic talking about logistics. He was so enthusiastic that we began to joke that Dad might just jump in the canoe with us on departure day. He was a former Alaska man who had spent his early twenties tracking grizzly bears, sitting out a five-day snowstorm, racing his Ski-Doo, hunting wild goats, and catching king salmon. He and Mom had lived outside Anchorage for three years in the late 1960s, though their experiences were vastly different. She had finished nursing school, raised two toddlers, and started work. Dad had worked too, but he spent his free time living the Alaskan male fantasy. He wasn't such a hunter anymore, but he loved the wilderness. Mom—well, think of her as Mother Hen. She liked all her chicks in sight, and here I was about to set off like Chicken Little to find out whether the sky would fall. Mama Buckles wasn't happy.

After that night, Mom chose to focus on the wedding. Talk of the trip was like white noise to her. She didn't engage in it or respond to it, and she never asked questions about it. So our conversations became non sequiturs that went something like this:

Me: "I talked to this guy in Maine who builds canoes, and Charly and I are thinking of going out there to build our own canoe for the trip."

Mom: "Will you bring squash for Thanksgiving dinner?"

But as the date neared and the distraction of the wedding faded, she knew she had to either participate or be left behind—and Mom has never been one to sit at home alone. Dad was making plans to meet us; my brother, Link, wanted to meet up as well. Mom also began to listen to Charly—really listen—and came to realize that he was not the Pied Piper about to lure her daughter away. He may not have known a lot about milking cows, baling hay, or even fixing a car, but he did know about traveling in the wilderness. As a registered nurse, Mom respected medical knowledge, and Charly knew wilderness first aid. She started to ask questions and to look at the maps. Slowly, she hatched her own plan: a family vacation along the trail for her and Dad's thirty-fifth wedding anniversary. She asked Charly for advice on the whens and wheres, and they pulled out maps and planned and schemed before deciding on Blind Pig Island on Namakan Lake in Voyageurs National Park, about an eight-hour drive from my parents' house. They would rent a houseboat, and we would meet them there the last weekend in May—one month into our canoe trip.

Two easy paddling days after High Falls, we arrived at Blind Pig Island and set up camp the night before the family was to arrive. The next morning nesting merlins woke us up, calling to one another regarding food delivery to their babies. After breakfast we fished, napped, read, and paced. I walked up a hill to look out at the lake, anxiously awaiting the family arrival. After ten trips up and down to look, we finally ate dinner then read, sketched, and paced some more.

Finally, finally, finally Dad, Link, and my sister, Stephanie, rounded the corner at dusk in a small motorboat. I jumped up. Charly jumped up. And we all began waving. They sang an out-of-tune rendition of "Love Boat," in reference to the *Duluth News Tribune* article, circled back around, and waved to Mom and Stephanie's husband, Dave, who were waiting in the houseboat. Mom drove around the point and headed to shore, where the guys and I tied off the houseboat for the night, grabbing hugs and exchanging quick bits of information. The houseboat had all the amenities: kitchen, dining room, shower, two bedrooms, and an upstairs deck that had, of all things, a slide that shot off into the water— a bit of Disneyland in the wilderness.

I walked into the kitchen and caught sight of my grandmother's rhubarb pie sitting on the counter. Pie crust is a simple thing: three parts flour, two parts fat, and one part liquid. The filling—fruit and sugar. It's the good intentions that make all the difference. No one else made pie like Grandma. I had stood beside her making dozens of pies for my sister's wedding dinner—three parts flour, two parts Crisco, and one part water. I've replicated her technique but never achieved the same results.

Rhubarb pie. Nothing could have been further from our world. I cut myself a slice, and the rest of the family, sensing they might miss out, pushed me aside for their pieces. Charly was second in line, then Dad, Link, Dave, Steph, and Mom. With the first bite, I tasted spring. That slice transported me to Grandma's farmhouse kitchen, watching her roll pie dough, pour in the filling, pinch the edges, slice a design in the crust, and for the final touch, sprinkle white sugar over the top. Just another dessert for the men working in the fields. I had my immediate family with me for three nights, and with the pie, Grandma had stopped on by for a visit as well.

Charly built a fire on the shore and we gathered around. "Let's hear some stories," Link said.

"It was a dark and stormy night . . .," I started, between bites of my second slice of pie.

"Nooooo," the crowd responded.

"It was, wasn't it Charly?"

"When?" He dipped his fork into his third piece of pie.

"Two Harbors."

"It was a dark night," he agreed.

"And it gets stormy later."

"Start from the beginning," Charly prompted.

"Of the trip?" I asked. The fire was crackling in the background.

"Bark Point."

"Oh, well, if you all want our first near-death experience: It was a hot and windy afternoon . . ."

And so we told them abbreviated versions of our short list of tales—rounding Bark Point, paddling in the dark to Two Harbors, portaging through the Boundary Waters.

"How about you guys? What have you been up to?" I asked.

"How's Sioux?" Charly interrupted.

"Sioux has been an . . . *interesting* addition to the family," Mom said.

"Yeah, well, Sioux likes to go in and out a lot," Dad said.

"The other morning—we must have left him out that night—I'm lying in bed. It's five in the morning. I have to get up in fifteen minutes, but I'm enjoying lying in bed, listening to the birds, watching the first light come through the window. And then I hear the cat. He's meowing, but I'm thinking, 'Let him howl. I'm not getting up.' The meows get louder and louder. I look up to where the sound is coming from—and there he is on our skylight looking down at us."

I petted Knock-Knock, who leaned into me, as I watched Charly and Mom's faces in the firelight, the two of them sharing a laugh over a black cat. This was progress. I had once told Mom I didn't think that she and Charly would ever be friends. They proved me wrong. And when I look back, I think the tension between them was really a fight for me—Julie the daughter versus Julie the wife. Mom feared I would become like Charly—serious, stingy, and intellectual. Charly feared I would become like Mom—extravagant, loud, and emotional.

Of course, what they both didn't know and were only beginning to discover, and what I knew all along, is that they were both so much more. And so was I. Mom had begun to see Charly's playfulness; Charly, Mom's more serious side. I suppose the unspoken battle between Charly and Mom is one we all play out with our in-laws. In-laws provide a peek at your spouse's future, the inevitable. When you're young, it's unsettling at best. You think that if you can only assert yourself more and remove the other person from the scene, the future will play out differently. It was the same tug-of-war I played with Herb. When Charly was with Herb, he talked economics and asked financial questions. I feared someday his Herb demeanor would stick.

"Okay. I've got a joke for you, Charly," said my dad from across the fire. Dad was in his mid-fifties, but still had a shock of brown waves crowning his head. If a caricaturist were to sketch him, he would dramatize his hair, like Jimmy Carter's, then add big square wire rims resting on a Romanesque nose. Dad's head would be sitting atop a torso the size of an old oak and resting on lanky legs. "I guess you'd call it a north woods joke."

We all groaned.

"Let's hear it, Garry," Charly said in support of his father-in-law.

"OK. There was a guy out fishing, and a five-pound mosquito and a ten-pound mosquito landed on him. One mosquito says to the other, 'Should we eat him here or wait till we get back to camp?' And the other one replied, 'Well, if we take him back to camp, the big one will eat him.'"

Charly and I camped on the island while the rest of the family slept in beds on the houseboat. For two days aboard the houseboat we told tales, played cards, motored around the lake, slid down the slide, fished, and swam. It was 1999, the summer of *El Niño*—sunnier and hotter than it should have been on Memorial Day weekend. During lunch one day, Charly broached the idea of another get-together.

"So what do you two think of coming up to Wollaston this fall?" Charly asked. We would be staying at Wollaston Lake for the winter and then continuing on from there in the spring.

"Well, yeah, I'm all for it. I don't know about Laraine though," Dad said, looking over at Mom's face.

"Tell me more about it," she said, eating a cracker with cheese.

"Well, you two would pick up our winter gear at Mike and Phyllis's and drive it north . . ." Charly started.

We had her. She was in. It was only a matter of when and how. I've never known anyone as passionate as Charly about the wilderness and anyone so open to life experiences as my mother. Mom had gone from not acknowledging the trip, to planning a weekend at Voyageurs, to committing to a four-day drive into the wilderness. Charly and Mom talked about routes north—ignoring Dad and me. Dad and I had gotten lost twice before in high-profile incidents—once while hiking (the map blew away and the trails were faint) and another while cross-country skiing (I have no explanation). So we were excluded from discussion that required planning with maps.

On our last night together, Link grilled steaks and potatoes over an open fire. Thunder boomed nearby, and just as he pulled off the last steak the rain let loose. We all ran inside the houseboat, even Knock-Knock. It felt downright decadent to have a roof over my head during a rainstorm. The next morning Mom fried eggs and sausage. Charly and I loaded our canoe for the ride to the dock to say our goodbyes. Link, Steph, and Dave were leaving; Mom and Dad planned to stay for a couple more days and then meet Charly and me in International Falls, an hour away by vehicle.

A reporter who had discovered that a Buckles had rented a houseboat at Ebels Voyageur Houseboats on the Ash River took a guess that it would be us. And while Charly and I may not have been a big story in some circles, I realized from my time working for a small-town paper that we were a scoop for this reporter. When I was at the *Ashland Daily Press*, I once did a story about a woman riding her horse from Arkansas to Alaska because she passed through town and I happened to spot her. I wrote about a Quebec man who was biking through the United States to raise awareness for something. If two canoeists had paddled by on a larger journey, I would have chronicled them too. The reporter didn't disguise his disappointment when he saw our canoe loaded aboard the house-boat. The so-called canoeists didn't make much of a photo without their canoe. He snapped a shot of us with Knock-Knock at the end of the dock.

7

Serendipity

After the goodbyes, Charly and I unloaded the canoe from the houseboat. With Knock-Knock in her bow position, we paddled northwest toward Rainy Lake via the Gold Portage to Black Bay. We enjoyed an easy afternoon of paddling smooth waters, talking about the weekend, the upcoming get-together with my parents in Wollaston, and the interview with the reporter. At the Rainy Lake Visitor Center, we stopped to find out the exact location of Mallard Island, our next destination. Mallard was the home of conservationist Ernest Oberholtzer. He had died in 1977, but a foundation had been established to preserve the unique place he called home and encourage the continuation of his varied pursuits. Mallard Island wasn't on the map, and the Park Service didn't know where it was located. We guessed it was the spot called the Review Islands, because the location fit.

While Charly called Herb from a pay telephone, I checked out the park's display of voyageur history. I wandered past the maps and sketches and dioramas. I picked up a brochure about an Oberholtzer Trail and walked outside to find it. I walked the short trail, and when I returned Charly was already sitting in the stern, poring over maps.

"Dad's having complications with his colon cancer," Charly said as he pushed off from the dock.

"What kind of complications? Did he say?" I asked, looking back to Charly for clues.

"Not much. It was a typical conversation with Herb Ray. He mentioned the cancer then moved on to financial matters."

I rolled my eyes.

"He must have said something," I said, taking a paddle stroke.

"Just that he and his doctor were talking, his treatment isn't working out, and he might need surgery again."

"So, he's out of remission. Should we think about going home?"

"Dad said to continue with the trip."

"Of course he did. Do you think he'd tell you if he needed you?" I asked.

"I don't know. What's our plan? What do we bag the trip for?"

This was a conversation we'd had for more than a year—a morbid, necessary conversation without a satisfactory answer. Who rated high enough to warrant our canceling the trip? Who really wanted to be the one that would bring us home? Before we left, Charly had said what he believed to be his final goodbye to his grandmother. I had done the same with my grandparents. We knew we wouldn't return for their funerals.

"You know the answer," I said.

"Remind me."

"We go home for the death or serious illness of immediate family," I responded.

"I don't know that Dad's that sick right now. I think it would annoy him to have us there, hanging around. I feel like doing this is better for his morale; he's so into the trip."

"Well, let's wait for more information," I said.

"He says he hasn't received any money from our renters yet."

"It's not even the first of June," I exclaimed, turning around.

"I know," Charly said, shaking his head and laughing. "That's Dad for you."

We were still traveling west along the American-Canadian border. We knew that we had missed Mallard Island when we pulled ashore and spotted a sign for camping regulations for Ontario Crown lands.

"Oops, wrong country," Charly said, pleased as punch at having overshot Mallard Island and landed in Canada.

It started to rain, the light had all but faded, and Knock-Knock shivered at my feet. Charly looked at the map as we bobbed in the water. We were near the Canadian border, so we were close. Charly turned us around and pointed the canoe toward an archipelago of four small islands. The smallest one was Mallard Island, pointing like a finger into the heart of Rainy Lake. I had written and asked permission to visit Mallard Island. A woman named Jean Replinger from the Oberholtzer Foundation had responded in the affirmative. We pulled up to the dock in the misting rain. I could tell we were in for a treat just by peeking at the funky architecture. The most immediate example was the wanni-gan—a floating kitchen from the logging days—that we later found out acted as the permanent dining hall for the island.

Before we could look around more, Jean, who had faded red hair and a charged spirit, greeted us at the dock. She began with fast-paced intro-ductions and then recited the rules of the island. We needed our own bed sheets. Composting toilets were located to and fro. We were on our own for meals. "No dogs allowed," she said, looking down at Knock-Knock, "but since you're already here, the dog can stay." She invited us to eat dinner the next night with her and the other volunteers who were readying the island for the summer. "You know Ober canoed north one summer," she started.

"To York Factory," I finished. "We read about it in *The Beaver* magazine."

She smiled, sizing us up. "Let's get you to your cabin."

Jean walked over the rocky trails like a wrestler, with a short but con-fident stride, all the while looking back over her shoulder at us and talking. She wore tan cotton pants, a long-sleeved black T-shirt, and a utility vest like the ones that photographers or fishermen wear with pockets for their gadgets. The amazing thing was that Oberholtzer had tucked nine eclectic cabins, plus an icehouse, toolshed, and outhouses, on this slice of granite shield—and it all seemed so natural. Jean led us along the granite spine to Front House, a two-story cabin with cedar half-log siding and an open porch to the west, a utility porch to the north, and a summer kitchen porch to the south. Inside there were shelves and shelves of books—all there to be touched, looked at, and read.

Oberholtzer died in 1977, leaving the island to friends who had formed a foundation to keep it going. The island now functions as a wilderness school, offering limited week-long classes on everything from Ojibwa language to painting to poetry, all meant to honor the man who had once lived there. A Harvard graduate, Oberholtzer arrived at Rainy Lake at age twenty-five diagnosed with rheumatic fever and only a short time to live. He traveled to Rainy Lake to pursue his passions for wilder-ness, the native people, exploration, and the arts—and stayed. Proving the doctors wrong, he lived to be ninety-three. During his fifty years on Mallard Island he amassed eleven thousand books, two pianos, a collec-tion of maps and photos, and a few canoes. I had learned about this island from a friend who had spent a week on the island writing a poem about Lake Superior, and from another friend who had spent time there working on an Ojibwa language project. Both had been invited guests with approved projects, and both suggested that we visit Mallard Island on our way through.

Author Bill Holm, in his book *Eccentric Islands*, had called this place an "island of civilized wilderness." Shaped like a lizard, Mallard Island is only four hundred paces, or a quick four-minute walk from the eastern tip of the tongue to the western tail. A bridge extends that tail another few paces and ends with Japanese House—a Zen-like square building that hangs over the water. I sat there, writing in my journal, as a flock of Canada geese flew overhead in a V-formation. They honked and rotated positions, one flying solo for a few flaps, then falling back in behind its mates. My first thought was that they were heading south for the winter. But of course it was only the end of May, so they were heading north. It had been hot for so long that I had lost track of the seasons.

The next morning, Jean moved us to Bird House to make room for electricians who were due to arrive. Bird House was three stories tall and maybe fifteen feet by fifteen feet. The roof was nearly flat. Oberholtzer and others used to sleep up there, Jean said.

Later we wandered through Ober's house, just across a footpath from Bird House, looking through his journals and books. Jean joined us in the afternoon, telling stories and answering questions. Jean had taught for forty-three years. She helped start Minnesota Outward Bound and expanded their program to include courses for girls. She taught winter camping skills, was an avid cross-country skier, had traveled all over the world, and now volunteered as program director for the island. Jean first came to Mallard Island in 1982 and was immediately hooked by the charm of the place and the plight of the boxes of books essentially left to the squirrels. Oberholtzer was a hungry reader and ordered books from around the world. Jean submitted a plan for caring for the books, and the foundation accepted. It took two summers with six people working five hours a day, five days a week, to reach the beginning stage of cataloging his books on Arctic literature, nature, poetry, and everything else. She told us that the native people considered the islands sacred. "There is magic here if you are open to it," she said, "Too many coincidences. Serendipitous things happen here."

At dinner that night with Jean and other Ober Island regulars, like writers John and Edith Rylander and Iowans Mary and Steve Holmes, our education continued. Oberholtzer was responsible for saving most of the Boundary Waters from being dammed and developed. He also completed an epic canoe trip in 1912 to Hudson Bay and back to Mallard Island—Jean has since edited Oberholtzer's journals and photographs from that trip into a book called *Bound for the Barrens*, published by the Oberholtzer Foundation. We would be retracing some of his route. They talked about other conservationists who overlapped at least part of Oberholtzer's era and with whom he corresponded: Aldo Leopold, Sigurd Olson, and Olaus Murie. Oberholtzer helped defeat a plan by the industrial giant Edward Backus to build a series of dams from International Falls to the Pigeon River. These dams would have flooded out most of the country we had paddled through on the way to Mallard Island, including Lac La Croix, Basswood Falls, and Curtain Falls. Instead of dams, Oberholtzer proposed an international wilderness preserve, and he dedicated twenty years of his life to seeing it through. He also helped found the Wilderness Society and worked toward the establishment of Voyageurs National Park.

The electricians never arrived, never called. Jean said she'd been waiting for an electrician for four years. I told her I knew of a more reliable one who loved to kayak and would love Mallard Island—my dad. Charly and I paddled to town and reconnected with Mom and Dad near International Falls, found a campsite, then headed into town to run errands, including mailing food to ourselves for pick up farther along the trail.

The next day, as we sat at a café eating lunch, Jean appeared and charged our table, smiling, with her hand out. Mom and Dad loved her from the start and vice versa. Jean seized the moment and suggested we all motor out to Mallard Island. Charly and I looked at one another, shrugged our shoulders, and smiled a what-the-hell smile. Dad and Jean toured the funky cabins to look at what needed to be done. Mom conducted a photo shoot. Mom and Dad made plans to return in August. Dad would wire the island pro bono. In exchange, he would get to stay on the island, hang with Jean, and kayak on Rainy Lake. As it would turn out, he and I would return an additional two times to complete the work, Charly would return for a week of hunting mushrooms and discussions on Arctic literature, and I would return for another week to work on this book. Serendipity.

Mom and Dad stood at the shore of the Rainy River with Knock-Knock. It was time for us to head north and for her to go home—too many flies and too much sitting around. Mom and Dad planned to drop her off with Mike and Phyllis, who would care for her for the next year or so.

"I'm going to miss you guys," I whispered into Dad's ear as I hugged him goodbye. "Thanks for everything."

"We'll be seeing you soon," he said, patting my back.

Knock-Knock took this pause in the action to find a hidden pile of rotting fish guts and roll and wiggle and roll some more, smearing the mess fully into her fur. The fish gut smell and her slimy exterior made it easier to say goodbye. I coaxed her into the van and closed the door as she curled onto the back seat. She always did love a good couch. Mom and Dad, within moments of our leaving, would drive to the nearest car wash and hose her down.

Meanwhile Charly loaded the canoe and I quickly got into the front. The river, which was running higher than usual, carried us away quickly as I waved goodbye. Mom and Dad stood on the dock, watching us leave.

"Watch out for storms," Mom shouted to Charly, voicing her latest concern.

"What are we supposed to do if we see one? Do this?" Charly joked, holding his paddle to the sky.

"Get out of the way," she yelled back, laughing.

8

In Sickness and in Health

The Rainy River flowed dark and fast, the river's history so palpable I could almost see the voyageurs paddling, hear them singing, and smell the smoke from their pipes. It was a short river—about eighty miles, connecting Rainy Lake to Lake of the Woods—with Indian burial mounds and gnarly oak, basswood, and cedar trees alongside farmsteads with cows, horses, sheep, silos, barns, and hayfields. Just as Mom and Dad faded from sight, we spied an eagle sitting in its nest with a chick, black and fuzzy against a blue sky. It was sunny and bug free, and we were heading downstream, so I took off my sandals, set down my paddle, leaned back, and read aloud the handful of letters from our mail pickup in International Falls.

From my friend Ted: *Dear Paddlers, Greetings. There is nothing on cable. It is 11:30 p.m. Sunday night and I feel far away from nature.*

From Charly's friend Miranda: *I'm in my first-trimester, fixin' our house and moving out of our apartment. I spend a significant portion of my day inca-pacitated from nausea and fatigue. I typically only throw up one or two meals a day—that's all. "This only lasts three months," people kindly point out. Have you ever been sick for three months?!!*

"Poor Miranda," Charly commented, dipping his paddle in just enough to keep us facing forward.

"Sucks to be her," I agreed.

Mosquitoes came out in droves that night. We had a two-person bug screen dome tent, but hadn't yet sealed it at the bottom. Charly had bought a bed sheet at a thrift store in International Falls to tear into four strips and sew to the bottom of the screen. Suddenly, it was time. We both dove under the bug screen, the mosquitoes following. They nipped at our ankles, our ears, and our wrists—any area left exposed.

We couldn't sew in the dark, but we could take temporary measures. I tore pieces of duct tape. Charly tore wide strips of the pea-green sheet. We both ran our hands along the duct tape, the screen, and strips of material, creating a seal. Slowly we killed the mosquitoes already inside, and their numbers dwindled. Panic subsided.

Once the mosquitoes departed and we were lying side by side, scratching here and there, I felt a tickle on my leg, and then my arm. I reached down and plucked a tick from my thigh, and then another, and another. Same with Charly. An army marched up our bodies. They, too, wanted blood, and they were potential disease vectors. We pulled them off each other and for crazy laughs pretended to eat them like baboons at the zoo.

The next morning we stitched and sewed until we had a mosquito-proof net, but nothing would deter the tiny ticks. They just became a part of trail life.

Further down the river, Charly spotted a canoe heading upstream with two men paddling steadily in rhythm. Canoes in the wilderness are like magnets, attracting one other. The four of us waved our paddles, nodded our chins, smiled, and yelled some greeting. We pulled up beside them and paddled backwards so they wouldn't lose too much precious upstream momentum. The one in front rolled a cigarette. Short with curly dark hair, he was handsome and charismatic and a storyteller of tall yarns. He told us his name was Doug. He pointed toward the back and introduced his paddling partner, Dana.

They were two Canadians, attempting a journey much more ambitious than ours: Edmonton to Prince Edward Island—a 3,400-mile trip in one summer. Their story was this: they were drinking buddies who got to dreaming and scheming about paddling across Canada. Their friends had predicted they would never do it, so to prove them wrong, here they were. We tossed questions and answers back and forth like a tennis rally. Where are you going? Where did you start? When did you start? Why? How? How was Lake Winnipeg? What about the rapids on the Winnipeg River? These two men had firsthand knowledge of what was to come for us, and we had information about where they were headed.

Doug inhaled a drag of his hand-rolled cigarette and gave us a run-down on liquor stores along the way. He'd paid attention. They had left on April seventeenth from The Pas on the Saskatchewan River and had already gone twelve hundred miles. In contrast, we had paddled about four hundred miles since May first. "We pushed ice all the way to Lake Winnipeg, where we finally got stopped by it," Doug told us. "There's an old cabin on Lynx Bay—check it out if you get the chance. We holed up there for a week."

"So you did the crossing?" Charly asked.

"It was a wild ride. We got caught in some huge waves, but I'll tell you I preferred Lake Winnipeg to Lake of the Woods. Too many motor-boats on Lake of the Woods," Doug said.

Dana, who kept his paddle in the water, was quieter but had more useful information. He warned us about a set of rapids above the White Dog Dam on the Winnipeg River. "There's five miles of big water; stay right," he said.

"We haven't portaged once this trip—he won't do it," Dana said, pointing with his paddle toward Doug, who only grinned a don't-listen-to-the-old-guy-in-the-back grin. Doug described one spot, called The Dalles, where they clawed their way up the side of the river through rapids. He laughed as he told the story; Dana grimaced.

Doug told us about the dam policy in Canada: since the dams blocked historic canoe travel, the workers were required to provide trans-port around the dams.

"But no one has hauled our packs—we've had to do it ourselves," Doug said.

"You're only the second canoe we've seen in twelve hundred miles," Dana said.

Doug nodded, obviously glad to see us.

"You'll be seeing more once you hit the Boundary Waters," I told them.

All of us would have liked to pull over, build a fire, and tell stories long into the night, but no one suggested it. It was too early in the day, and the day was too nice. Maybe if it had been raining or windy or closer to dark, we would have spent a few hours together. But we had to be con-tent to have met, if only for a few moments.

That afternoon I pointed to a domesticated spot on the shoreline. Charly and I pulled over and walked up the side of the hill to a town park. It had a trail and a shelter. I walked back to the canoe to get our lunch, and we sat—legs outstretched, green grass tickling our bare toes—eating dried fruit, nuts, sausage and cheese, a spoonful of peanut butter, and a square of chocolate. Charly and I both leaned back in the grass, our heads in the shade of a birch tree, no mosquitoes anywhere, our stomachs and feet in the sun, and took a nap. I slept a refreshing fifteen minutes, then sat up, drank my last gulps of water, and looked around to refill my water bottle. I normally filtered my water, but if I could find water at this park I wouldn't have to. Charly woke and walked with me to take a look. We found a water pump painted turquoise.

"Nirvana!" I exclaimed and gladly began pumping.

"I don't know, Jules. Take a look," Charly said, pointing down at a crack in the casing around the well.

"You're kidding, right?"

"It's getting direct runoff."

"You are so paranoid." I said, laughing as I dipped my Army surplus canteen under the flowing water.

"I'm not taking a chance."

"Too bad, sucker. Guess you'll be filtering your water."

Charly and I approached a farm in the evening. Several kids ran out to the riverbank, and I asked them if they had any suggestions for where to camp. "Camp here," they screamed. And so we shared a pasture with sheep and a golden palomino horse. It was a picturesque farm of international origins. The mother was from Switzerland and the dad from Alsace-Lorraine. They had seven boys from toddler age to a thirteen-year-old. A boy named Daniel, who had Down's syndrome, came out while we set up camp. He spoke five languages and was visibly appalled that we could only manage English and a bit of Spanish.

His mother, a slender beautiful woman who did not look like she had borne seven children in the last thirteen years, came down later. "My kids won't give me peace until I come and say hello," she said. She told us that campers and canoeists often chose the same spot that we had. She also confirmed that this summer on the Rainy River was one of the buggiest in recent memory.

Charly strung up our tarp and set up the bug net while I prepared chili for dinner. We'd been soaking the dried beans in a pot all day. I fried venison sausage bits and added water, dried tomato powder, dried peppers, the chili beans, dried tomatoes, and dried onions. Charly and I walked with our steaming bowls to the edge of the river and watched the water flow by in the setting sun. We swatted mosquitoes until their numbers grew and chased us under the bug net.

I didn't feel well when we went to bed, and by the middle of the night I felt worse. I stumbled outside the bug screen to throw up. I was naked, and mosquitoes attacked my pink, brown, and white flesh. Everything inside of me—the dried fruit, nuts, sausage, cheese, and chili—flowed out, sounding something like a farmer slopping his pigs. The palomino horse snorted nearby. It was a clear, dark evening. I looked up at the stars, hands on my knees, panting as if I'd just run sprints, and then heaved again. I'd never been so sick. Flu and colds usually pass me by. The only time I'd ever thrown up was in the first grade. I was sitting at a school lunchroom table across from Laura Langhus eating watery tomato soup and grilled cheese sandwiches. Laura and I were best friends and co-choreographers, developing dance routines in her living room to *I Am Woman*. I threw up my grilled cheese sandwich and watery tomato soup in the lunchroom, and for the next thirty years never touched another grilled cheese sandwich.

Charly lay inside the tent, listening. "I've never seen anyone get so sick on the trail," he said, pride in his voice.

"Thanks." I took his statement as a great compliment. "Don't you feel sick?"

"Uh-uh," he said in the moonless dark. "I think it was the well water."

"Ugh."

He turned on his headlamp and pulled out the *Wilderness Guide to Medicine*, which recommended 7-Up and crackers.

"That's helpful," I replied, knowing that the nearest town was twelve miles away. "Next."

I took three more trips out into mosquito land, attempting to side-step my former contributions to the pasture, before the Pepcid and a Benadryl took hold. Charly woke at daylight and packed camp. I took another Benadryl, which made me sleepier, and I kept nodding off as I paddled toward town, my head drooping then jerking up as I awoke.

Looking like some Raggedy Ann reject, I leaned on Charly for the fifty-yard walk from the dock to the public park in the town of Rainy River. I collapsed on the grass and immediately fell asleep. I smelled of vomit, shit, and sweat. Charly bought 7-Up and ice cream and found a public shower. I drank the 7-Up. He ate the ice cream. "I need to sleep," I muttered. He showered and returned, nudging me awake with his hand on my shoulder. I showered and returned to my grassy spot, collapsing to the ground for another two hours.

"Mommy, look at the lady on the ground," said a child to her mother. I didn't move. A guy mowing the lawn started circling closer and closer, creating an outline of my limp shape. I stood and stumbled to the canoe.

"There are cabins for rent ten miles downstream," Charly said, rear-ranging our gear in the canoe. "Let's make it there, and you can sleep on a bed tonight."

Ten miles to a bed inside away from the mosquitoes; I had an incentive to keep going. I paddled one stroke after another. Ten miles. Ten miles. Ten miles. By evening we were there. The cabin had lime-green shag carpeting and smelled like a forgotten butt-filled ashtray. I didn't care. I fell into bed and slept. Thunderstorms rolled in late—it had rained most days or nights that we were on the Rainy River—and I turned to my other side and slept some more. For twelve hours I slumbered. Charly read magazines and watched the one station available on the television. I woke the next morning to the sounds of breakfast.

"How do you feel?" he asked over his shoulder, stirring something in a pan.

"Better. Much better."

"Oatmeal?"

I ate three bites, took two ibuprofen, and then packed. I helped carry our gear, load the canoe, and paddle toward foreign lands.

When we left the Rainy River, we left the United States and officially entered Canada via Lake of the Woods. I had applied in advance to cross into Canada and had received a remote border crossing permit that let us cross without a visit to customs. Aboriginals called Lake of the Woods the "lake of the islands." There are fourteen thousand islands, give or take a few, creating an illusory endless shoreline. Charly, who with his bushy beard and wild eyebrows was beginning to look like Festus, the gold prospector on the old TV show *Gunsmoke*, hopped into the bow of the canoe. He wanted me to navigate for a change of pace, and the navigator steered from the stern. Working our way from south to north on Lake of the Woods required full concentration. I had to match islands against the map to keep track of where we were, and after a while they all began to blend together. Eric Morse writes in *Fur Trade Canoe Routes of Canada, Then and Now*, "A look at the map shows the need for most diligent navigating; in fact, the voyageurs seem to have got lost more often in Lake of the Woods than in all the other miles of their long voyage put together."

I began looking more at the compass than the map. Charly must have suspected as much. "Are you keeping track of where we are?" Charly asked.

"Huh?" I asked, using a classic Buckles stall technique.

"You heard me."

"I'm pretty much just heading us straight north," I told him.

Even though I was looking at the back of his head, I could tell he was gritting his teeth.

"You can't just head us north."

"Why not? That's the direction we're going."

"Because we need to know where we are."

I rolled my eyes. Charly took the map to pinpoint our location then handed it back, pointing just below a cluster of islands.

At lunch we stripped down in the sunshine and dove off flat rocks into warm water. We were back on the Canadian Shield. No more muddy banks and mosquito hoards. The glaciers had polished granite into shapes that looked like humpback whales. In the afternoon Charly and I hiked to the top of Painted Rock Island and took in the expansive view. A small pile of rocks, a tipped over pole or prayer flag, and a little stockpile of wood indicated that we were not the first to be drawn to this spot. I sat down to sketch, and Charly walked around photographing wildflowers: orange tiger lilies, wild roses, and pink and yellow flowers that looked like shooting stars.

The wind gods bless paddlers by giving them tailwinds. And that's what we had our third day on the lake. I steered the canoe through the maze of islands while Charly rigged a sail using a tarp, a sapling trunk that acted as the mast, his paddle, and the spare paddles. We donned our life jackets and snapped on our protective canoe skirt. Charly sat in front, holding the pole, while I steered from behind.

We typically paddled about two miles an hour. With the wind's help we doubled our speed. It was like shifting into fifth gear, pressing on the gas, and letting the car rip at one hundred miles an hour instead of the usual fifty. Exhilaration coupled with fear as we cruised on the back of two-foot waves. For breaks from the wind we ducked behind islands when we could. We were finishing a long crossing when we spotted a very large powerboat—so large we couldn't see the driver. It was cruising into the main channel.

"Do you think they see us?" I asked Charly.

"I think we'll miss it," he replied.

Just then the boat turned left and headed straight for us. We both frantically tried to wave off whoever was driving the yacht-like boat, but it didn't turn away. Charly scrambled to take down the sail and untie his paddles from the tarp as the boat slowed in front of us, kicking up a three-foot wake. We were already riding big swells. I anticipated one of two possible outcomes: One, the swells and wake would flip the canoe, we would get wet, recover, and share a laugh if hypothermia didn't get us. Or, two, the swells and wake would flip the canoe, the boat would run over us, the propeller slicing off one or more of our limbs, and the trip would be over.

"Get the fuck away from us!" Charly screamed, desperately trying to wrangle his paddle out of the sail mast.

"Charly!" I exclaimed, ever an advocate for politeness even in the face of impending doom.

An older woman who looked like a retired schoolteacher pulled up beside us, *let go of the steering wheel*, and leaned over the boat. Charly flipped.

"Get away from the canoe! Get away!" he yelled over the wind, waves, and motor while bracing with his paddle.

"Charly, get a hold of yourself," I hissed.

"Are you all right?" asked the woman. She had gray hair swept into a bun and wore glasses and a white visor.

"We *were* all right. Thanks. Please move away," Charly replied, the sarcasm in his voice as thick as the woman apparently was. I feathered my paddle, sculling it back and forth, trying to steady the canoe as the motorboat's wake rocked us.

Suddenly the woman realized her mistake. Embarrassed she said, "Oh, we'll pull away." She returned to the steering wheel. A man in the boat, presumably her husband, never moved from his seat. They motored to the side of our canoe, and we paddled straight away, the tarp hanging loosely in the middle of the boat.

My heart beat fast and strong and my knees shook, but I broke into laughter. "You swore at a little old schoolteacher."

"I felt like Luke Skywalker without my Jedi light saber," he said, referring to having his paddle tied up in the sail. Charly started to laugh and suddenly we were laughing so hard we both had tears streaming down our cheeks as we rode along on swells.

We continued sailing the rest of the afternoon until the wind created three-foot waves, then we switched back to paddling. The closer we got to the town of Kenora, Ontario, the fewer camping opportunities there were. We passed by an increasing number of homes, motorboats, and people and ended up camping at Anicinabe Campground, eating Pringles from the campground store at a picnic table in the dark.

We had sailed and paddled thirty-one miles that day. Even though we were camped on a slope and campers talked and partied around us, we both fell deeply asleep. In the morning we walked toward town to scout the historic Rat Portage. Walking through a residential area, Charly pointed to a canoe trailer, noteworthy in a motorboat town.

"I wonder if there's someone around who knows something about the portage and the Winnipeg River," he said.

"Knock on the door and find out."

And so he did, which is how we met retirees Dave and Sharon Roberts. The trailer belonged to their daughter, who was canoeing at the time. Their son-in-law, John, who was in the house, worked for the Ministry of Natural Resources, mostly in the Lake of the Woods region. He knew everything about Lake of the Woods and the Winnipeg River and gave us advice on routes, rapids, and portages. John and Charly pored over maps—a great unifier among men in the bush. I made small talk with Dave and Sharon. Dave was a retired elementary school principal. They lived in Kenora in the summer and spent winters in Tucson, Arizona. Others apparently did the same: Kenora's summer population of one hundred thousand shrank to ten thousand in winter. The primary industries supporting the town were split between tourism and the paper mill.

John offered to give us a ride around the portage if we could be ready in forty-five minutes. We ran back to our campsite, packed in record time, and paddled to the boat launch. John, Sharon, and Dave waited for us, and we drove past the Rat Portage and through the town filled with little shops and painted murals. The threesome dropped us off five miles down the Winnipeg River and waved as the river pulled us away.

9
Duff Day

In *Fur Trade Canoe Routes of Canada, Then and Now* Eric Morse wrote, "The Winnipeg River was unquestionably the grandest and most beautiful river the Montreal Northmen saw on their whole journey from Lake Superior to Lake Athabaska." An impressive river with grand rapids and falls, the Winnipeg dropped 274 vertical feet in elevation through a series of waterfalls and rapids from Lake of the Woods to Lake Winnipeg—a stretch of 200 miles. In the 1960s, Morse experienced the same river that we encountered, including most of the dams. Instead of providing transport for voyageurs, today's Winnipeg River produces electricity for the provinces of Ontario and Manitoba and for export to the United States. In fact, our lights back home were lit by the power of the eight hydroelectric dams of the Winnipeg River. These eight dams flood all but 21 of those 274 feet. The river begins in Ontario with the Norman Dam at Kenora, flows past the White Dog Dam, then winds itself into Manitoba through Point du Bois, Slave Falls, Seven Sisters,

MacArthur Falls, Great Falls, and Pine Falls, then feeds into Lake Winnipeg.

Even in its tempered condition the river felt wilder than anything we'd seen so far on our journey—with fewer people and less evidence of campsites. I was the first to spot the two-foot standing waves that Dana had warned us about, visible from a mile away. Charly was the first to hear them. Here the river slipped over a ledge into a smooth wave, lifted into a long wicked curl, and then turned spastically white.

Charly steered us to shore at a rocky spot above the rapids, where I stopped the canoe short of the rocks and gingerly hopped out, then helped pull Charly's end to shore. There's nothing like paddling a canoe built of wood and canvas to give one an appreciation for what the voyageurs endured. They paddled birchbark canoes that never touched shore, lest they need repairs. So, in this case, the voyageurs would have jumped into water up to their waists to maneuver the canoe. Charly secured *Le Strubel*, tying off on a large boulder, and we scouted the rapids by walking the full length of them.

"They're not nearly as bad as I thought they would be," I said.

Charly nodded in agreement. "We can line the canoe," he said.

Lining, or tracking, the canoe meant we would only need to portage the packs. We could float *Le Strubel* along the edge of the rapids while steering from shore with ropes attached to the bow and stern. We portaged Josephine, Bertha, and the rest, then returned to our red canoe. Charly tied a line to the stern. I walked in front, holding the bowline to control the front, while Charly walked behind controlling the stern. The purpose of lining a canoe is to avoid lifting and carrying eighty pounds of wood and canvas awkwardness over slippery rocks to the other end of a set of rapids. This was also good practice for longer sets of rapids where we could line *Le Strubel* and have her carry the gear. I walked carefully, alternating between looking at my feet to avoid a broken ankle and watching *Le Strubel*, while listening to Charly's commands of whether to loosen my rope or tighten it, keeping in sync. It's a physics thing that I'm not even going to pretend to understand. I take directions well. The trick, according to Charly, is to use the river's current against the angles of the boat to steer in or away from shore, without letting the current get ahold of the boat.

At the bottom of the rapids, I walked into thigh-high water to work the canoe around some rocks. An eddy grabbed the canoe and would not let go. I feared losing control of *Le Strubel*, and so I held on tighter.

"The river will give her back, just loosen your grip," Charly coached.

The rocks were slick and I struggled to maintain my footing, holding tighter.

Le Strubel bobbed in an eddy, facing into the rapids. There she stayed like a belligerent toddler, refusing to return to safety. For what seemed like ten minutes, I held tightly.

"Loosen your end," Charly continued as he pulled the stern tighter.

And then as quick as a handshake, the current grabbed *Le Strubel's* behind, turning her around, and we pulled her to shore. I carefully stepped down from the rocks and waded into the water; the dam below had turned this area into something like a bathtub, with a ring of slimy green around the edges. I held the sides of the canoe while wading in up to my waist, two-foot swells creeping up my back. Charly lifted the packs from the rocks where they waited and set them into the canoe.

Next stop: the White Dog Dam. The dams, so large and menacing, freaked me out. I couldn't let go of the unfounded fear of getting sucked into the powerhouses. The maps marked the portages to get around the dams, but the maps had been wrong, so we approached each one with caution. I sketched wild irises while Charly scouted the portage for accuracy. He reported back, and we hauled Bertha and the rest of the girls up the trail and around the dam to the other side.

Below the dam we glided past the village of White Dog on the White Dog Reserve. The place looked like something straight out of a quirky European film. If I were to direct a movie, I would reconstruct that hillside, that town. The people of White Dog had an aesthetic contrary to their wild and unruly surroundings. Someone had arranged his or her laundry by color. Whites hung to the left and blended into yellow and then orange and blue at the far right. The laundry, held by clothespins clipped neatly at the corners, blew larger than life on the hillside against green freshly mowed grass and slate-colored clouds. Typical northern needs-a-coat-of-paint houses slumped along the top of a ridge overlooking the river. We didn't stop at White Dog, but even now I wonder about that person who hung laundry by color.

A day later Charly ran out of steam. His notes from that day read, "Talked Julie into letting me nap after only a few miles." Like I did on Lake Superior, I wanted to make miles. I had an incentive—the Winnipeg Folk Festival, a rousing weekend of folk music. We had driven there twice before, seen Ani DiFranco, the Nields, and dozens of other bands. I had deluded myself into thinking that we could make the festival (with about a dozen logistical barriers yet to be worked out), so wanted to keep moving. In addition, a day off is not taken lightly in canoe tripping. Paddlers tend not to "waste" calm, sunny days, because who knows what the weather will bring the next day. It could turn out that the day off in sunshine requires one paddled in the rain or wind. Canoeists believe they'll curse themselves by vacationing on the nice days. At least this canoeist does. But after a morning of pushing through what felt like thick honey, making only five miles, feeling serious muscle strain in my own arms, and listening to Charly beg for mercy, I conceded that we could take the next day off.

One morale boost that day: we crossed the Ontario-Manitoba border, marked by a wooden sign with Manitoba's emblem, a buffalo. This was west. Thinking about how far we'd already come made us both giddy. We'd paddled our way across Wisconsin, Minnesota, and Ontario, and now were on to Manitoba. The landscape changed almost immediately. It was not quite so rocky here, and we could almost smell the prairies. We paddled through narrow stretches with flat rocks poking up through the water, creating eddies. Along the shore grew brilliant-green oak, aspen, and pine woodlands. We started seeing motorboats from a fishing resort in the area.

Charly steered us toward Little Echo Lake, a small lake off the beaten path that would hopefully get us out of the motorized zone. Right away we spotted a five-star camping spot on a hill about one hundred feet above the lake. We climbed to the top, looked out at the view, then looked down at all our packs that we'd have to schlep up the hill and thought again. "Let's see if there's something else on this lake," Charly suggested. We paddled around the shallow murky lake analyzing sites like tourists scoping for just the right hotel or bed and breakfast. One had too many empty beer cans and fish remains. Another lacked dry wood. In the end no site seemed as appealing as the first, and so we lugged Josephine, Holy Boy, and Bertha, our daypacks, and Madame Boudreau up the hill and left the canoe at the bottom.

I sat in the fading light, writing a letter to my parents at ten o'clock at night. A campfire fueled by jack pine knots crackled, snapped, and popped, flinging hot red cinders up into the evening air. No flashlight. No candles. I inhaled the smoky pine-filled scent of our first bona fide campfire. The campsite had an abundance of wood, and we'd had the energy, time, and desire to expand our usual cooking fire. Charly had caught a pike and fried it for dinner. The wind blew through the tops of the trees making them sway and sing; the sky was pink and orange at the horizon. Charly assembled our bedroom for the night by unrolling two air mattresses, zipping two sleeping bags together, and spreading out a flannel sheet inside. I heard a few motorboats go by in the distance— late-night fishermen most likely. Loons warbled and an eagle flew by. Finally, at dark, we crawled beneath the flannel sheets and said good night.

I slept late, rolled over, and slept some more. Duff day. Canoe speak for vacation day. Charly fished, hiked, ran up the hill to get the camera to photograph a snapping turtle. "The hugest I've ever seen," he exclaimed, holding his arms in a large circle for emphasis. "A god-damned tortoise," he said. I ate granola under the bug tent and slept some more. I finally got up at nine and Charly urged me down the hill to look for the snapping turtle, but she was gone. There were smaller turtles in our camp trying to scrape holes in nonexistent soil to lay their eggs. It was a high-water year on the river, and the turtles were forced to lay eggs on the rocks. We hadn't seen a beach for a long time. It was painful to watch them, but there was nothing we could do.

Charly set up the tarp for shade. I baked a stellar batch of cinnamon rolls. Pelicans flew by at nearly eye level from our hilltop perch. We both spent the day listening on and off to Canadian Broadcast Corporation programming: "The Second Greatest Disappointment: Honeymoons in Niagara Falls," "Best Broadway Musicals," "Interview with Air Traffic Controllers," "Firsts." We listened to what were becoming favorites: *Dead Dog Café* and updates on daily roadblocks set up by First Nations people in response to grievances they had with the Canadian government.

CBC interviewed a band called Blacky and the Rodeo Kings. The band members each do their own thing, but had gotten together twice to cut albums. For their last album, they sat around a table, ate red meat, drank beer, and played their favorites.

The interviewer: "Doesn't it cut down on quality to record in your kitchen?"

Their answer: "Clarity of sound is overrated. We were going for spirit."

"We gotta check them out," I shouted over to Charly. I sketched an orange tiger lily and yellow honeysuckle. I wrote letters and caught up with my journal.

By firelight that night Charly read a poem he'd written.

Little Echo Lake

I love the sounds you learn living in the bush
Wing beats, for example, like the sound of loons
or eagles or crows flying overhead.
Just learned white pelican. Sounds like seagulls
screaming off in the distance when they fly over.
Or the sound of a turtle digging a nest for eggs,
slowly and quietly
scraping.

A duff day was just what we had needed. We left early the next morning, logging twelve miles by lunchtime. We spent most of the morning filling one another in on segments of CBC that the other had missed or discussing programs we both had heard. "Remember your first bicycle?" I asked.

"Mmm. No."

"Really?"

"You remember yours?"

"No."

"Well."

"Okay. First car?"

"Blue 1977 Suburban. We all chipped in and bought it for our big canoe trip. Drove our stuff north, brought it back . . . hey, you're lily dipping up there."

"I'm listening," I protested.

"You can listen and paddle at the same time."

"Alright, alright, I'm paddling. So you brought it back and . . ."

"And we got nine hundred dollars more than what we paid for it."

"Your first car experience would be a money-making one."

"What about your first car?"

"A green Chevy Impala."

"And?"

"Three hundred dollars. Cashed in a savings bond. Doubt I got anything back out of it," I said.

By late afternoon we parked our canoe above the dam at Point du Bois, a company town for Manitoba Hydro, and scouted the portage. Charly spotted the liquor store recommended by Liquor Store Doug and decided to buy a bottle of red wine. As we walked back, a well-worn brown truck pulled up beside us. The driver, a mustached man wearing a baseball cap, rolled down his window and asked, "You canoeists?"

"Yes," we said in unison.

"Doing the portage? How much stuff you got? I could give you a lift," he said without taking a breath.

His name was Gord Johnson, a forty-something guy with the weathered look and build of an outdoorsman. He was just getting off from his shift at the dam. He drove us to our canoe, and we loaded everything into the back of his truck. Charly stood in back holding down the nose of the canoe while I rode up front and learned these facts: The dam was one of the oldest in the system, built in 1911. A person had to work for Manitoba Hydro to get a house in town. The population averaged 100 people with an all-time high of 144 and low of 22—depending, I guess, on the amount of work available. Gord ran the tramcar that shuttled supplies from Point du Bois to Slave Falls. There was no road access to Slave Falls Dam, located down river. "It's a great job," he said.

After a five-minute truck portage we unloaded the canoe and our packs. Typically the entire river ran through the Point du Bois powerhouse, and the falls next to it remained dry. But not when we were there. The river was so high that the powerhouse was full and water poured over the half-mile-wide smooth pink granite steps. Gord invited us to his house to look at maps and have a beer. We had already covered twenty miles for the day, so we accepted. He wanted to know everything about our trip.

"The bush. It's magic. It's in my soul," he said wistfully.

Gord served cans of Labatt's Wildcat, rolled a smoke, then brought out maps of the region. He had a stuffed loon in his living room. He told me that his old man had caught it accidentally in a fishing net. Gord's shelves were filled with trinkets from the region—rocks, arrowheads, the kinds of things a wanderer, curious about the world, always finds. Gord pulled out an archaeological report, "Studies in Manitoba Rock Art." I flipped through the typed pages with hand drawings of petroforms. They looked like a series of random rocks to me. A longer look and the rocks took shape: turtle, snake, human, square—all arranged by people long ago. Petroforms are usually found on a flat slab of glacially polished granite. No one knows who made them or why, Gord said. Archaeologists think they could be as old as eight thousand years. Gord told us that there was one downriver on a side stream called Tie Creek.

The Winnipeg River came alive in Gord's living room. The history predated the Voyageurs and even the Cree and Ojibwa people. He told us legends like the one about Slave Falls, our next stop along the river. The story goes that a slave woman wrapped herself in a deerskin robe, stepped into a canoe, and went over the falls to escape life with a cruel master. Gord sent us off with an out-of-print map that detailed the river route and history. We camped on a little island above Slave Falls Dam.

The next morning Charly was in an unexplained foul mood and tossed hefty Josephine on the yoke of the canoe and the yoke broke. It had already been showing signs of stress, and the sixty-pound pack did it in. We ran a set of rapids and went down backwards—my fault, of course—and his foul mood deepened. Charly wanted to search for Gord Johnson's petroform on Tie Creek, but the novelty of chasing streams to their beginning had worn thin for me, and I didn't want to. I wanted to make miles. Tie Creek curves back and forth and back and forth, and my mood worsened with each and every bend. I didn't yell, I just grew more and more silent. By then, we knew each other's silences up and down and inside and out—pondering silence, pleasant silence, daydreaming silence, and stony cold silence. While Charly understood this to be a silence of the latter variety, he chose to ignore the chill. I did think a lot about Slave Falls and about the endless legends of Indian princesses that jumped to their death. A similar legend was told in my hometown of Viroqua. *I could do a master's thesis on leaping Indian princesses*, I thought, but did not share with Charly. And so on we paddled back and forth in silence through the winding river until a beaver dam ended the search.

"Let's call it quits," Charly said.

"Okay."

I cheered up as we cruised down Tie Creek back to the Winnipeg River and told Charly about my new idea for graduate work. I created a memorable meal that night at Otter Falls, maybe to make up for killing the petroform excursion with my silence. I marinated dried shitake mushrooms, onions, and rosemary in the white wine Charly had bought in Point du Bois, sautéed them in butter, and then added hydrated spaghetti sauce. Charly boiled the noodles. We clinked our stainless steel mugs filled with Point du Bois wine in a toast and ate what tasted like a gourmet meal of fresh ingredients.

Gord Johnson's map showed two routes for the next day. The river broke into two channels: the Blanche River and the Pinawa. We chose the Pinawa Channel since the map noted that the voyageurs preferred it in high water because there were fewer rapids. Pinawa is a Cree word meaning "calm channel." And it was. It was a small river with lots of birdlife and without any motorboats. It had vertical mossy granite walls and there was just enough water to float us over the shallow rapids and rocks.

There were more people at the Pinawa Dam than we'd seen all summer. The dam had been decommissioned in 1951 and converted into a park. Teenagers jumped from the top of the dam, which looked like a Roman ruin, while younger kids played in smaller pools of water and adults soaked next to them. It was ninety-some degrees. We needed to portage the canoe and packs, but no portage existed, so we hiked and hauled for three and a half hours, jumping into the water with our clothes on to cool off. Finally we loaded *Le Strubel* and continued down the channel and through the reservoir of Lac du Bonnet in the early evening.

It was June twentieth, and the tourist season had started at this reservoir. People wearing bathing suits rode carefree in motorboats, motored on Jet Skis, floated in inner tubes, and lounged in the shade. And this sounds crazy even to me, but for that day I started to think that it must be nice to take a weekend off and play. Even though we'd just enjoyed a duff day atop a hill, paddling had begun to feel like work. Ten, twenty miles a day. Make camp, take down camp. Paddle, paddle, paddle all day long. It wasn't a bad job, but still, it felt like a job.

Tourists meant tourist shops and restaurants.

"I bet we could find a burger—and fries—around here," I suggested.

Likely sensing my all-we-do-is-work mood, Charly yelled out to a young guy throwing sticks to his black Labrador. "Where can we get a burger?"

"Camp Hide Away," the guy shouted back. "It's a few miles down on the left side of the river."

We paddled by lake houses one after another, arriving at Camp Hide Away at eight thirty. I walked to the trailer office/restaurant/store and found Terry, the owner, playing cards with friends. Terry looked like a voyageur—short and square with a crew cut and a few crooked teeth. He was obviously looped. He swayed when he stood. We exchanged basic information. He laughed when he heard we had paddled from Wisconsin to his establishment. I asked about burgers. "Sure, we can cook a burger for you. Come on in. I'll turn on the grill." His two daughters appeared like mythological nymphs and began cooking. Charly walked in and said, "Hello."

"I'm pretty sure you are the first to canoe from Wisconsin to the Hide Away. Though we did have a kayaker stop by. He'd been out one day. One day. He wondered what we had to offer. I told him, 'We have a lounge,' and the guy perked up. He stopped in for a couple of beers, his legs obviously in pain, and then paddled away. You want a sled dog?" Terry asked, abruptly changing the subject, already bringing us each a beer.

"Does he paddle?" Charly asked.

"No, but he loves the water. I'll give you the harnesses and everything," he continued.

"We're only looking for paddlers right now."

Terry's friends bought us another can of Labatt's as we sat down at the booth. Terry had worked in construction for eighteen years in Winnipeg before buying Camp Hide Away. He'd owned it for six years. He was like most bar owners I knew—amiable, hard drinking, and a fine storyteller. As he filled out a campsite card for us he asked for the date. Reflexively I reached down my shirt for my watch, which had hung by a string around my neck since the Boundary Waters.

"What, do you have a calendar tattooed on your tits?"

I turned ketchup-red as I looked at my watch. His daughters saved me by delivering my burger with French fries. We won them all over when we reached for the vinegar and dripped it on our fries—a Canadian tradition borrowed from the English. "No one in the States has vinegar on their fries!"

The burgers hit the spot, but the camping didn't: twelve dollars for the privilege of sleeping on hard ground under yard lights next to a road on a hot and muggy night. And the showers required quarters, which we didn't have. We woke early and slipped out before anyone stirred.

On the summer solstice evening Charly stripped off his clothing and jumped into an eddy just above a long waterslide called Whitemud Falls. I tuned in our solar radio to the CBC, ate Pringles from a can that I had picked up at Camp Hide Away, and listened to the weather report: wind and possible thunderstorms. We hiked both sides of the slide looking for a way to portage, but couldn't find a trail; and with the granite walls there was no way to line the canoe. We had only one choice—to run the rapids. Charly felt anxious about the whitewater, and if Charly felt anxious, I felt anxious. We decided to delay the inevitable and camp. Besides, it was already dusk and we had landed at a gorgeous spot. Just before I got ready to pop corn for dinner, I spotted something swimming toward us, moving precariously above the rapids.

"It's a bear," said Charly.

"No, it's a moose," I said.

"Too small to be a moose."

"I think it's a moose."

The animal was headed directly for our rock. We crouched down so we wouldn't scare the moose-bear. The unidentified mammal perked up its ears: black bear. Before the bear could reach shore, the current sucked it over the ledge and downstream right past us. The bear looked so helpless in the swirling water.

"Oh, no!" I couldn't help but shout out.

"Eddy out!" Charly yelled to the bear. It looked our way, ears straight up in the air. Just then, an eddy took hold and swung the bear around into the swirling current close to shore. The young bear lumbered out of the water, shook itself off, sniffed the ground, and sauntered into the woods. Good lesson in eddies, I noted.

We stayed up late, swatting mosquitoes and eating popcorn in the reddish sunlight still remaining at ten o'clock. Charly didn't sleep. The sound of the rapids kept him awake, his stomach churning.

He is not the first man to be kept awake by the sound of rapids. Sigurd Olson writes in *The Lonely Land* of lying near a set of rapids on the Churchill River. "I awakened once during the night and lay thinking of the approaching day and the warnings we had had. Running rapids in familiar country is one thing, running them in a strange land where rock formations as well as the speed and depth of the water are different, is another. . . . One bad move in white water and the expedition could end before it really got underway."

So Charly, like Sigurd Olson, and many others, I'm sure, flipped back and forth in a restless, unsatisfying sleep. Meanwhile I slumbered deeply through the night.

"You need to have some fun in rapids," I said, lying next to Charly the next morning.

"Is that what I need?"

"We need to get inner tubes so you can see just how stupid you can get and still survive," I said. I did not grow up paddling canoes. I did, however, spend most summer days floating the creeks and ponds of southwestern Wisconsin farm country, dodging cattle.

"Hmmm."

I ate granola for breakfast. Charly declined due to his sour stomach. We reviewed our strategy: follow the slick tongue down the left side and be ready for anything past the first bend.

As we set off down Whitemud Falls, Charly shouted, "Act like a bear!"

The rapids were a blast. We rode the smooth tongue like an amusement park ride and made good time cruising downstream, landing at the last dam on the Winnipeg River before lunch. Just as Dana and Doug had told us, workers from the dam stood outside ready to help us around the dam. Five workers in all, obviously thrilled with a break in their routine, loaded our gear into a truck and drove us and our gear around the dam.

With the dam still in sight, we spotted two paddlers in a canoe, heading upstream. Strong paddlers, making miles at a brisk pace. I don't remember their names but can still see their bright youthful faces: two women who had just graduated from college. They were paddling across Canada in two parts, over two summers. They had started in The Pas and were headed east to St. George, Newfoundland. They planned to start in The Pas the next summer and head west to Tuktoyaktuk, Northwest Territories. They had stickers from hometown sponsors plastered all over their canoe. We talked portages, campsites, and points of interest. They liked Lake Winnipeg, although they thought it was windy. "You want some dried fruit? We left about twenty pounds at the campground in Pine Falls," one of them said.

"I was going to ask you the same," I laughed. "We'll probably be leaving another twenty pounds. It's been such a hot summer, who can eat that much dried fruit?"

"There's a Subway in Pine Falls," one of them told us.

The women didn't have a good map of the Winnipeg River, so Charly passed along the one Gord had given us, and we said our goodbyes.

Pine Falls was an industrial paper mill town that smelled of rotten eggs. Next to a plant spewing smoke into the air and gunk into the river were stacks and stacks of black spruce not much larger in diameter than my thigh. "How could it possibly be profitable logging in such a remote region?" Charly commented. "We're mowing down the boreal forest to wipe our asses." For the record, and this is something Charly would want clarified, he avoids indoor toilets and never used toilet paper the entire trip, preferring leaves and sphagnum moss.

Pine Falls was the location of our first food pickup and another chance to get mail. Charly had mailed the food box from International Falls. Friends and family had also been given the address and anticipated date of arrival. I had contacted the post office in advance to tell them to expect general delivery mail, a typical arrangement for canoeists. We still had food, but wouldn't be passing through another town of much size for at least twenty days.

We walked to the post office and picked up our boxes and mail. It was ninety-six degrees with a howling wind. My face looked more like a Craisin with every scorching day. Charly found a pay phone and called his dad while I entered the air-conditioned Subway, ordered sandwiches, and sat at a booth waiting for him.

"Dad's trying a new treatment for colon cancer, but it sounds like a colostomy might be unavoidable," Charly said as he sat down.

I studied his silent profile—bushy beard, defined cheeks, greenish-gray eyes, and high forehead—and tipped my head to see his face. He looked up at me and then away.

"I should be there with him," Charly continued, rubbing the bridge of his nose as if he had a migraine.

"Do you want to go home?" I asked.

"So I go home and then what?"

I shrugged.

"He's so pumped about our trip," Charly said.

We both stared at our sandwiches. I couldn't think of anything else to say. Charly didn't offer any more, so I unwrapped my sandwich and started to eat. He did the same.

For the rest of the afternoon we read through our pile of mail. We were more connected with many of our friends and family members during that summer than ever before or since. We had time to read letters, think about them, and respond.

From Charly's Uncle Dick: *The 2000 presidential race is starting to heat up, and it is duller than I can ever remember. The candidates that are substantive are dull, those that have a thimble full of magnetism are intellectually challenged.*

From our friend Landis: *All is well here with the normal settling in of our summer routines. Our transition time went tremendous this year with both of us unemployed for one month so we could get on with the real work, as Gary Snyder would put it. I wonder what this culture would be like if everyone were unemployed for one month out of the year. I can't help but think there would be more balls thrown, walks taken, hugs given and birds appreciated. Such simple changes to change it all.*

From Dawn: *Sorry I don't have more for you. It's embarrassing how crazy things are here. Andy works all the time (literally) and as the weeks of not seeing him roll on, the stress of it mounts.*

And from Herb: *Dear Charly, Have torn myself away from my crossword puzzle this morning because I swore to myself that I would get a letter off to you. Actually it's closer to noon and I had finished the puzzle and was cleaning the chrome on the stove burners. But it's a beautiful, sunny, low eighties day and after I finish this letter I plan to do a little sunbathing.*

I looked up. "Cleaning the chrome on the stove burners—why am I not surprised?" I teased, taking a bite of my industrialized tuna salad sandwich.

Charly grinned, obviously pleased by the memory. Herb had once driven five hours north to attend my parents' thirtieth wedding anniversary bash—a full-blown barn dance. With everyone outside playing volleyball, throwing horseshoes, and talking and laughing, we had found

Herb in the kitchen scrubbing the stovetop. My mom joked that she had no idea that it was supposed to be white.

We read these letters aloud, jotted letters in response. I stood to call home while Charly wrote to Tembec Inc., the corporation responsible for the piles of black spruce logs. By coincidence, a forwarded copy of the *Earth First! Journal* arrived in our Pine Falls mail, featuring a piece on Manitoba's threatened boreal forest, specifically Tembec Inc.'s plans for expanded logging north of Pine Falls.

No one answered the telephone at home, so I called Mom at work. She was in the midst of a crisis—a real crisis, she was a cardiac nurse—but was able to take a few moments to tell me that Sioux the charismatic cat was missing. He had disappeared while we were all at Voyageurs National Park. Mom and Dad had hung signs and talked to the neighbors, but he was gone.

"It's my fault," I told Charly. "I knew he would take off without someone around, and I knew Mom and Dad were coming to see us. I should have boarded him."

"If Sioux's disappearance is the biggest tragedy of the trip, I can live with it," Charly said, and I agreed.

As the sun started its descent, we left the deliciously air-conditioned Subway and walked toward the town park, where we camped for the night. The next morning, Charly handed over dried fruit and two blocks of cheese to a bemused and confused family who stopped by the park. We loaded up, floated past the Tembec pipe discharging a sickly yellow pulp-mill effluent into the river, and paddled toward Lake Winnipeg.

10

The Talk

Lake Winnipeg is a schizophrenic lake, geologically split down the middle with granite on its eastern shore and limestone on its western shore. If you look at a globe, only a handful of lakes are shown. Lake Winnipeg is one of them. Shaped like a meat cleaver in mid-chop, the blade is on the northern end and the handle is on the southern end. Canoeist and author Eric Morse called Lake Winnipeg "a mean lake, for which it is difficult to find much affection." Journalist Eric Severeid, who at age 17 traveled 2,250 miles, mostly by canoe, from Minneapolis to Hudson Bay and later authored *Canoeing with the Cree*, gave up on paddling Lake Winnipeg and instead opted for a ride aboard a steamer. Looking out as a northwestern gale blew through he wrote, "At last all the tales of sudden death on Lake Winnipeg had been confirmed. The thought of being out there in the canoe made me turn pale."

We followed the Winnipeg River onto Lake Winnipeg in a rainstorm. The clouds and sky took on an unnerving, greenish-orange tone I'd never seen before and haven't seen since. I'd never seen a tornado, but I'd seen and felt tornado weather—a green-tinted stillness that screams, "Run!" Paddling from the comforting confines of a river, where I could see both shores, onto a large lake with a tornado sky had me looking over my shoulder. We paddled to shore, rigged a tarp along the brushy shoreline, and watched what turned out to be just another day on Lake Winnipeg.

There were no casual campers, no recreational fishermen, and no boaters out for an afternoon ride. The reason: the lake is too big, too feisty, too muddy, too shallow, and too rough. Winnipeg, from the Cree word *win-nipi*, translates as "dirty water" or "murky water." There was so much silt that we had to let the water settle in a bucket before filtering it to drink and cook. Only a few thousand people lived in clusters along the shore. For the most part, small bush planes and an occasional distant commercial fishing boat were the only indications of human habitation.

On our fourth day on the lake we paddled into Loon Straits, a town of eight people, and pulled up to the dock of a log house with a Canadian flag. As we climbed out of the canoe and onto the dock, a short woman with silver hair shouted, "You must have read the book. We get a lot of voyageurs stopping here."

It turned out that canoeists Joanie and Gary McGuffin had mentioned stopping here, at the home of Anne and Carl Monkman, in their book *Where Rivers Run*. Canoeists had been stopping by ever since. "I just pulled a fresh bannock from the oven and put on coffee," Anne said. "Come in and have some."

Charly and I knew we shouldn't stay long, that the lake was calm and the skies a soothing blue. But heck! We hadn't talked to anyone but each other for a week. We walked inside and sat down at the kitchen table, which overlooked the dock, our canoe, and the lake. Anne poured coffee and I didn't stop her. There was something about the gaiety of the moment—the way she invited us in without hesitation, pulled fresh bannock from the oven, carried the pot of coffee from the stove to the table—that seemed so perfect. And if I had said, "No, thanks, I don't drink coffee," it would have altered the mood. She would have responded, "Oh, can I get you tea or something?" The moment would have been lost forever. Charly must have felt this as well because he accepted his cup without hesitation, even though he didn't like coffee either. We passed cream and sugar between us as well as a glance saying, "Hey, we're drinking coffee." And it wasn't bad. I sipped slowly and even accepted a second cup while tearing off pieces of the soft and chewy bannock—bread made with flour, baking soda, salt, and lard.

Carl was a true man of the North. His list of jobs included commercial fisherman, carpenter, woodcarver, bush pilot, postman (which involved driving a boat several miles across the lake), plowman, and road grader. Anne was a Mennonite of Russian descent who handled the household duties and was researching a book about their town. Loon Straits had once boasted 150 people—mostly with the surname of

Monkman—but everyone left in the 1960s when the fishing industry took a dive. No industry. No jobs. Plus no one left for anyone to marry because they were all related. Electric lines and a road connecting Loon Straits to the outside had arrived just three years before we did.

Charly and Carl headed to the woodshop to work on a new oak yoke for the canoe—another bit of serendipity. Anne and I moved to the living room, and she told me about the family history and about other paddlers—like the French priest who had stopped, stayed a day, and left, heading north. The next afternoon he returned, apparently turned around. "I wondered why the sun beat on the wrong shoulder," he had told her.

Another paddler came and stayed too long. "We finally had to ask him to leave," Anne said. "He seemed lost in the world." And yet another pair of paddlers didn't pack any food because they tried to live off the land. "They were very hungry," Anne chuckled. Their last meal before arriving in Loon Straits had been turtle soup. When we finally left, Carl handed us a package of frozen walleye fillets. Anne handed me a new pocket-size Bible. "You never know when you'll need it," she said.

Well, we did have the crossing ahead. We had two options with this lake. One, we could paddle up the entire eastern shore, along the northern shore, and back down the western shore to our destination, Grand Rapids. This option added another week of travel—and it would be windier on the east side of the lake since the prevailing winds were from the west. Or, two, we could paddle up the eastern shore, cross at the narrows, and continue up the western shore. The second option was the more efficient, but the more risky because all the water from the cleaver's handle passes through the two-mile narrows. Two miles would take us up to an hour. A lot could happen in an hour.

The day after leaving the Monkmans, we approached the crossing as the sun was sinking to the horizon through a splattered orange sky. A navigational light used to warn boaters of rocks blinked on the other side. It was useful as a focal point. We secured our gear and snapped on the red canvas spray deck. Charly took stern. I sat in the bow. The wind ran east to west, pushing us across. I wasn't scared. I wasn't panicked. I wasn't even counting. This was fun. Sometimes the things we dread most and worry about longest turn out to be nothing. We crossed Lake Winnipeg, the eleventh largest freshwater lake in the world, in an exhilarating thirty minutes, even surfing on big waves near the end.

With the stress of crossing Lake Winnipeg gone, I had little to occupy my mind. The big open sky melded with the expansive lake. The light, wind, and space combined with the silent rhythmic paddling and prompted a type of madness to set in. With no distractions, my mind was like a scratched record, replaying scenes from childhood over and over again. Hey, Steph, wanna take a wagon ride? A push down the gravel pit hillside. Mom! Trip to the hospital. Steph at age two in a full leg cast. I wondered about friends from long ago, enemies real or imagined, old boyfriends good and bad, classmates with whom I had lost touch. Where were they? What were they doing? How were they? If I'd had their addresses, I would have written letters to everyone I'd known since kindergarten.

I thought about having kids. When Charly and I first met we were in our twenties, and at that time I didn't want children, mostly because I didn't like them. I thought of them as short, snotty, whining alien creatures, and I couldn't imagine why I would want one of my own. I didn't want to change diapers, and I didn't want to spend my nights with a crying child. Charly didn't want children for more political reasons. The planet was already overpopulated and overtaxed. He thought it irresponsible to bring another child into the world for no reason other than society expected it.

But I was in my twenties then. At thirty-three something had started to shift. I was starting to think kids weren't so awful. I had started to think that a baby running around our woods sounded, well, nice. I wasn't sold on the idea, but I wanted to know it was an option. We'd had conversations a few times that usually went like this:

Me: "If we're not going to have children, let's do something more permanent. Taking the pill every night is ridiculous."

Charly: "I'll get a vasectomy."

And there it would end. I had talked to friends whose husbands had vasectomies about their decisions to not have kids, but still I couldn't come to a decision of my own. I couldn't end the option. Maybe this is intrinsic to my nature. Just like I couldn't let go of this canoe trip, I couldn't let go of the possibility of children. I didn't like dead-end roads. Anyway, with the half-hearted offer of a vasectomy, the conversation would end. I didn't encourage it and Charly didn't pursue it.

On Lake Winnipeg my mind wandered from the past to the present to the future and back. I wrote letters I would send later. I asked Dawn to read a eulogy at my funeral, and told her that I wanted to be cremated with my ashes spread at the family farm and at the Sioux River Beach as bagpipes played "Amazing Grace." I wrote a eulogy for my grandfather, who wasn't dead yet. I wondered in my journal how much one needed to relive the mistakes of the past before ranting like a lunatic. A few years after our trip, I had the pleasure of sitting next to a Jungian psychoanalyst. I described for him my mental state on Lake Winnipeg. He said he wasn't surprised; for an extrovert Lake Winnipeg was like a sensory-deprivation tank.

"People go mad in the desert," he said. "But, of course, you had Charly."

And I did. Even though I felt like I was losing it at times, my mind had never been so open to ideas, conversation, and literature. I started mentally writing my own novel, telling Charly the story about a mother and her dying anorexic daughter. My mother had once told me about a patient, a young woman who would probably die from starvation, and that the mother of the patient could do nothing. I couldn't get the image out of my head. We lived in the fattest nation on the earth, and yet we had young women starving themselves to death; we lived in the most medically advanced nation, and yet there was nothing to be done for a patient determined not to eat.

On the Fourth of July, we paddled alongside miles of limestone cliffs intermingled with long stretches of beach. The cliffs reminded me of the sandstone cliffs of Lake Superior—tall with trees holding tight on top. The limestone was a pale yellow, bleached white in some areas and stacked like little bricks that looked like an old castle in disrepair, complete with moss creeping up the side. We startled a beaver snoozing on a low limestone ledge and then took a photo before it clumsily jumped into the water.

"Not often you catch wildlife snoozing," Charly noted, always pleased to find a wild animal unaware.

For lunch we stopped at Lynx Bay, an old abandoned fish camp, and found Doug and Dana's names scratched into the door of the main cabin along with a collage of names from other windy days. We added ours: Julie Buckles and Charly Ray, July 1999, Lake Superior to the Arctic Ocean.

That afternoon we paddled near a long sandy stretch of beach.

"How about if we get out and pull the canoe?" I suggested, eager to move my legs.

"You pull and I'll steer."

The pulling was easy and the walking joyful. And steering was not necessary because a light breeze held the boat just offshore, so Charly pulled out his copy of Tolstoy's *Anna Karenina*, chosen for its density. I had brought *Two in the Far North*, a memoir by wilderness advocate Margaret E. Murie, and Louis de Bernieres' novel, *Corelli's Mandolin*, simply because they were at the top of my reading list. Lake Winnipeg provided our first moments to read. We discussed the characters of these books like they were members of our own family. Charly leaned back in the canoe and read aloud from *Anna Karenina* as I walked the canoe as if I were walking a well-mannered dog. Two major developments: Anna told Vronsky that she was pregnant. Vronksy competed in a steeplechase, made a fatal error, and broke his horse's back.

"Things don't bode well for Anna," I said.

I had read *Anna Karenina* in college, but quickly and under pressure. It was terrific to reread it with the luxury of time. I could only imagine the necessary pleasure that books once brought to people before movies, television, radios, and the internet. *Anna Karenina* transported me to turn-of-the-century Russia, a cosmopolitan place filled with tea parties and calling cards, where people danced the mazurka and spoke in French, English, and whatever else was in vogue.

Wind. We constantly stopped for wind coming off the nearby prairies and swirling around the big lake. Most days went like this: Start. Stop. Rest. Read. Start. Stop. Write. Sketch. Start. Stop. Start. Stop. We were actually using a page torn from an atlas for a map because no detail was needed. At twenty miles to the inch, our progress was barely visible. We paddled all day and looked back at the spot where we broke camp that same morning. The western shoreline rarely varied, so few landmarks existed to prove our progress. We sat windbound on Lake Winnipeg, our plans foiled, while the music played at the Winnipeg Folk Festival.

The few variations stood out from the monotony. White sand beach and a set of wolf tracks. White limestone beach vanishing into the skyline. Yellow sand beach, a boat wreck, and a black bear poking its head above the brush line. The bear trotted away, and Charly and I swam like we were on a Caribbean honeymoon. I cooked dinner on a rocky beach, and a white-tailed deer scampered down the shore. Charly set up camp, heard a snort, and turned around to face a black bear. He wasn't sure which one of them was more freaked out.

Charly's skin took on a leathery look. I had major biceps and weather-weary hands. We both applied balm to our hands nightly to keep them from cracking and bleeding. I felt downright crusty from the wind and sun. My fingers, hands, and wrists began to go numb from all the paddling, too stiff and sore to even hold a pen.

Charly and I paddled in silence most days, occasionally noting something unusual to look at. "Eagle at three o'clock," Charly would say. If I looked straight ahead that was twelve o'clock, directly to my right was three o'clock, behind me was six o'clock, and to my left was nine o'clock. We would have sung, but neither of us could hold a tune, nor could we remember more than segments of a song. To belt out a few lyrics—even a word—was cruel and unusual punishment because it would stick for days. I paddled for three days straight with the musical phrase, "Motoring. What's your price for flight?" in my head because Charly had said, "Let's motor."

Silence would be broken with random conversation.

"Do you replay your life's mistakes in your head?" I asked, turning around to look at Charly.

"Is that what you're doing? Like what?"

"I mean, what are you thinking about back there, Festus?" I laughed.

He was rubbing his wild beard, now bleached to blond with reddish tones.

"I've been on two other expeditions. I had a lot of thoughts then. I guess I worked them out. I thought a lot about my mom on the second one. She had died the November before. I felt guilty for working so much to earn money for the trip the last summer that she was alive. But I haven't had any of that this time."

"Then what are you thinking about?" I asked.

"What we should do when we get home. Should we have cows?"

Charly never could make up his mind if he wanted to be a nomadic hunter-gatherer or a farmer. So it didn't surprise me that while we were living the nomadic life, he would daydream about the other.

"Hah. Mmmmm. Maybe one. That's all we would need for ice cream, cheese, and milk," I said, enjoying the distraction. "But we'd have to be there to milk her twice a day."

"Can't you train them to milk once a day?" he asked.

"I know farmers who milk three times a day, but I've never heard of anyone milking once a day."

And so the game went—goats, pigs, chickens, horses, and crops.

"And what about kids?" I asked.

"What about them?"

"Should they be there on the farm?"

There was a long pause, with only the dripping of water off the paddle.

"You want kids?"

"I don't know, maybe."

"One or two?"

"Two, I think," I said, breathing, smiling.

"Well, someone's got to do chores."

I didn't turn around, but I could hear the smile in his voice. As usual, Charly surprised me. When I think about it, we made all our biggest decisions either in a canoe or on a portage. We made plans to travel to Maine to visit Helen Nearing during our first paddle together on the Potomac River. We decided we would move in together on a four-day canoe trip in northern Wisconsin. I threw out the marriage idea on a portage in the Boundary Waters. And now, paddling the expanse of Lake Winnipeg for twenty days in all, we had committed to the possibility of kids.

11

Elvis is in the House

"Have I ever told you about eating whale tail in Arviat?" Charly asked.
"Probably, but tell me again."
We had left Lake Winnipeg, portaged around the Grand Rapids Dam, and were now paddling across Cedar Lake toward the Saskatchewan River, a massive river that drains most of Canada's western prairie and even some of Montana. Paddling Cedar Lake was like floating over a graveyard. What appeared to be flat limestone islands thick with cedar trees were actually the tops of former hills. The lake had always been there—a rich resource for the Cree fishermen and trappers. But in 1963, with the installation of the Grand Rapids Dam, Manitoba Hydro had flooded the waterfalls, rapids, land, and—we would find out later—a village further upstream.

"My buddy Ricky and I were hanging out in Arviat on Hudson Bay for a few days waiting for a plane ride to Churchill, where we'd catch a train back to the States. A woman came running by with a wash basin, and this guy—a soapstone carver—told us, 'The whales are in.'"
"What kind of whales?"
"Belugas."
I looked down at the murky water pooled up in Cedar Lake behind the dam. Piles of dead trees lined the shoreline as far as I could see.
"We heard boats and gunshots, then saw two guys standing in front of the boats with rifles. They tied ropes to the tails and pulled the belugas to the crowded beach."

"What did you do?"

"We just stood back and watched them fill washbasin after washbasin with whale meat. Ricky and I were so into the culture and soaked every bit of it up—this was special."

"I bet."

"Some kids asked us if we'd like some whale tail, so we sliced off a piece with my Swiss Army knife."

"And?"

"Ate it."

"And?"

"Bland, rubbery."

"Good joke on the white guys."

"I've never been sure what to think," Charly laughed.

The beaches on Cedar Lake were made of limestone flakes, sharp in their newness, creating a challenge for landing our canvas canoe. Charly devised a system of hopping out of the canoe before we reached shore and positioning two of the ubiquitous pieces of driftwood, polished smooth by the elements, to make a roller ramp. I kept the boat steady and paddled forward onto our homemade ramp, later hopping out so we could roll the canoe above the sharp shards and place it further up onshore. Once we parked *Le Strubel*, we began hacking through the tangled trees onshore with an axe and a saw to carve out a spot to sit for lunch and to camp at night.

The next day we paddled toward Easterville, the only town on Cedar Lake according to our map. Charly wanted to gather clues for locating the Saskatchewan River on the other side of the lake. When Manitoba Hydro flooded Cedar Lake, they flooded the Chemawawin Cree Nation's village called the Old Post, which had been located at the meeting point of the Saskatchewan River and Cedar Lake. Whether the residents of the Old Post agreed to the deal remains disputed. Manitoba Hydro relocated the Cree people next to the small Métis village of Easterville, where they remain.

Easterville looked rough—run-down government housing, gravel and mud streets, no trees. An old man sat in a chair near the dock, a tape recorder in his lap playing bluegrass tunes. He stared blankly ahead grinning, sometimes laughing. I stayed at the dock watching the canoe while Charly walked to town to find someone who could provide directions to the main channel. Dropping my feet over the edge of the dock, I massaged my forearms—I suspected a minor case of carpel tunnel syndrome from all the paddling—and watched kids crawl, leap, and swim in the water. Some younger kids walked over to ask for a ride in my canoe. I smiled but shook my head no. A commercial fisherman approached, and I asked him about the location of the river. "Over there," he said, pointing with his chin in the general direction, but that much we already knew.

The next day, we passed the former mainland village of The Post, where a group of traditionalists had returned home to reclaim their town. They didn't offer any more help—just pointed their chins in the general direction. We'd have to find the river on our own. No small feat. It was a five-mile crossing to the river delta, which itself sprawled across another five miles or so of old river channels and islands. Flat, flat landscape without relief to mark anything. It is such a vast wetland that the Convention of Wetlands, an international initiative, recognizes it as a globally significant wetland—the largest freshwater delta in the world. Charly navigated most of our route with 1:250,000 maps, where one inch equals five miles. On the map the river channel is obvious, a thick blue line. But our canoe view showed only brushy islands, clumped together and stretching uniformly to the horizon north and south. We made our way for seventeen miles, stopping and starting to calibrate with the map, then five more miles through tall grasses. Through a combination of luck and skill, Charly found the current and steered us right to the mouth.

We had been heading upstream since Grand Rapids. Now we were heading upstream and against some serious current.

"Let's camp at the first spruce tree," Charly said toward evening, hoping for some dry ground as he surveyed the sprawling river delta. I fantasized aloud about a mowed lawn with a picnic table. Four hours later the sun skimmed the horizon, but midsummer twilight left plenty of light to paddle by. We gave up on the spruce tree and stopped to look at a few possible sites along the way, only to discover a torture chamber devised by beavers. The toothy rodents had chewed the alder thickets into lethal punji-like stakes, all about a foot high. Sleeping there would necessitate a major clearing effort with power tools. With the din of mosquitoes growing, we began to consider paddling through the crescent moonlit night. The river, nearly a mile wide, allowed us to paddle *Le Strubel* up the middle and escape most of the mosquitoes. We attempted to land a few times, but the whine of the mosquitoes chased us back to the middle of the river.

But then around a bend, like a scene out of an old Sunday evening Disney show, Charly spotted, of all things, a dock—an oasis in a desert of mosquitoes and sharpened stakes.

I rubbed my eyes.

"Look, Honey, maybe there's a picnic table," Charly joked as we neared the dock.

I rubbed my eyes again and looked out at a mowed lawn, cabin, sheds—and a picnic table, complete with a red-and-white tablecloth. Even though it was late, it was still light out, and I was not hallucinating. Unsure if anyone was home or not, we tied the canoe to the dock and walked hesitantly toward the cabin, swatting mosquitoes as we went. Charly knocked on the door while I looked around, amazed.

A man opened the door a crack, a twelve-gauge shotgun in his hand. By this point in the trip, I was not terribly alarmed by the firearm, and besides, I didn't care. I wanted to sleep and to escape the mosquitoes. A shotgun seemed a minor obstacle.

"I thought you were a bear," said the man, lowering the shotgun and opening the door wider. His name was Charlie LaVallee, a small man with black hair, dark complexion, and smiling eyes. "Canoeists?"

We both nodded.

"Mind if we camp in your yard?" I asked.

"Sleep here," he said, pointing inside at the floor. He didn't have to offer twice. We ran, skipped really, back to our canoe for our sleeping gear. The mosquitoes were so thick that we left everything in *Le Strubel*, just taking time to tie the canoe to the dock and grab our sleeping bags and air mattresses. His cabin was meticulously neat and tidy. On a stand next to his La-Z-Boy recliner sat a rotary phone and candy dish.

"Do you have phone service?" I asked, surprised by the telephone.

"No. My wife just thought I should have a phone. Bought it at a garage sale."

We laid out our sleeping pads and sleeping bags and crawled inside. It all seems so strange in retrospect—approaching a stranger's home and within five minutes setting up camp on his floor. I would never do it any other place, certainly not in an urban setting. But on the Saskatchewan River it made perfect sense.

"You two all set?" he asked.

"We're great," I said, scratching a mosquito bite on my ankle.

"Thanks so much," Charly added.

LaVallee lit a mosquito coil next to the woodstove and then lay down on his squeaky mattress in the cabin's corner.

The next morning over a cup of coffee, he told us that we had arrived at Pine Bluff, Manitoba, or what remained of it. It had once been an old trapping and fishing village of Métis—people of Aboriginal and European descent, and LaVallee had grown up here. In the 1930s and 1940s it was a town of eleven hundred people, five stores, and a school. Everyone had moved away, including LaVallee, but he kept the cabin for weekend use.

His yard was a popular camping spot for canoeists. He told us that the two women we had met on the Winnipeg River had stayed at the cabin too.

"How far do you go in a day?" he asked.

"Fifteen to twenty miles."

"You must be patient to go so slow."

I hadn't thought about the trip as an exercise in patience, but it was. I was learning that with one paddle stroke at a time, you could paddle your way across a continent. "I'll see you on the river," he said as we loaded our canoe and paddled away. "I have to go to town in a few days." By town he meant The Pas, located seventy miles upriver. He offered to give us a ride but we declined, ready to move on.

The Cree Indians called the Saskatchewan River *kisiskaciwanisipiy*, translated as "swift flowing." After only a few days on the river, Charly and I renamed it the Big Muddy Buggy—silt-laden water with steep muddy banks topped with thick brush. Plus we were paddling against the swift current that was moving at about six miles per hour. We ate lunch in the canoe and camped as late as we could because there was little to enjoy onshore. We didn't bother with cooking fires. Instead we stopped at dusk, set up the tarp and bug net, and jumped inside to eat peanut butter and crackers or granola and dried milk.

Three days and forty miles later, Charlie LaVallee motored up behind us. Looking even smaller in his large commercial fishing boat, he wore a red life jacket and a big smile. "Going to town," he said.

"Really," we replied.

I wouldn't ask, but I was hoping his offer still stood.

"Be there in an hour," he said.

It would take us two more days against the swift current.

"Hmmm."

The mosquitoes buzzed around my ear.

"Think I could fit your bags in my boat."

"Let's do it," I smiled.

We loaded our packs and canoe into his fishing boat and were soon blasting upriver at twenty miles per hour, grinning all the way. He drove us to the town dock, and Charly handed him a bag of wild rice as a gesture of thanks.

One of Manitoba's oldest and most historic cities, The Pas (pronounced pah), population fifteen thousand, provided our urban experience of the trip. We came for a night and stayed for five. A billboard posted on the outskirts of town claims The Pas as a "tourist paradise." Overstated perhaps, but it had its charms. Where else do you experience four men practicing Scottish bagpipes along the riverbank at sunset, a Ukrainian Orthodox church behind them?

People disagree about the origin of the city's name—some believe it is from the Cree word *W'passkwayaw* for "wooded narrows"; others think it is the French le *pas* for "step to the north." Local historian Clem Jones said it was a combination of both.

Clem owned the Kinsmen Kampground where we camped. Within an hour of our arrival, he had led us to a clump of nearby spruce trees to show us a scar in the trunk of one. "Here's where the Hudson Bay Company barges used to tie off," he reported. Noting our interest, he invited us for a personal tour aboard the *Lillian B.* up the Saskatchewan to the Carrot River. We stood next to Clem and were the only two people on the boat—this was a VIP tour. However, because he wanted the practice, he stayed in character, pulling down the microphone and using the loudspeaker to point out historic sites and wildlife as if there were twenty people on board. He ran daily riverboat tours, occasional bird-watching excursions, and the city tourist information center. In his former life, Clem had worked for the Royal Canadian Mounted Police, running dogsled teams on search and rescue missions.

It was on that tour that we sighted two men cruising in a lightweight racing canoe.

"That's Gib McEarchem and Ken Bell," Clem told us as they glided past with speed and ease, their strokes strong and confident. "Gib's a real interesting guy, you'll have to meet him."

Clem dropped us off at the dock where Ken and Gib were getting out of their canoe. Tall and athletic, Gib had striking white hair and a beard that would win him a blue ribbon at a Kenny Rogers look-alike contest. Ken was a broad-shouldered athletic type, probably half of Gib's age. It didn't take long for the four of us to become friends.

"Do you know where we could buy some paddles around here?" I asked. For nearly a thousand miles Charly had been using his sturdy but heavy Mohawk paddle. For five hundred miles I had used a light but flimsy paddle we had bought for a few bucks at a lumberyard in Pine Falls, before Lake Winnipeg. It seems odd now that we had overlooked good paddles considering we built our own canoe, but as we'd clambered through the pile of pretrip details, paddles had been an afterthought. We knew we needed paddles. The Pas was our first chance of finding some.

"Nah, no one has decent paddles. We'd have to get them from Winnipeg," Gib said, looking at Ken. "How long are you in town?"

We walked over to our canoe, locked inside Kinsman Kampground's fenced compound. Gib looked it over closely. He correctly assessed our E.M. White Guide wood and canvas canoe as a freight canoe, meaning big and sturdy, but not very fast. And our paddles, well, "That's not a paddle," Gib said of my lumberyard special. "That's a pushing stick. You'd break this with one good stroke."

I didn't doubt that Gib would. Turns out he had raced canoes professionally for twelve years in his youth. In 1967 he led the Manitoba team to victory in Canada's centennial Trans Canada 104-day, 3,300-mile canoe race. *Paddler* magazine named the race one of history's most epic expeditions. Gib was also a world-class cross-country skier and had raced in the first wave of the Birkebeiner, a fifty-two-kilometer cross-country ski marathon in northern Wisconsin that my dad and I skied every year. A bush pilot for thirty-odd years, Gib fought forest fires from the air in the summer. He either skied or headed for Mexico in the winter.

"Don't worry, you won't leave The Pas without good paddles," Gib said. "You need to do laundry? I'll pick you up tomorrow."

Later I stood in the bathroom of the Kinsmen Kampground staring in the mirror. I hadn't really caught an image of myself since the restaurant at Lac la Croix. The elements had significantly changed my looks. My face was baked and my hair blond. I had lost or redistributed about twenty pounds, and my biceps had evolved. I sheepishly raised my arms, looking around to make sure no one walked in, and flexed my right arm. Wow! Then with more gusto, I pulled my short sleeve up on my left arm and flexed hard. I had the arms of a weight lifter.

The next morning Gib and Ken picked us up for laundry and a tour of the airfield, including planes capable of scooping six tons of water in seconds. Gib's "house" was the highlight. He lived in a converted school bus decorated in eclectic fashion. Parked next to the worker headquarters at the airstrip, the yellow-and-black bus had a kayak and a Moosehead beer sign strapped to its side and moose antlers in the front.

That afternoon we read the newspaper—headlines reported the disappearance of John Kennedy Jr. Later we picked up our last resupply of food and our last batch of mail for the summer and then sat at our campsite reading letters aloud.

From my friend Ann, the one who dogsledded five hundred miles to Nome to tie the knot: *I envy the peaceful, even boring nature of your days of paddle, paddle, paddle. When my friend John and I paddled the Koyukuk River in the Brooks Range I can remember coming to a road house somewhere along the way and attaching myself like a leech onto any warm body who wanted to laugh and tell stories and exchange news. John was a somewhat serious fellow and I must have needed more comedy in my life. I persuaded him to stay another day so I could lounge around in the living room on beat up old arm chairs and drink stewed coffee with eggshells and listen to stories from the old farts who lived there.*

From Charly's sister, Kati: *The wedding was fun. Dad talked to everyone he could about your canoe trip. He is a very proud papa these days.*

From Charly's Uncle Dick: *We were so sorry to learn that your Dad's colon cancer is no longer in remission. I know how hard this must be on the two of you, being so far from him. Please keep us posted—your Dad is not a great communicator when it comes to his health, as you no doubt know.*

From Herb: *Dear Julie . . . Thanks for your note. I smiled at your comment that things were harder at times and at others easier than you imagined. I guess that's life in a capsule. Things you dread often turn out to be little or nothing. Things you think are no trick at all rear up and bite you.*

On our last night in The Pas, we stood in a loud, dark warehouse of a karaoke bar, drinking Budweiser. Ken and Gib had promised that for karaoke night an Eskimo man, or *Inuk*, would enter as Elvis, stay as Elvis, and leave as Elvis, never giving up the act. I had to see for myself. Gib showed up dressed in cowboy boots and cowboy hat, as if he weren't tall enough, and spent the evening avoiding certain women. "Good disguise," I joked with Ken and Charly.

The room began to fill, and gradually people approached the microphone, slaughtering innocent songs. We leaned against the bar breathing second-hand smoke for an hour or more before Ken reported, "Elvis is in the house." And sure enough there he was, all five feet of him. With his chest pumped, he walked slowly to the microphone and sang "Blue Suede Shoes." He didn't sing particularly well, or look, or even dress like Elvis. But he had the aura and attitude of the King, and he made us all smile. Charly and I walked out into the night at closing time and saw our first northern lights of summer, streaks of green and red hula hoopin' across the sky.

12

No Beginning, No End

The next morning, true to Gib's word, we left The Pas with first-class wooden paddles—Bending Branches brand from Wisconsin—light, strong, and sleek. Gib not only sent us off with paddles, he also handed us the keys to his brown van. "I'll come get it later," he said. We loaded the canoe and packs and drove fifty miles up the road to the Sturgeon Landing on the Sturgeon-weir River, foregoing another week on the Big Muddy Buggy. The Sturgeon-weir is a tributary of the Saskatchewan. Eric Morse writes in *Fur Trade Canoe Routes of Canada, Then and Now*, "To the voyageurs, who remembered only going up its rapids, it was the Riviere Maligne. Coming down it was sheer joy. The Sturgeon-weir is not recommended as an up-route, since the river's rate of drop (at four feet to the mile) is nearly an ideal gradient to come down."

Well, we had to go up and up we went. The Sturgeon-weir ran clear as a gin martini—Charly's preferred cocktail—the bottom flat with pock-marked limestone. It was shallow, steep, and rocky. Charly experimented with poling instead of paddling. He stood in the back of the canoe pushing with a long slender balsam pole he had carried along since Cedar Lake just for this purpose. He'd talked about it with Maine canoeist Garrett Conover, a fan of poling, when we were in Maine building our canoe. Charly wanted to try poling, and this was the river for it. He wore freshly washed tan cargo pants and a long-sleeved cotton shirt he'd picked up at a thrift store along the way. His hair was long and bleached and sprung out in all directions. He looked young, fit, and sexy as he pushed us up river while I paddled.

Charly switched back to paddling, and I hopped out of the canoe and pulled *Le Strubel* around and over rocks to avoid slicing her open on the limestone. I walked under a bridge that connected part of a Cree reserve to the rest of the reserve on the other side, looking up at a dark-haired kid on his bicycle looking down at me. I felt strong, rested, healthy, and happy—and it seemed my forearms had gotten enough rest. The numbness was gone.

Up the river we went walking, pushing, poling, and paddling. Grinning and giggling, we were thrilled to be back moving again in water that was neither too high or too low and working as an efficient team. The limestone shelves were a pleasure to walk on. No slip, no slide, no ankle-busting rollers—just shallow flat limestone with skid control. The water felt warm against my legs and the sun hot on my shoulders. We made our way up a long set of rapids by lining the canoe. I walked ahead around a bend where the water ran swiftly. While Charly pushed, I pulled, and suddenly *Le Strubel* burst forth. We both grinned ear to ear. That afternoon on a break at Birch Portage, sprawling out on an extravagant slab of limestone, I started reading *The Honk and Holler Opening*, a book sent by my friend Ann, who said she wanted to send something that "had absolutely nothing to do with the north woods." Charly napped. A man and woman floated by in their canoe, heading downstream, and stopped when they saw us. They were from Minnesota and were on a sixteen-day canoe trip. The man wore a T-shirt from the Birkebeiner.

"You do the Birkie?" I asked.

"Yes. We have a cabin near Seeley," he answered.

"We live just north of there."

"Small world."

"You're the second person I've met in the last week that has skied the Birkie," I told him, thinking of Gib.

We continued tromping upstream like draft horses for the rest of the afternoon. We pulled over to take a break in the shade. "Gib was telling me that there's a Saskaloppet race, kind of like the Birkie, in LaRonge in March. I'm thinking I could get Dad interested in doing it with me since we'd be sort of . . ."

"Hey, listen," Charly said, pointing skyward.

"For what?" I asked, giving Charly an I-was-talking-and-you're-being-rude look.

"Plane."

"And?"

"Might be Gib."

We both peeked out from under our shade trees and saw a big bright-yellow water-bomber plane.

"It is Gib!" I exclaimed. We waved but he couldn't see us in the shade.

"Nice to know he's up there looking out for us," Charly said.

Three windy days later, we walked through one last boulder field and pulled the canoe to deep Amisk Lake, the divide between the lower and upper parts of the Sturgeon-weir River.

"Three days to do twenty-two miles. Not bad," I joked.

"I knew that was going to be a tough stretch. I wasn't disappointed."

We returned to paddling exclusively, albeit into the wind, next to big flat rocks and tall limestone cliffs topped with black spruce. We crossed the windy lake, digging deep and keeping our heads down, and the next day we found the river again. We cruised by a few cabins with flimsy corral-like structures and a sign that informed, "Fishing is closed October–May due to pressure on walleye."

"That's a good sign," Charly said.

"How so?"

"It means motors can navigate this section of the river in summer, which means the river is deep enough to paddle."

He was right. We paddled along with nary a rock in our way. That afternoon, as bedrock shifted from limestone back to the pink Canadian Shield, we passed by a graveyard with several dozen white crosses. There was a reserve marked on the map but no sign that there was a village, except for the cemetery. Someone maintained it enough to keep the brush down and crosses white. A child-size church sat at the center, overlooking the graves.

"It would make sense that there was a village here," Charly said. "We're just downstream from Stanley Mission, the site of the oldest church in Saskatchewan."

Because we were ahead of schedule, and because we had already finished thirteen hundred miles with only four hundred remaining before we reached Wollaston, we decided that if we found a good campsite we'd take a day off. Scoop Rapids fit the bill. A narrow rapids spilling over granite, Scoop Rapids had pelicans for entertainment and an established campsite complete with fire pit and saw-carved seats. In his book *The Lonely Land*, Sigurd Olson writes that "according to the Crees, travelers could always dip out a fish from a shallow pool at the lower end [of Scoop Rapids]. Someone long ago, they said, had left a scoop net there for that purpose, each user leaving it in the same place for the next one coming through."

Charly and I unloaded the canoe then paddled below the rapids.

While Charly fished, I watched pelicans dive, fight, and scoop fish. The comical birds jockeyed for position at the eddy below the last drop of the rapids. The current flushed out a school of minnows, and the pelicans stuck their ridiculously long bills, heads, and necks underwater, their bright-orange feet kicking in the air. Then it was back to jockeying for position.

The next morning Charly caught a walleye, eyed the greedy pelicans, and decided to gut it immediately. We hunted for mushrooms, sometimes sinking knee-deep in the soft, moist mossy forest floor. Mushrooms sprouted everywhere—slippery jacks, puffballs, boletes, and strawberries and cream that looked just like its name. Charly inspected each individual mushroom, judging freshness. If deemed worthwhile, he identified them with his book, determined if they were edible, and then gave them the nod or the drop. We picked a quart of blueberries and ate all we wanted on the spot. The temperatures cooled and the bugs disappeared.

A contingent of travelers walked into camp that night, planning to portage around the rapids. Two young men were guiding one's dad and his German friends. Charly invited them to camp with us, and they didn't hesitate. One of them had swamped a canoe earlier, so three of them were wet and none of them had eaten dinner. They unloaded a semi-load of duffel bags and gear plus six coolers. They were out paddling for five days, the son told us, but only going thirty "clicks," or kilometers. He commented on our tarp setup, which he called a "hootchie."

Rain pounded on our canvas tarp, every bit as intoxicating and comforting as our steel roof back home. Our German guests and their friends sang songs into the night as Charly continued reading *Anna Karenina* by candlelight, and I soaked up a *National Geographic* I had purchased in The Pas. One story featured the Yellowstone River, and soon Charly and I started talking about another canoe trip—down the Yellowstone. The German chorus and rhythmic sound of the rapids and raindrops lulled me into deep slumber, atop a comfortable bed of sphagnum moss.

Moving camp the next morning felt as routine as making the bed or doing the dishes. Somewhere between Lake Superior and here, this excursion began to feel less like a trip and more like a life. We were gypsies on the go. We slipped out of camp before our guests stirred. Pelicans continued to bob, dive, jockey, and float. River otters, too curious to swim away, hissed at us as they swam in circles. A young black bear on the other side of the river rooted for berries, and we slowly crossed over for a photograph. It lumbered to shore, scratched its ear, and lay down with its paws stretched out in front. But then it caught our scent, scrambled to its feet, and ran away through the woods.

We passed two canoes carrying three men and a boy just before the last rapids of the day.

"Are you from Minnesota?" one asked.

"Wisconsin."

"Close enough. I noticed your Wintergreen jackets. I'm from Duluth."

"Washburn," Charly laughed.

"I read about your trip in the paper," he said.

"Small world," I said.

He and his crew—two older men and his son—were out on a ten-day trip from LaRonge to Flin Flon. They had a copy of *The Lonely Land* and were reading it out loud to one another each night.

"Good to meet you," I said as we pulled away.

"Hey, have you heard about the Frog Portage?" he asked.

"No, is it pretty bad?" Charly asked.

"You'll be surprised . . . "

Two days later we neared Pelican Narrows, the second-to-last town on our route before reaching our winter home at Wollaston. We spotted graffiti on granite rocks—"'99 Jason Vern, '99 Tamishe, Robbie, Wes"—and knew we were near. We ate lunch and took a nap. "Go in from a point of strength," Charly said, reciting the mantra we used for entering towns along the way.

We paddled to the town dock, located next to a small beach with broken glass. I had the feeling I was playing out a scene from an old western. Stranger rides into town. Townspeople take notice. They stop, turn around, peek past the kitchen curtain, and shut doors in preparation for trouble. Pelican Narrows was an end-of-the-road Cree reserve where English was the second language. We walked down the shaky dock past old snowmobiles parked for the summer; past laundry hanging on lines in no particular order; past shacks, boarded-up houses, and powerlines; past dark-haired children, to the Northern Store (formerly called the Hudson's Bay Company). A small group of men and woman who stood near the entrance watched us enter the store that carried standard WalMart fare—huge televisions, diapers, and groceries. The apples were wrinkled, the blueberries outrageously priced at four dollars a pint and available in the wild not far from the front door. On the other hand, bananas from Ecuador could be had for fifty-nine cents a pound.

A woman walked next to us. "Is that your little red canoe?"

"Uh huh," I responded, nodding my head in the affirmative.

"Where you come from?"

"Wisconsin."

She did not respond.

"The United States," Charly added.

"Ohhhh."

We purchased stale flour, Tang, eggs, and butter before paddling out of town. We camped that night above a set of rapids and slept to the sounds of running water, restless bird life, motorboats, and distant gunfire—presumably some hunter. The next morning we enjoyed a lazy couple of hours around camp. Charly slept as long as I did now. With Lake Superior and Lake Winnipeg behind us, neither one of us got nervous enough to force the other to go. We laid everything out on sun-soaked rocks to dry, then jumped into the lake and bathed. I trimmed Charly's bleached locks, watching them fall to the mossy ground. He trimmed the sides of his beard, which made him look biblical.

Later that day, we paddled past a cluster of cabins at the narrows of Wood Lake. An older Cree woman hoed her garden, and two boys cut grass with sickles. Wild rice grew at the edges of the river. We were at the northern edge of our home ecosystem. The boys ran to the dock to ask where we were going. They had not heard of Wollaston Lake or Wisconsin. We were in the twilight zone—no one knew where we were from or where we were going except for an occasional Minnesotan.

We kept pushing our way upstream as the river dwindled smaller and smaller, winding back and forth until we came to Frog Portage. The locals had laid a set of tracks complete with a cart to roll boats and gear across the portage. "This *is* a surprise!" I exclaimed. We loaded our packs and gear and pushed it the half mile over surprisingly flat ground, considering that were crossing a height of land that separated two watersheds. Historically the Frog Portage was critical to the fur trade, providing an important pathway between the Churchill River and the Sturgeon-weir. The book *Canoeing the Churchill: A Practical Guide to the Historic Voyageur Highway* reports that explorer Alexander Mackenzie in the 1700s told a story about the Frog Portage. He wrote:

"It is necessary to cross the Portage de Traite, or, as it is called by the Indians [Cree] . . . Portage of the Stretched Frog-Skin, to the Missinipe [River]. . . . The Missinipi, is the name which it [Churchill River] received from the [Cree], when they first came to this country, and either destroyed or drove back the natives, whom they held in great contempt, on many accounts, but particularly for their ignorance in hunting the beaver, as well as in preparing, stretching, and drying the skins of those animals. As a sign of their derision, they stretched the skin of a frog and hung it up at the Portage."

The government historical marker—shot full of bullet holes—told a similar story in three languages: English, French, and Dene (formerly called Chippewyan). It was amazing to walk to the other side of the trail, see the Churchill River, and realize we had paddled from Wisconsin to the Churchill River.

"Looks like the desolate north," Charly said, pleased.

13

The Desolate North

Billy seemed sulky and when I told him to cook some oatmeal, I thought I heard him say "Damn the oatmeal." For supper he only ate bread and cocoa, giving no explanation. I was very tired and went straight to bed.
– Ernest Oberholtzer, 1909 trip journals of his travels with Billie Magee

The Churchill River! I grinned and Charly grinned as we loaded packs into the canoe. The Churchill River said to us, "Hey, kids, you've come a hell of a long way." This was true north, way north, and up north. I looked at the historic river that the voyageurs, Cree, and Dene had paddled for hundreds of years—hunting, moving furs, and bringing home supplies. The trees alongshore were charred from fire in the recent past. The river ran low, exposing ten vertical feet of rocky shoreline with a bathtub ring where the waterline had been.

The voyageurs would have taken a left at Frog Portage and paddled upstream to Lac Ile-a-la-Crosse, where they spent their winters. We took a right, pointing *Le Strubel* with the current for the first time since the Winnipeg River. We planned to paddle down the Churchill for only twenty-one miles to the Reindeer River and then head upstream to Reindeer Lake. Paddling with the current but against the wind, we stopped after two exhausting miles at the mouth of the Pickerel River, a river Charly had traveled during his first northern canoe expedition in 1984— a 17-day, 190-mile trip.

"Big adventure for a sixteen-year-old suburban kid," he said.

"Do you recognize it?" I asked.

"Not really, but it feels familiar."

We sat out of the wind below the long flowing rapids that feed the Churchill, while our pizza baked in the Dutch oven. The air cooled my skin—no humidity with just a light breeze in our protected spot. The sun ducked under puffs of clouds, then out again into the deep-blue sky. I alternated between my tattered wool sweater and my cotton T-shirt, depending on the clouds.

Boyhood summers vacationing at Coon's Lodge in northern Wisconsin had sparked Charly's initial interest in wilderness. To be precise, the fishing got his attention. He caught his first fish on Trout Lake at Coon's Lodge, and he and the perch were hooked. "When I close my eyes and think of home, I can definitely smell and feel Winnetka, but just as much, I smell and feel Coon's Lodge," Charly had told me earlier in the trip.

By all family accounts, Charly became obsessed with fishing. He and his friends fished the nearby pier at Lake Michigan as well as the golf course water-hazard ponds. To earn money for fishing tackle purchases, young Charly dug up nightcrawlers and sold them to bait stores. He tried to convince his mother to pay for his bait with the reasoning that if salmon cost seven dollars a pound and he caught a six-pound fish, it was well worth her investment of a few dollars for bait. She bit and bought the bait for him. His buddy Jim, of the musk-ox story, returned from a June church group trip to the Boundary Waters with stories of catching more fish than the group could eat. So when Charly's church youth group organized an August Boundary Waters trip, Charly signed on. But by August the fish had retreated to the bottom of the lakes to beat the heat, and he got skunked. Still, he fell in love with the country.

Charly started searching for a wilderness canoe camp and found it in Camp Manitowish, located near Coon's Lodge in northern Wisconsin. He registered for their "Pioneer Trip" and the next summer headed to Saskatchewan and to this spot. Following the Camp Manitowish wilderness tripping trajectory, the following summer Charly hiked the Beartooth Mountains in Montana for twenty-two days. And the summer after that, for his "Expeditionary Canuk," he paddled for forty-nine days, seven hundred miles from Wollaston Lake to Hudson Bay.

"That's when I started dreaming of paddling from home to Wollaston Lake," he said.

"And here we are," I said.

"You know what I do remember?" Charly asked. "I vividly remember catching a northern pike the size of my leg at some falls. Kettle Falls, I think.

I awoke two mornings later to the sound of silence—loud, loud silence. Two days of howling wind had forced us to stop, start, wait, and start again. We'd only gone thirteen miles since we started down the Churchill.

"Hear it?" I asked Charly, who was curled against me.

"The wind died."

"Let's go."

It was so quiet, I could hear the humming of dragonflies and flapping of a loon's wings overhead. Another loon called through the mist. We packed quickly and pushed off. It wasn't even six yet.

"It feels like we're flying through the clouds," Charly said, looking down at his compass to get a reading. We were heading across Uskik Lake, which is a few miles wide, and couldn't see much shoreline with the thick mist rising off the river. Charly anticipated a portage around Kettle Falls and didn't want to be on the wrong side as we approached.

"Look there," I said, pointing with my paddle at a small island thick with spider webs dipped in dew, lit by the sun, refracting through the fog. I paddled in the front, breathing in the coolness. It was only the first of August and it felt like autumn, like Halloween weather, when you can see your breath and know that the snow will fly soon, but not yet. I could hear ducks splashing. I could feel their restlessness, their anticipation. They would start heading south in the next few weeks. I looked back at the iridescent webs, pushing my paddle easily through the water.

The fog lifted like a theater curtain, letting the sun take center stage, and I pulled off my sweater. A sleeping pelican floated near shore. An eagle sat in a burned-out tree, then took off on a fishing expedition, the tree swaying from its force. I heard the rush of Kettle Falls well before we landed at the portage. Charly grabbed Josephine and started over; I took Holy Boy and followed. He stopped and, like a bird dog, pointed to a patch of blueberries. I started picking and shoving blueberries into my mouth. Tart, tangy, and juicy blueberries. Fresh, flavorful, firm blueberries. Blue on the outside, pinkish-white on the inside. The wild ones are smaller than commercial berries, but they pack so much more punch. Small blue marbles of absolute heaven.

"There's enough here for breakfast," I yelled to Charly and pulled a Nalgene container from my daypack. I wore rubber knee-high boots, my

Army surplus pants, and a tie-dyed T-shirt. I didn't bother to drop Holy Boy. I was so strong and so excited about the blueberries that a forty-to-fifty-pound pack on my back was just a slight inconvenience.

"I can't believe you," Charly said, referring to the pack. He had gone to the other side of the portage, dropped Josephine, and returned. "I knew you were part black bear, but this is ridiculous."

"Go get more Nalgene containers," I said. There were so many berries that I finally dropped Holy Boy and filled two quart containers. Charly filled our mugs. We both snacked on pin cherries and a few Juneberries then harvested rosehips for tea.

At the other side of the portage, overlooking the rapids, I poured a bowl of granola and piled blueberries on top. We had finished the portage and now relaxed, enjoying the literal fruits of our labors, my fingers stained purplish blue.

"So, is this the spot?" I asked, stretching out on a rock to take a nap.

"The what?"

"The historic falls where Charly Ray caught his monster pike."

There was a long pause, then he said, "Must be Atik Falls."

We paddled a short distance to Atik Falls. Pelicans bobbed for minnows in the roaring rapids. This was our exit ramp for the Reindeer River. I looked back at the Churchill River, watching it ribbon its way down a long river valley. Charly jumped into a deep hole below the rapids and I followed. The water, cool and clear, left my skin tingling in the hot summer sun.

"This isn't it either," Charly laughed.

"We're on a quest to find the famous fishing spot."

"Maybe Steep Hill Rapids."

The shoreline of the Reindeer River region had burned recently, leaving a charred landscape of little black sticks over new green vegetation. We paddled upriver all afternoon past blackened trees. "The land of little sticks" is often used to describe this country near the treeline. About three hundred miles north of us lay the border of the Northwest Territories and Nunavut, where the trees no longer grew due to cold and wind.

"There's more water in the Reindeer. It looks as big as the Churchill," Charly said, pushing his paddle into the stream to get a depth reading. "Gives me hope we'll find good water upstream. And I bet we'll see a moose along this stretch."

"I'm beginning to doubt that they exist. We haven't seen one since . . . since . . . I don't know, that one swimming near International Falls?" I asked, taking a paddle stroke.

"We're off the main highway and onto the back roads, Baby. We'll see a moose."

A tailwind helped push us upstream the next day.

"Let's rig a sail," Charly suggested.

I steered the canoe toward shore. Charly pulled out his axe and cut down two small trees and stripped the branches. He pulled out a dark-blue tarp from Madame Boudreau. The poles formed a cross and the tarp was attached to both, taking the shape of, well, a sail. It worked. The wind, not nearly as strong as the day we sailed on Lake of the Woods, pushed us forward, and no motorboats threatened to run us over. Charly used his feet and hands to hold the contraption, while I kept paddling and steering.

We sailed beneath a power line stretched across the river. "I don't remember a power line," Charly said, referring to his Pioneer Trip. "When did they put that in?"

We paddled and sailed until dusk, camping that night at Steep Hill Rapids. Charly fished the rapids. I was hungry—too hungry—and grew agitated, pacing behind Charly, who was fishing instead of cooking.

Recognizing the signs, Charly suggested, "Hey, Hon, why don't you eat something?"

"I'd rather wait for dinner," I muttered and left to go set up our bed for the night.

He caught two walleye then with painstaking care, cleaned and filleted them.

"When are you going to fry those fish?" I asked, hands on my hips.

"Uh. Now," he said. Crouching next to the stream, he rinsed blood and scales from his hands. "Why don't you have a snack?"

"I'm sick of goddamned dried fruit and nuts," I said, sounding something like Linda Blair in *The Exorcist*. It wasn't a logical or true statement, considering I'd eaten picked-off-the-bush blueberries and fresh fish the past few days. I stomped off to inflate the air mattresses. I continued muttering about the lousy campsite. The bed was lumpy, rain-soaked, and tilted. The rapids too loud. Charly fried the fish, and we ate in silence, the tender flavorful white meat filling me until I felt foolish.

I licked my fingers and looked at my feet, composing an apology in my head. Charly showed no interest in starting the conversation. He watched the river and purposefully chewed his food—one bite, then another.

"Sorry, I kind of lost it," I said.

"Eat something next time."

I gritted my teeth. I stared hard at a stick circling in an eddy, held by the current. My eyes followed its futile journey as I debated whether to continue the squabble, holding on like that eddy, or whether to just to let it go. I ate the last of the blueberries, tasting their subtle sweetness, and stood to do dishes.

The weather shifted in the night, bringing cool temperatures and a stiff northern wind. We crossed the river and climbed the short but aptly named Steep Hill Portage. On the other side, we faced a sea of two-foot whitecaps. "Let's leave after lunch," Charly said. With a few hours to kill, I decided to start a fire, heat water, and string up our black plastic shower bag. I poured hot water into the bag that also doubled as a dry bag, then set about finding a tree that was tall enough and sheltered enough for a shower.

Charly wandered off to look for mushrooms. I looped a rope over a sturdy branch, pulled until the shower was at the right height, and looped the rope around the tree trunk. While doing this, from the corner of my eye, I spotted the largest, plumpest, rosiest wild raspberries I'd ever seen. I started to pick and eat and pick and eat. I ate a pint, or maybe a quart—enough so I could focus on my shower, dry off, and dress. Once clean, I returned to picking and plucking, and I filled every container I could find.

"Look at you, little bear," Charly laughed, finding me in the midst of a brambled mess.

"Look at these!" I exclaimed.

And he was impressed. For the trip, Charly rationed himself to two photos (slide film) per day. Digital photography? Not even in our vocabulary then. He used one of those precious shots to photograph my overflowing containers. A photo that would have sent Martha Stewart up the Reindeer River. The wind blew. We ate lunch. The wind blew. Charly hunted for mushrooms. The wind blew. I organized my daypack. The wind blew. Charly caught two more walleye for dinner. He used his second photo on a group shot of walleye, mushrooms, and raspberries. This was a fresh food frenzy. For dinner that night, we dined on fried fish and mushrooms served on a bed of couscous, then treated ourselves to tapioca with fresh raspberries for dessert.

"Looks like we're camping here tonight," I said, eating a spoonful of tapioca.

"Not a bad place to be windbound," he said over the roar of the rapids.

"I don't suppose this is the site of the alleged big fish."

Charly shook his head. "I don't know where I caught that fish."

We stayed for two days of windy, cloudy, cold weather. With so much time, I took another shower, cooked hashbrowns and sausage, made chili, boiled tea water. I picked raspberries, keeping all the containers full. I did laundry and inventoried our food. It looked as if we'd have enough for another twenty days, which was how far we were from Wollaston. How strange it was to be twenty days away from our winter destination.

A local fishing guide pulled onto our beach. He had a camp with two cabins two miles away. I asked him about a cross I had noticed marked on the rocks near the rapids. He told us that about four years ago, two drunken guys were horsing around in their motorboat. Their motor gave out, and they were swept down the rapids without life jackets.

The third day we woke to a still-cool, foggy morning. I picked more raspberries for the trail. Charly caught another walleye and fried it for breakfast, serving it with wild rice and raspberries and leftover tapioca on the side. Rested and full on fresh fruit and fish, we quickly paddled to a pictograph that the guide had told us about. It was small and looked like part of the rock had broken off. I could only distinguish a pine tree and what could have been the tail of a fish. It started to rain, so we ducked into the forest. Wearing our anoraks, red and tan, we sat on thick green moss with a light rain misting down on us. We didn't talk, just sat and listened to the rain. I knew we were near town because I could hear howling dogs in the distance.

14

Attend!

"Want to see my dead rabbit?" asked a small Cree boy, holding out a shoebox.

"God, no. Don't open that lid," I responded.

Five grade-school-age boys played on the dock at Southend, a small village built on a hilly island at the south end of 150-mile-long Reindeer Lake. The boys hadn't heard of Wisconsin, but they knew Wollaston. "You're *paddling* all the way there?" the boys asked wide-eyed.

"All the way," I smiled. From our perspective, we were in the home stretch. I took a quick survey of the town. The store was at the bottom of the hill, near the dock, and the houses worked their way upward. Teenage boys sat in a motorboat on their way out to catch fish, and to hunt moose if the opportunity arose. One kid told us he shot six a year, mostly in the summer and fall.

"We haven't seen a moose in eleven hundred miles," I said.

"What do you do with the hides?" Charly asked.

"Mostly give them to the elders," he replied. The teenagers motored away, and Charly and I walked toward town, past the young kids with the shoebox .

After weeks of solitude, Charly and I seized up in the face of so much stimulation along with the pressure of a deadline. Everything closed at five and it was already late afternoon. We needed to divvy up who would do what and in what order. After thirty minutes of negotiation and debate, we decided I would head to the post office and then the grocery store. Charly would go directly to the Ministry of Natural Resources to find information on routes through Reindeer Lake.

As we walked up the road, a stranger pointed Charly in the direction of the Natural Resources office. I headed to the post office and met a man walking with two huskies. Dressed in a classic green wool vest that looked oddly out of place here, he introduced himself as the brother of Tommy, who owned 140 sled dogs tied up outside of town. We had passed the dogs earlier on our way into town. They looked well fed and cared for, a relief considering the endless stories I had heard of dogs let loose on islands—and sometimes forgotten—for the summer.

"I'm interested in maybe putting together a small team for the winter," I told him. Charly and I had dogsledded with our friends John and Mary Thiel, the same friends who had given us Knock-Knock, and had thought about setting up a kennel ourselves.

"There's twenty-two racing mushers at Southend and a few in Wollaston," he said. "You'll find dogs. People are always selling and buying."

I picked up two packages at the post office—one from Dawn and another from our neighbor Judy Peyton—then walked to the Northern Store to call home. I dialed from the pay phone located inside the door next to the candy machines. A handwritten sign said that cigarettes had not come in for two weeks. Dad answered the phone and must have had a map nearby because he knew exactly where I was calling from. People walked past, curious about the stranger in town. Dad filled me in on Grandpa's ninetieth birthday party at the farm. Charly walked past, apparently back from the Natural Resources office, and bought a Mr. Big bar and a Drumstick ice cream cone. I told Dad I needed to go and would call him again when we got to Wollaston.

With fifteen minutes until closing, Charly took the phone, showing me that a mouse had beaten him to the inside of his Mr. Big and that his Drumstick had no cone. I walked inside. The store didn't sell vanilla extract, whole-wheat flour, or more than one flavor of Pop Tarts, but it had three sizes of canvas wall tents—a fact that delighted Charly to no end. I bought a few items. Charly had to cut off his conversation with Mike because the store was closing up, so we returned to the Natural Resources office, where Charly had spotted a phone booth. The pay phone had been ripped off its cord, but the staff inside let Charly use their phone.

I was sitting in the canoe ready to open my two precious packages when two girls approached. More than anything, I wanted to sit by myself and read those letters, but I didn't want to be rude. After all, this may be my last chance for interaction with another human being other than my husband for twenty days. They were the daughters of the town's Pentecostal priest and said they had moved twenty or more times in their lives. The two girls peppered me with questions about Charly, the canoe, the trip. Then they left, returning with a backpack. "We're going hiking," they said as they walked off.

I returned to the beautiful letter sent by Judith. She had sketched a slice of Bayfield apple and a Lake Superior seagull feather onto thick purplish paper. Judith had loopy legible handwriting, and she twirled and swirled words from home around the sketches. Spring rains had flooded our valley, the strawberries had ripened and plumped to extraordinary sizes, and neighbors' gardens looked huge and lush. *Listening to the news of the disappearance of JFK Jr.'s plane this morning, I can report with relief that everyone you and I know seems to be thriving.*

I tucked it away, smiling, and pulled out a letter from Dawn. *Hey girl, LOVE your letters. They transport me and make me manic like you obviously are."*

I grinned some more and read and reread both letters, taking in all the news from home—both trivial and important. Charly returned from an hour of talking through details of home life—rental issues mostly. Finally, in the fading light, we paddled out of town.

"Dad says he's heading to Ober Island the last week of August, and they're still planning to come up at Halloween." I reported.

"How was your grandpa's party?"

"Great, of course. I guess they had a hundred or so people at the farm."

"Sad you're not there?"

"Yeah. But happy to be here too. What did you find out from Natural Resources?"

"Good news. The grayling start thirty miles or so up the Reindeer— 'fish 'em in the shallows,' they told me." The presence of Arctic grayling was yet another sign of our northern progression.

He continued with his report between paddle strokes. "That power line we passed under is Sask Power's line to Black Lake. It's been put in since my Pioneer Trip. They recommended that we take a shortcut through Reindeer Lake, up Numbian Bay to Nokomis to Swan Bay. I'll show you on the map when we get to camp."

We stopped for the night just out of sight of town, the northern lights circling and dancing above. I wore my extra-large blue-striped men's flannel pajamas. Charly wore a short-sleeved T-shirt and his pointy brown wool hat brought back from Peru by his dad. We ate the spoils of my shopping excursion —smelly sardines, mustard, and crackers—inside the bug net and under the tarp. I know—the worst possible trail etiquette, unless one wants to lure a bear. But what the heck!

I announced that, for a change of pace, I would get up first the next morning and make breakfast. Charly roused me at sunrise by asking a long string of detailed questions—"How are you going to make the crepes? What pan are you going to use? Do we have all the ingredients?"—until I couldn't stand it anymore and got up. The sun filtered through the fog traveling down lush green hills and valleys and wrapping around Big Island, where Southend was located. Charly lay in bed, watching me combine and mix fresh eggs, flour, hydrated milk, salt, and butter and fry crepes over the fire—just a few seconds on each side. I rolled them and served them with freshly picked blueberries and melted butter and sugar.

Loons yodeled continually in preparation for their flights south. "I think I've been out too long," I said. "The loons are really getting on my nerves. Some peace, please!" Charly laughed and started a series of jokes about hunting loons.

Later in the day, after a soaking thunderstorm, we paddled near little waterfalls and rivulets trickling against solid granite into the lake. Everything was washed clean and green and sparkled in the sunlight. We skinny-dipped at lunch and I paddled topless, much to Charly's delight, in the afternoon. For three months he had not seen magazines, billboards, movies, television, or even many live women; so in his eyes, I was the sexiest thing on the planet. We listened on and off to the CBC into the evening: the Russian economic crisis and the Canadian farm crisis, "Dead Dog Café," and a program about how everyone has a twin or soulmate somewhere.

"Who do you think is most like you?" Charly asked.

"Mom."

"Really?"

"Really."

"I don't think of you two as anything alike."

"You're kidding, right?"

"Name a few things."

"My love for reading. My need and appreciation for female friends. Love for travel. Curiosity about the world. I could go on."

"Hmmm. Well, that's interesting that you would say that. I don't think of my dad and me as being anything alike."

"Hah."

"Tell me how we're alike."

"You're both cerebral, analytical, fair. You both really like to have things done correctly. You're not crazy about chaos or noise or messes. Your interest in politics, current events, foreign affairs, and economics. All your dad."

"I suppose . . . "

After a brutal day of portaging the local so-called shortcut fighting a flock of black flies, we camped on a small island on an unnamed river. Charly fished while I sat and scratched the back of my neck. He was gambling with a favorite lure, hoping for a wary walleye or even a grayling, so he didn't use a steel leader to protect his lure from a toothy, aggressive northern pike. I watched as the pike broke the line and swam off with the lure. Charly cussed, then quickly put on a pikey Rapala with a steel leader and cast the line, counting on the fact that pike are fairly dim in the backcountry. Charly had the last word, catching the pike a second time—his favorite lure still dangling from the pike's mouth. He fried the dumb pike with some hawk's-wing mushrooms and dried onion and made wild rice cakes on the side. We ate on the point of the island, watching grayling surface for the evening hatch of flies on the river.

"How about a game of canasta?" I asked.

"I hate canasta," he replied, deadpan.

I laughed at his insider joke. The second winter that Charly and I lived together, we reserved a primitive winter cabin in the Upper Peninsula of Michigan and invited my parents and Charly's dad to join us. Dad and Herb skied downhill. Charly and I skied cross-country. Mom stayed at the cabin and read a novel. That evening, the room lit with lanterns and candles, Mom sat at the head of the wooden table and told us about canasta, a card game that she had learned from her grandmother. She pulled from a cloth bag a single-spaced legal-size page of instructions that she had typed. She had made copies for everyone. We were all tired, but Dad, Charly, and I rallied, making eye contact, nodding when appropriate.

Herb didn't respond. He leaned against the wall, willing his body as far away from the group as the light allowed, hunched over, reading a thick Robert Ludlum paperback. Mom handed out the rules, placing Herb's on the table in front of him and waxed on about her sentimental associations with this complicated card game. Charly, in an effort to engage Herb, said, "Dad, didn't you used to play canasta?"

Herb glanced up. "I hate canasta," he replied and returned to his book.

As we were paddling the next day I leaned back in the canoe and shouted in my best theatrical diction, "Attend! We have heard of the thriving of the throne of Denmark, how the folk-kings flourished in former days, how those royal athelings earned that glory." Dawn had sent *Beowulf* at my request. Charly and I couldn't really make sense of this first epic adventure of English literature, but it sounded great when read aloud.

Floating next to cliffs, Charly jigged for trout. Some guy at Southend told him to use pike guts—but no luck. Charly speculated that perhaps the pike-guts advice was a good local joke on tourists. I read more of *Beowulf* aloud until I sensed no one, meaning Charly, was listening any longer. I set the book aside and leaned back, closing my eyes and listening to water lap against the canoe.

Since we planned to layover for a few days, we debated about our campsite that night like we were buying our first new car. Eventually we decided on a long sandy beach on Reilly Lake. Munching on granola and blueberries for our beachside dinner, we watched fish rise to the surface.

The half-moon, already in the sky, brightened as the sun descended, loons cried, and a plover walked by. There were so many fish rising to the surface that the water looked like it was boiling. They were so close to the beach that Charly couldn't sit still any longer. He picked up his rod, tied on a spinner, and cast. The line hit the water and a fish grabbed the bait. Charly expected grayling; he got a good-size northern pike. Charly threw it back. He cast again. Bam. Another northern pike. He caught and released a few more before he leaned the rod back against the bush.

"Canasta?" he asked.

We lay in our sleeping bags, playing cards.

"Okay, here's the deal. Tomorrow morning, let me sleep in," I said.

"Sure."

"No, I mean it. No chatter. No, 'What should we do today?' No, 'What do you want for breakfast?'"

"No problem."

The next morning I slept until a decadent eight thirty. I woke alone. Looking out through the bug net, I watched Charly putter—stacking wood, sorting through packs, and starting breakfast. I walked out and gave him a kiss. "Thanks," I said.

"It nearly killed me."

"I know. I'm going blueberry picking," I said, picking up a Nalgene container.

"In your pajamas?"

I walked near camp until I found a patch of grape-size blueberries. They were so plentiful that it took only fifteen minutes to fill a container. I heard the crackle of fire and smelled the smoke.

"How about crepes and blueberries for breakfast?"

"How about it!"

I washed laundry and hung it out to dry. I swam and bathed and read and sketched and wrote in my journal. I ate fish, blueberries, and mushrooms. We played canasta on the beach in the afternoon. A big flock of geese flew overhead, heading south, and we knew it was time to head north.

15

Final Stretch

At Swan Lake I rested on a log and looked down at my black-and-blue legs, which had been scraped raw by rocks. I could feel the start of a yeast infection from being in the Swan River all day and a renewed sunburn on my nose and cheeks from the scorching sun. For the past eight hours Charly and I had pulled and tugged the canoe up a series of rapids and into a stiff wind. There were no portages, and most of the landscape had recently burned. Unlike the Sturgeon-weir, the Swan River had no flat pockmarked limestone on which to walk. It was filled with big boulders, small boulders, and sharp boulders hiding in tea-colored water. Stepping from one boulder to the next in water that changed in depth from two inches to six feet and back again, I smashed my knees and shins and once fell in over my head.

Sensing my this-is-your-idea-of-a-honeymoon mood, Charly compensated by prattling on about how in 1957 Eric Morse retraced Thompson's route, starting at Southend and traveling through Reindeer Lake, up the Swan and Blondeau Rivers, across Wollaston, and down the Cochrane River. "We're camped at the very site where Morse and his fellow paddlers had rested for the night," he told me while sautéing hawk's-wing mushrooms and boiling Tom Kha Kai soup from a mix.

I stood silently, sorely, slowly to search for berries. Charly watched me walk away and looked relieved when I returned with a container of blueberries. "Nothing like a few berries to improve the mood of a Buckles," he joked.

I smiled a thin smile, picked up another empty Nalgene container, and continued walking.

"Tomorrow will be easier. I promise," he shouted.

All that stood between us and Wollaston Lake now was the Blondeau River, a smattering of little lakes, and the Muskeg Portage—about three days of paddling and portaging. Explorer David Thompson first discovered this route for Europeans in 1796. He was hired by Hudson's Bay Company to find a shortcut for the major fur-trade route, which ran from the Churchill River to the Athabasca River, and included a twelve-mile portage. But it turned out that Reindeer and Wollaston Lakes stayed frozen longer in spring—too late for the fur companies to transact business efficiently—and so Thompson's shortcut was never used. Historically, native people and trappers traveled the route. And so did fishermen. At one point, it served as a winter road for commercial fishing access to southern markets. Today the little traffic that there is comes from recreational canoeists. This small section of the Blondeau River and Muskeg Portage was the only section of our twenty-seven-hundred-mile expedition for which Charly had bothered carrying 1:50,000 scale maps that featured five times more detail than we'd had on our other maps. For additional guidance, Charly had garnered trail notes from previous canoeists.

We woke to a north wind, low clouds, and cooler weather and paddled into the wind across Swan Lake to the quiet, winding Blondeau River, a sleepy, boulderless stream that meandered back and forth and back and forth at a turtle's pace. For lunch we walked to the top of an esker. Eskers are the remains of glacial river bottoms. Long ago at this spot, rivers ran over, under, or inside mile-thick glaciers. When the glaciers finished melting, the riverbeds became winding sandy hills that look like giant snakes from the air. I picked blueberries; Charly looked for mushrooms. Black flies attacked, so we ran to the canoe, jumped in, and paddled *Le Strubel* like she was a getaway vehicle until the bugs blew away.

"Never get out of the boat. Never get out of the boat," Charly said, quoting a line from *Apocalypse Now* where Willard and Chef get out of the boat looking for mangos and meet a tiger.

Around the bend, a cow moose stood eating in the middle of the narrow river. I stopped paddling and froze. *She's going to hit us,* I thought, but could not speak the words aloud. Her massive physique—all head and legs—blocked our passage. A moose is like a dairy cow times four, only dangerous. Moose have a reputation for pounding other mammals to a pulp with their hooves. I saw my first moose when I was a kid living in Alaska, but I don't remember it. My first moose memory as an adult was with Charly. Camped in the Quetico in Canada, we awoke to two moose mating across the bay. They went at it all morning. We could hear the bull moose thrash through the woods, making a sound like a chainsaw. Then he'd emerge and head toward the cow moose as she drank from the lake. She wanted nothing to do with him, so would rebuff his advances, and he'd go back into the woods, thrashing about and so on. Those two moose were tiny in the distance. This one was huge and right there in front of me.

I heard Charly in the back of the canoe rustling for the camera. I remained frozen, my paddle midstroke. I could have at least back-paddled, but I couldn't move. The moose looked up, water dripping from her chin. She lunged gracefully toward the bank and then into the woods.

Two moose calves stood up in the grass on the bank, turned, and followed.

"My god. That's the closest I've ever been to a moose," I said, blood pounding in my ears. "Did you get a picture?"

"No, I didn't have enough time."

"I thought she was going to trample us."

"Might have, with those moosettes nearby."

As if a mother moose with twins weren't enough for one day, a few rapids later we spotted a bull moose, water dripping from his massive rack as he dipped for weeds. Charly wanted to get closer to get a photograph, so each time the moose plunged his massive head under the water for a bite, I paddled us closer.

"Shhh. Be quiet," Charly advised as I paddled, trying not to let water drip noisily off my paddle. "Get closer."

"Shhh. I'm working on it."

"Shhh. He's going to hear us."

I paddled in stop-and-start motion until the moose looked up and spotted us. He trotted back into the woods.

"How do they get through the woods with those antlers?" I asked.

"Practice, lots of practice."

The next day we needed to find our exit ramp on the Blondeau, a portage that would lead us to a series of lakes, the Muskeg Portage, and eventually to Wollaston. We were in high spirits and moving fast. The trip notes said we'd find our portage after seven portages up the Blondeau. The water was higher for us than it was for the author of the trip notes, and we were able to paddle up rapids without needing to portage. So we were unsure of how our count matched with his. "I think that was five, hey, Jules?" Charly asked.

"Hmmm. I'm not sure."

"That looks like it could be the portage, but I don't think we've gone far enough."

"It can't be. It's been such an easy morning."

We came to a waterfall, about five feet high.

"Seems odd the trip notes don't mention a waterfall," I said.

"Unless this is just one of the portages."

Charly climbed to the top of an esker to look around.

"I don't know. We might still be right."

We portaged everything around the waterfalls, and the river started to get shallower and wider. We got out and pulled the canoe forward. Then the river narrowed and the paddling was good.

"Jules, let's pull over so I can take another look," Charly said.

He climbed the esker; I sat in the canoe.

"I think we're here," he said, pointing to a place on the map. "We must have blown by the portage, and we're miles up the Blondeau."

"Is there another route from here?"

"It might be possible to blaze a trail to the next lake," he said, studying the map. "There's only a bit of land between the Blondeau and Middle Lake."

By going this way, if it worked, we would skip the first four lakes in the chain between the Blondeau and Muskeg Portage and pop out onto Middle Lake.

"Never turn back," I declared.

"That was probably Hubbard's motto," Charly laughed.

Hubbard, remember, was the mastermind of the ill-fated 1903 Hubbard expedition into the unexplored Labrador wilderness. Lost, Hubbard and two companions spent a summer and fall living off fish and wild peas until Hubbard died and the others were found.

The river grew wider and shallower with big round boulders sticking out of the water like a parking lot of VW buses. We continued on, alternately wading and paddling upriver, portaging occasionally, until the river became too narrow for the canoe.

"I think we're on this thin blue line that will take us to Middle Lake," Charly said. "So, we might be able to portage over the hill and hit it."

"Then let's go."

We loaded packs on our back and hiked for a half mile, looking for Middle Lake. No sign of the lake. We turned back, still carrying Josephine and Holy Boy, and set up camp, eating a cold dinner and our last candy bar. The bugs descended, and a light rain started to fall. Charly tossed and turned all night worrying about losing our way. I was giddy with the prospect of adventure and slept like a puppy. After the monotony of paddling, this was fun. We were headed in the right direction—only three or so miles from Wollaston—and we were okay on food.

The next morning Charly skipped breakfast. I ate granola. I came up with the idea that we should try to pull the canoe up and around the bend and then come back for the packs once we made it to Middle Lake. We loaded a few of our lighter items—Madame Boudreau and our day-packs. I pulled. Charly pushed. There were so many boulders that we could barely maneuver *Le Strubel* through. Around the first bend, there was another bend and around that bend, yet another. Around every bend, I expected to see our destination lake. Instead I was met with less water, more boulders, and rapids. Charly went ahead to scout the head-waters of the Blondeau, but returned defeated.

"Jules, we gotta turn back."

"I know," I said, my head drooping.

"We gave it our David Thompson best."

"I know."

My soaring adventurer spirit sank. Instead of explorers forging a new route, we were lost cattle, retracing our steps, too aware of the portages and rapids ahead. On the bright side, it was a hell of a lot easier heading downstream than up. We were able to run quite a few rapids, and walking *Le Strubel* meant putting the brakes on rather than forcing her forward. We ate lunch again at the five-foot-high waterfall. Shortly after, we found the remains of an old log warehouse—a former trading post that appears on a historic 1834 map I had given Charly for his thirtieth birthday—and an old blaze marking our portage, the same spot Charly had noted the day before.

New growth from a burn had turned the area into a jack pine Christmas tree farm—and the start of the trail was impossible to see. We used a compass to keep us moving straight east. Charly walked in front with Josephine, limbing occasional jack pines with his axe so we could maneuver the canoe through and leaving blazes so we could find our way with the second load. I followed with Holy Boy and my daypack until we reached the first lake, and then we returned for the rest of our gear. Gliding into the water felt like paddling on top of the world. With the land dropping away to the Blondeau Valley to the east and to Wollaston on the west, we teetered between watersheds. We camped on a tiny island on the second lake, in a bed of Labrador tea bushes. Charly found an old stovepipe and the remnants of an old cabin, now wrapped in moss.

Morning came, and through wind and bugs we traveled the third and fourth lakes, reached Middle Lake at last, and then skimmed across the fifth lake. "We'll be at Wollaston by tonight," one of us said, and the other agreed.

The Muskeg Portage, located between the fifth and sixth lakes, started out dry and easy. *Big deal*, I thought, carrying Josephine and my daypack on my back and Holy Boy on my front. And then my foot touched the ground and kept going. Lifting my foot, I heard a distinct sucking sound. I stepped again and my other foot disappeared. *Ah, so this is why it's called the Muskeg Portage.* I dumped Holy Boy and my daypack then continued through this boggy stretch with just Josephine. Charly was ahead of me carrying eighty-pound *Le Strubel.* I watched him sink in up to his knees. I sank to my knees with every step. Charly stopped for a break, the canoe sitting atop the muskeg.

"Let's try it in stages," he said.

I dropped Josephine and we returned for Holy Boy and Bertha. Slowly, moving like old packhorses, we picked up and moved packs then stopped and returned for more. Sensing vulnerability, black flies bit and buzzed around our ears and eyes. It was growing late and my energy waned. Charly dropped waist deep in muskeg three times with the canoe. I stopped to take a break.

"I can't move another step," I said.

"I'll scout and see how far this goes on."

My hero.

Charly returned with news of dry earth. I stood, and Charly helped me load Josephine. We reached a hard-packed trail, but before I could celebrate, I kicked up a nest of yellow jackets, hornets with a sting that feels like a combination of an electric shock and a tiger bite.

"Run! Run!" Charly yelled.

I dropped my pack and ran screaming for a half mile. I felt one sting, then two, then three. The hornets stopped stinging me, but I kept running.

"Come back," Charly yelled.

I stopped, looking for a swarm of bees, but there were only blackflies. I walked back, sweaty, sore, and burning with multiple stings.

"I've never heard you yelp before. You sounded like a puppy that's had her tail stepped on," Charly commented helpfully.

We portaged to the seventh lake, silent in our defeat. It was a bit anticlimactic not to make Wollaston after such a painful day. I spotted a bear as we pulled to shore. Charly set up the tarp and bug net while I foraged for blueberries and huckleberries. Somber in mood, we explored our surroundings and found an old camp with wood pieces, probably from an old log cabin. Three portages to go before reaching Wollaston.

It rained the next morning, and we took our time breaking camp, both of us sore from the day before. My bee stings ached and my blackfly bites itched, but on the upside, my yeast infection had subsided. Charly fried blueberry-and-huckleberry rice cakes and then baked corn bread for our lunch. We paddled and portaged against the wind and into frothy waves. We knew we'd be windbound at Wollaston Lake, so there was no need to rush. Charly clocked the wind at forty-five miles an hour. On our next-to-last portage, I had to walk ahead of Charly holding the bow of the canoe steady in the wild wind while he carried it. We stopped at the top of the hill and looked to the east. And there was Wollaston in the distance. I threw my arms up, making a W; Charly shot one of his two precious photographs for the day. Such a strange and exhilarating moment to stroll over the hill and spy our short-term goal: Wollaston Lake. We had paddled seventeen hundred miles—the distance from Chicago to Havana, Cuba.

Wollaston is large and clear with countless islands and bays. It is 120 miles long and 60 miles wide—roughly the size of Massachusetts without Cape Cod. It is the largest lake in the world to drain naturally in two directions. The northwest corner drains to the Mackenzie River and Beaufort Sea in the western Arctic. The northeast corner drains to the Reindeer River—where we had just paddled upstream—down to the Churchill River, and on to Hudson Bay.

We were at Wollaston Lake, but we were stuck. The wind continued to howl at forty-five miles an hour, kicking up tremendous waves. We set up camp; cut boughs for extra bed padding; and picked cranberries, huckleberries, and blueberries. Charly engineered a shelter, using the canoe for one of the walls. He tied off eighteen lines from the tarp to create a sleeping space strong enough to withstand the wind. Geese and loons headed south, and we woke to a forty-six-degree morning.

"You know this is fulfilling my childhood fantasy—windbound, running out of food, picking wild berries to survive," Charly said.

"No kidding," I laughed. "We're living out my Laura Ingalls Wilder fantasies."

We had run out of jam, granola, peanut butter, chocolate bars, fruit bars, bacon, Tang, tea, crackers, and dried fruit. We were low on flour, oil, and sugar, but still had plenty of wild rice, couscous, cornmeal, cocoa, and powdered milk. For three days, the two of us concocted every kind of rice cake possible—blueberry, cranberry, and huckleberry for starters. My legs were bruised and cut, my arms still hurt from yellow-jacket stings, and all my muscles ached for a rest, but I couldn't stop smiling. The Swan-Blondeau stretch had been the hardest part of the trip, but it felt deliriously good to have made it to Wollaston. We were stuck, but I didn't care.

16

Honeymoon Destination

Peter and John Elander welcomed us to Wollaston Post.

A dark-haired teenage boy wearing jeans and a white T-shirt stood with his younger sister on a sandy beach at the edge of town. A dozen or so scrappy-looking sled dogs chained to posts barked and howled behind them. This was the town of Wollaston Lake, known locally as Wollaston Post, located on the eastern side of the lake. With no roads, the only way in or out of town was by air or water.

"Where are you going?" the boy asked. His sister stared silently.

"Here," I answered, pointing toward town, and then laughed because it sounded funny to say "here" after months of saying "there." For now, we weren't going any further north. He and the girl looked at one another.

"Where did you come from?" asked the boy.

"Wisconsin," I started to tell them, but then said, "The United States."

His lips pursed in a gesture of recognition and admiration. "Long way."

"A real long way," Charly echoed, helping me pull *Le Strubel* onto shore.

"Where is the Northern Store?" Charly asked. We wanted to buy some groceries then head toward Minor Bay Lodge, where we had made arrangements to stay for the winter.

"None here, but there's a store . . . I'll teach you," the boy said, picking up a stick and scratching a map of town in the sand.

"Here and here," he said, making indents in the sand.

The town was wrapped around a narrow mile-long bay shaped like a finger pointing south. We paddled around the point toward the town dock, past penned-up dogs, tied-up dogs, and loose dogs. We paddled past parked snowmobiles, abandoned trucks, lines of laundry waving in the wind, motorboats pulled onto shore, and power lines stretching over run-down government houses arranged in a skewed grid. I spied a few people watching us as we paddled toward the town dock. This was motorboat country. A canoe in town rated attention.

Across the bay two men stood on a small private dock waving and shouting, Canadian and Danish flags hanging behind them.

"Do you think they're waving at us?" I asked.

"Of course they are."

"I think we found the Monkmans of Wollaston," I said, referring to Anne and Carl at Lake Winnipeg.

"Should we go over there?" Charly asked.

"Food first. I'm starved."

As we docked, a truck skidded to a stop. A middle-aged guy—lean, white, with a red bandanna holding back his hair—hopped out and asked the usual who, where, and how questions. His name was Doug. He was apparently the welcoming committee, sent by the two men we'd seen across the bay.

"That's Peter and John over there. If you like, you can camp at their place," he told us, pointing in the direction of the private dock where they still stood. "We're having a picnic tomorrow, and there's a square dance tonight."

Neither of us said anything. We hadn't talked to anyone but each other for three weeks and couldn't quite catch up to the accelerated tempo of his introduction.

Finally I said, "We need to grab a bite to eat. Do you have any recommendations?"

"The Confectionery. Just follow this road," he said, pointing up the street. Then he jumped into his truck and departed as quickly as he had arrived.

If Charly and I were to arrive in say, Chicago, and from across the street two guys started to wave and shout, and then a third guy approached to tell us that the two guys—a father and son—wanted us to camp in their yard and that we were invited to a picnic and there was a square dance that night, we would have done the same as any sane

American: averted eye contact and propelled ourselves forward at an increasing speed until the intruders disappeared. But in the last four months, we'd become accustomed to being approached and befriended by random strangers at town docks: Gord in Point du Bois; Anne and Carl Monkman in Loon Straits; Charlie in Pine Bluff; and Clem, Ken, and Gib in The Pas. We were so used to it that neither of us even commented on Doug.

All of my thoughts were on the Confectionery. Doug *had* said confectionery, hadn't he? I rambled on about this confectionery and all its possibilities while Charly remained silent and skeptical. A confectionery, as defined by the dictionary, is the practice of making candy or a store where candy is sold. I imagined a quaint building filled with sweet-smelling handmade candies, rows of turtles and truffles, sodas, and milkshakes. A kind young woman wearing an apron would stand behind the counter, a bit of cocoa powder on her cheek, ready to serve. I envisioned Diane Lane and divinity.

We approached a square dingy building that could just as well have been government housing.

"There's your confectionery, Honey," Charly remarked, pointing to the dirty building without a charming awning or cute sign. It could not possibly have Diane Lane or divinity inside. I was hit by the smell of grease and cigarette smoke as I opened the steel-grate security door and walked past a wall of graffiti. One corner inside the Confectionery was devoted to marshmallows, Tang, candy bars, and soda. A few people at tables turned to look at us. We smelled of campfire smoke and wore our frayed, faded, and smudged trail clothes—the same clothes we'd been wearing for four months. Except for our skin color, we didn't look particularly out of place.

Our hiking boots clunked on the floor as we approached the counter. A sign read "No deep fryer food available."

I pulled a generic black and white menu from a stack on the counter, and we both checked out the short list of non-deep-fried foods. An older woman who looked nothing like Diane Lane stood behind the register.

"How about a milkshake?" Charly asked.

"No milkshakes," she said.

"How about pie?" he tried again.

"No pie."

"What do you have?" I asked.

"Cheeseburgers and pork chops."

I looked around for the *Saturday Night Live* camera. Charly went with the pork chop then chose a table near a row of telephones, thinking we'd call home and tell them we'd made it to Wollaston. But then Social Director Doug walked into the restaurant, over to our table, and sat down as if we were old paddling partners. He started talking. He talked as if he had just broken a long vow of silence. Or more accurately, he talked as if he had finally found someone new to share his stories. Doug had taught school in the Arctic for years, and then two years ago he quit and moved to Wollaston. He had come to Wollaston to help his brother, who owned the Welcome Bay Store—one of the stores the teenage boy had marked in the sand map. It seemed important to Doug to explain the native people, called the Dene, to us. Doug's analysis was the most earnest of the many explanations we would hear in the next seven months. His assumption was that we would judge; he wanted to lighten the judgment.

"Every now and then one of the guys comes in drunk. Maybe his friends have passed out; maybe he's sick of drinking. And he'll say, 'Doug, give me a canoe,' I say, 'I'll rent you one if you put a three-hundred-dollar deposit down.' Then he'll say, 'Don't have three hundred dollars.' So I say 'Okay. I'll give you that one over there, it just needs a little work to fix it.' And he'll say 'I don't want to fix it, just rent me a canoe.'

"They just want to get in it, you know, and float in the lake off from town. You just need to go a little ways off and turn around, and the town has its humanity again. They just want to be away from the poverty and despair that you feel in town," he finished, studying our faces.

We both nodded as if we understood. We had not even been in town an hour, and I felt drained from too much conversation. As nice a story as it was, we never once in our seven months in Wollaston saw a canoe other than our own—in the water or on land.

"You planning on getting a snowmobile?" Doug asked as I wiped cheeseburger grease from my lips.

"Don't think so," I responded. Charly shook his head no.

Charly and I walked back to our canoe in the fading light, untied it from the town dock, paddled across the bay, and tied up to the dock at the Welcome Bay Store, a huge square building of peeling green paint and plywood, with bolts on the doors and steel screens on the windows. Inside, small items associated with alcohol and chemical abuse, like vanilla and hairspray, were locked behind glass counters. A pound of butter cost $5.95; a gallon of milk, $7.95. I was relieved that we had packed our own food for the winter. Doug's brother, Jim, stood behind the counter, a telephone lodged between his shoulder and ear. He didn't really look like Doug at first glance. For one, he had a full head of curly black hair, but his gray eyes revealed a brotherly resemblance. Jim rented cabins and sold snowmobiles, hardware, and groceries. He called himself the capitalist of the family. He also had a hankering for wilderness travel, and so said his creeping smile when he heard about our trip.

"Where'd you come in on Wollaston?" he asked, briefly hanging up the phone.

Charly relayed the *Reader's Digest* version of the trip while I loaded a basket with flour, sugar, Tang, and butter.

In darkness—our quick visit had become a major detour—we paddled a few hundred yards up the finger-shaped bay and introduced ourselves to the waving father-and-son team. Our arrival was the equivalent of an RSVP to the camping invitation. John Elander stood tall and solid, with blond hair, a wisp of a mustache, square shoulders, and a face rounded with middle age. He wore a baggy green sweatshirt, blue jeans, and a baseball cap.

"You know, Will Steger and Paul Schurke passed through here when they were training for their expedition to the North Pole," he told us. He had an energetic way of telling a story—flinging his arms and raising his voice.

"Really?" I asked, having recently read *North to the Pole*, the book about their sled dog trip to the North Pole.

"Jim and I put them up for a few days. Were those guys glad to get a shower!" he laughed. He went on to tell us that Steger and Schurke had been following a snowmobile trail. During the night a huge snowstorm covered all traces of the trail, so they had to snowshoe, poking their ski poles into the snow until they hit the hard pack of the snowmobile trail and slowly working their way along the trail.

I liked John immediately and identified him for what he was: a Man of the North. If I were lost in the wilderness and could make one phone call, and Charly weren't home, it would be to John Elander. Later, Charly looked at his research notes for Wollaston and found John's name. Someone had told us to find John once we got to Wollaston, and here he had found us. John had come to Wollaston fresh out of college, twenty years before, assigned as a Natural Resources officer.

"Back then, the road maps of Saskatchewan ended at LaRonge," he told us as we sat around a bonfire in his front yard. "I'd never heard of Wollaston Lake. When they assigned me here I had to find a map that went beyond LaRonge. When I found it, I thought, 'Holy shit! That's the end of the world!'"

He quit Natural Resources after two years and started the Welcome Bay Store with Capitalist Jim. They ran it together for ten years, then split as business partners. John managed Athabasca Airlines and scheduled who, what, and when for the barge that connected Wollaston Post to the road to LaRonge. John also held the positions of fire chief, emergency management leader, and Sask Power emergency contact.

Wollaston was remote but not completely inaccessible. It had one airstrip and two small airlines as well as a combination barge and ferry that ran twice a day during the summer months. To get to LaRonge, the nearest town with pavement, people had to fly; or they could take the 28-mile boat ride across the lake, then drive 260 miles down the gravel road. In winter, people drove or snowmobiled across the lake on the ice road instead of traveling by ferry.

The next morning I heard the wind, looked out, and saw waves kicking into the bay. We weren't moving. John ducked his head under our tarp, noticing everything in our camping outfit. He handed me coffee in a thermos. In the daylight we could see his cabin, the oldest building in Wollaston Post. Made of jack pine logs notched at the corners, it had been constructed in 1948. Wollaston Post was little more than fifty years old. I think of the United States as being a young country, but Wollaston Post reminded me that Canada is even younger. John told us that an old trapper, Mel Jamison, built the cabin. Jamison and his wife made a good part of their living selling home brew to the Dene—five cents a bottle, a two-bottle limit per person.

"You two interested in showers?" John asked.

"We need 'em?" Charly asked, gathering our breakfast items. I stayed in the sleeping bag.

"Sure, so you can tell stories about the grungy canoeists grateful for a shower to the next people who happen through town," I chimed in.

John giggled. "I'm going to like you two. Eat your breakfast, drink your coffee. I'll take you over to Derek's house, then give you a tour of town." John's cabin didn't have a shower.

"Who's Derek?"

"He works for the other airline."

"Doesn't look like we're going anywhere today," I said, nodding my head toward the lake.

"What did you think of that wind a few days ago?"

"We were sitting at Compulsion Bay, eating the last of our flour, sugar, and just about everything else," Charly said.

John laughed. "That was the strongest wind we've seen here for a while. Blew those jack pine over in front of the house. Clocked it at eighty kilometers in some areas."

"It was kicking our ass. I used every rope we had to tie off the tarp," Charly responded.

The town's main road curved around the finger-shaped bay. Several shorter roads intersected but didn't go more than a few blocks. Every road was a dead end until the ice road formed. The Hatchet Lake Band of Dene lived on the points of land at the entrance to the bay. Private and federal crown land surrounded the rest of the bay. The division between reserve and nonreserve land was marked as clearly as if someone had spray-painted a blaze-orange line along the boundary. Reserve land was denuded of all trees; and the rest was wooded. I never heard a good explanation for why the Dene cut the trees around their houses. Charly speculated it was to keep the bugs away.

John took us on a driving tour down the single main road around the bay, pointing out the main attractions: grocery store, post office, gas station, Confectionery, Welcome Bay Store, RCMP office, elementary and high schools, airport, and community center. About twelve hundred people—80 percent of them Dene and 10 to 15 percent Cree—lived in town.

John drove us to a high spot overlooking the lake, glanced at his watch, and panicked because he didn't see the barge. This meant the captain had decided against traveling with the propane trucks on the big waves, which meant John would have to juggle the barge schedule for the next few days. Propane tanks took priority, so someone would have to be booted from the next run. The school needed to get propane before the freeze-up period—the weeks while the ice was forming. Those weeks were like purgatory, he said. The barge quit running, yet the ice road wasn't ready—so nothing came in or out except by plane.

We understood, we said. Back home on Lake Superior, Madeline Island relies on a ferry for its supplies. The locals depend on an ice road in winter, and so they wait for freeze-up and anticipate the icy drive back and forth between the island and the mainland. Of course, Madeline Island was only a few miles from the mainland. Wollaston Post was 28 miles from a 260-mile long road to LaRonge.

We heard a plane.

"Oh, that's one of mine," he said, looking skyward, and we hopped into his truck and headed to the airport.

Charly and I looked at one another and smiled. John was a madman and we loved it.

At the airport a sign on the chain link fence warned, "All stray dogs will be shot," and a sign inside the fence said, "Beware! Loose dogs on runway." John's airport consisted of a trailer at the end of a small-town-size runway. John booked six passengers twice a day—that's all the plane could fit. He had a desk, computer, telephone, and fax machine. The lobby included a few scattered seats, but no bathroom. John showed us his recently vandalized red two-seater plane that sat wounded at the end of the runway.

"No insurance and no one went to jail," he said, shaking his head.

Next we hit a machine shop to find out more about the status of the barge. The barge had turned back because the waves were too large. At home, John made phone calls rearranging barge passengers. John's cabin was a typical bachelor pad, except for his mother's romance novels on the bookshelf. Despite the rustic exterior, the cabin had all the markings of civilization: a satellite dish on the roof, a large television that was always on, and two telephones—one for work and one for himself—that rang often.

John's dad, Peter, walked in from working in his garden of potatoes, rhubarb, carrots, beets, and flowers. He had Coke-bottle glasses and a thick Danish accent. Peter joked that their kitchen table never needed wiping after a spill. "It leans so much it self-cleans."

Peter served a stew of potatoes, carrots, and caribou-beef sausage.

"You plan to get a Ski-Doo?" John asked of our winter plans, scooping a bite of stew.

"No," I replied.

"How are you going to get around?" he asked.

"Where do we need to go?" Charly asked.

"You'll want to socialize. Come into town, visit Rick over at the lodge, make the rounds."

"We'll ski," I said.

He gave us a look that I would later recognize as one of restrained hysterical laughter. "Okay," he said, and shrugged.

John and Charly talked about maps, arrangements, and ideas for winter. I watched a rerun of *Northern Exposure*—the one in which Joel makes dinner for his friends, uses canned mushrooms instead of real ones, doesn't clarify the butter, and is surprised when everyone stops talking to him.

"What cabin are you going to stay in?" John asked about our Minor Bay Lodge arrangements.

"No idea. Randy didn't say," Charly replied. "You know, what I'd really like to do on principle is stay in our wall tent."

"A wall tent?" John said, raising his eyebrows and looking at me. Again, his eyes fell into sidesplitting laughter. "Not here. It stays at forty below for days and sometimes weeks. You can't stay in a wall tent."

"We'd burn a lot less wood."

"You'd freeze."

"How much wood do you think we'll need?" I asked.

"Ten cords." John said.

"How is it burning softwood?" Charly asked.

"jack pine up here is like hardwood. Small sticks but really old, so the growth rings are tight. And you burn green wood in with the dry,"

John and Charly took the four-wheeler to visit the RCMP, Canada's police department, and Peter brought out wine from hiding. Wollaston was a dry town, so booze was coveted. Peter told me that an eleven-dollar bottle of Mickey's rye sold for fifty dollars on the black market. A bottle of hairspray cost thirty dollars. Some locals used it for a buzz.

Peter poured a glass of red wine for me and then sat and told me in his thick Danish accent about life as a young man in Denmark during World War II. He had been part of an underground resistance movement and was planning to blow up a rail yard when he was caught by the Germans and sent to a concentration camp. He escaped and walked toward Denmark, staying in the countryside to avoid more trouble with the Germans. He came to Canada in the 1950s, when John was eight years old, to find a better life. Canada was at that time encouraging immigration of workers to help in the booming economy.

Charly and John returned to find us laughing and sipping wine in candlelight with flowers on the table. "Ohhh, what's going on here? A little competition, Charly," John said, scrunching his shoulders and poking Charly.

Charly grinned. "It's hard to compete with this," he said.

Charly and I fell asleep to the rain drumming on our tarp roof and woke to calm waters. John had already gone to work. Peter stood on the dock as we pushed off. Charly had reached Randy from Minor Bay Lodge, but he was in Winnipeg. He had already left for the season. He said he left a cabin unlocked with a note inside with instructions.

"Stop and visit Felix and Linda Fischer," Peter said. "They're on the way. On Estevan Island. They're the nicest people you'll ever meet. They'd kill me if I didn't tell you to stop and visit."

We paddled out of town like we paddled out of all the other towns along the trail—not really expecting to return. We knew we'd likely see John sometime over the winter. He was resourceful and would find us. But we had no clue just how much our lives would intersect with Wollaston Post and the cast of characters we had met in the last forty-eight hours.

17

Estevan Island

After a morning paddle, we kept with our always-go-in-from-a-point-of-strength trail motto and ate lunch before we tied off at the private dock at Estevan Island. We walked down a rock-bordered trail past a hand-crafted wooden sign with "The Fischers" spelled out in birch twigs. Three grouse sat perched on the sign.

Someone I assumed to be Linda emerged from the cabin, carrying a horn in her hand. She raised the gold instrument and blew. She would later explain that the horn was her version of red-pepper spray—a bit of safety on the island. Before we could say hello, a man I assumed to be Felix charged from the woods. One thought entered my mind and never left: gnomes. Short, friendly, bustling gnomes.

"People in town told us we should stop by," I offered as way of introduction. I had pictured gray-haired, hunched-over retired people, not these horn-blowing, woods-charging people.

"Hello," Linda said.

"Hello, hello. Now who sent you? How did you get here?" Felix asked, brushing debris off his hands.

"We paddled from Wisconsin. Peter and John sent us," I responded.

"In a canoe? Oh my, oh yes, come in. Tea? Coffee?"

"Whatever you're pushing," Charly said, glancing at me.

"Tea would be great," I said.

"You paddled all the way from Wisconsin? So, let me see, you would have started on Lake Superior," Felix said, filling a tea kettle from a large white water jug.

"Then we hitched a ride into the Boundary Waters and followed the border lakes to Rainy River, then Lake of the Woods," Charly continued, pulling up a chair. Linda sat at the head of the kitchen table.

"Winnipeg River, Lake Winnipeg, Saskatchewan River," I added.

"And from there, the Sturgeon-weir, Churchill River, Reindeer Lake, Swan and Blondeau Rivers, and on to Wollaston," Charly finished.

"Lake Winnipeg? Can you believe this, Linda? They paddled all the way from Wisconsin? You know, we had paddlers here earlier this summer. They had a big heavy canoe and stayed a few days," Felix said.

Felix brewed coffee and boiled tea water, and Linda brought out cookies.

"You know the other thing about Wisconsin? Linda and I try to go a national park every year. We've always thought about . . . isn't there a national park near you?"

"The Apostle Islands. Our backyard," Charly said.

"You two will stay for supper? And how about the night?" Felix asked, pouring black coffee into mugs. "We'll be eating fish haddie and a green salad, right Linda?"

Charly and I looked at one another. "Sure, we'd love to," I said, then glanced over at Linda, who didn't look well. The polite thing to do would have been to decline, but it felt so good to be in Felix and Linda's company. I hadn't been around a woman since the afternoon in Anne Monkman's living room two months earlier. I wanted to soak in some female conversation, however brief, but then Linda excused herself and went to bed for the afternoon.

Felix and Linda's cabin was bigger than our cabin back home and, at least in one way, more modern. They had a gas stove and a wood cookstove in the kitchen. We had only a wood cookstove. They had cabin lights that ran on propane and a gas-operated generator, which they used sparingly to run their mobile phone. The original trapper's cabin was now the kitchen. People had tacked on rooms over the years—a living room, a bedroom, a mudroom, and a two-story addition that could sleep eight.

The three of us moved into the living room, ducking our head in the doorway cut out of the old log cabin. Felix added small logs to the Ben Franklin–style woodstove and sat on a blue vinyl overstuffed chair. There was a small table, a dartboard, stacks of magazines, and a row of Western pulp fiction on a shelf. A mounted black bear head overlooked the books. Charly and I sat on a stiff couch covered with a satin shiny peach-colored bedspread. A bulletin board filled with pictures of people holding up large fish was a testament to the long parade of visitors Linda and

Felix entertained all summer long, including their five kids and ten grandkids.

Felix was an avid outdoorsman, athlete, canoeist, and fishing guide. He loved fishing and fished every day in summer. He had played broomball until someone broke his sternum when he was fifty-two. His hand had nearly been cut off by a boat prop when he flipped out of his boat on Wollaston Lake. And he had broken his pelvis while cleaning out a duck nest a few summers before. He told these stories with a chuckle and a hint of embarrassment.

"So, did you spill the canoe?" he asked.

"We never tipped," I said, shaking my head.

"Probably the closest we came to losing it was on Lake Superior," Charly said.

And we told him a detailed account of our near-spill while rounding Bark Point.

With each story we told, he was reminded of one of his own.

"Did you paddle over Cedar Lake?" he asked.

"Nasty shoreline, kind of depressing," I said, remembering the displaced village.

He told us about three guys who fished every year at Cedar Lake. One year they decided to change their routine and try another lake. They told their wives where they would be and left on their four-day weekend. At the last minute they got lonesome for Cedar Lake so returned to their routine. "But they never called and told their wives," he said, pausing for emphasis.

They set up camp on an island and went fishing. The motor quit. They tried and tried to get it started, but it wouldn't start. Fortunately for them the wind was with them, and they floated to the end of the island, tied up the boat, and bushwhacked the two miles to camp. The next day they set up three bonfires, a sort of SOS. Days passed.

Meanwhile a search-and-rescue crew looked unsuccessfully for them at the other lake, where they'd told their wives they would be. The guys worked for the same firm, and the firm said it would foot the bill to continue the search. Their wives thought they were dead. The search expanded, and a crew went to Easterville, the only town on Cedar Lake. They asked if anyone had seen anything suspicious. "People said no. But then one guy spoke up. 'I've seen one strange thing. There's been three fires from that island over there every day.'"

Linda emerged later in the afternoon, lighting a cigarette. She was a petite woman, standing maybe five feet tall and weighing no more than ninety pounds with her blue jeans and long-sleeved red shirt on. She wore wire-rimmed glasses and had bangs, with the rest of her hair swirled into a bun at the top of her head. She looked like a woman who had worked hard for everything she had.

"Felix wants me to quit," she commented as way of apology for the cigarette. She had an accent I can only describe as Saskatchewan, pronouncing Felix with a short *e* so it sounded like Fellix instead of Feelix.

"For your health," Felix added.

Linda sat down in the red vinyl chair next to the large window in the living room. It was the spot that promised the best light. She started to work on a carving. She carved figurines year round and sold them mostly to locals. Felix was a woodworker as well. The figurines were of men of the north, paddling and portaging canoes. She showed us one woman she had done, washing clothes in a washtub.

In the fading light, Felix led us on a tour of the grounds: a bathhouse made of see-through greenhouse plastic, a log outhouse, several garden beds bordered by rocks and fenced to keep out wild hares. Spruce grouse pecked at cranberries and blueberries that grew in abundance in the forest openings. Bird feeders and duck boxes adorned the nearby trees. Tamarack and birch trees, tinged golden, held evidence of autumn. It was an amazing oasis to have stumbled upon.

Turning fish and vegetable scraps into compost, Felix had built the soil enough to grow lettuce, dill, beans, peas, cabbage, potatoes, celery, rhubarb, chives, sungold tomatoes, cherry tomatoes, and strawberries. He told us his garden did well because of all the light. He compared notes with his sister in Saskatoon, a ten-hour drive south of Wollaston Lake, and while her garden started out faster, Felix's garden caught up by midsummer.

Felix leaned down, picked a small yellow tomato, and handed it to me. I didn't like the taste or texture of tomatoes, but out of politeness I tried it. That little yellow sungold tomato changed my eating life. It was an explosion of flavor as good as my favorite fruits. I don't know whether it was because I had lived on dried fruits and vegetables for the summer or whether my taste buds were just ready, but I became a tomato lover that day.

"There must have been a fire around here," Charly said, a comment on the same-age trees surrounding the cabin.

"About fifty years ago this whole point burned," Felix said.

Felix led us on a short hike up a path behind the cabin. We climbed to the top of a gray granite hill. Shimmering water and islands of spruce trees spread out for as far as I could see. Estevan Island was so large that all the land I could see to my right and behind me was part of it.

For dinner we ate fish haddie (a stew) and a fresh green salad with tomatoes. This was bona fide home cooking, using food from the land. For dessert Linda fried *fitzkeckle*, donut-like breadsticks rolled in sugar.

Felix and Linda told us they lived in Pilger during the winter. They had sold their construction business, retired, and bought the Estevan Island cabin fourteen years earlier. They didn't own the land, but leased it from the Canadian government. It was called a wilderness lease, which meant they had to meet certain criteria—no electricity, no business out of the cabin, and no other houses within a certain distance.

They had both worked at Minor Bay Lodge, where we planned to stay. Felix had worked as a fishing guide. Linda had cleaned rooms.

"The industry has changed. It used to be family oriented, now it's about guys going after the big fish," Felix said. "I don't like guiding as much any more—too much pressure for the big ones."

"You must have to deal with all kinds of dynamics when you're guiding," I commented.

"I feel more like a counselor sometimes," Felix said. "I had a father and son once. The ex-wife had turned the son against the father, so the boy wouldn't speak to the father; and if he did, he wasn't nice."

"So what did you do?"

"I focused on the fishing. Tried to get the boy interested in catching fish."

"Did it work?"

"Not very well. He was so twisted up and angry. I felt bad for both of them."

"Do you know what cabin Randy left open for you?" Linda asked.

"No, he didn't tell us," Charly said.

"I hope he didn't leave the pilot's cabin," she said looking at Felix. "I bet he left the pilot's cabin."

"What's the pilot's cabin?" Charly asked.

"Oh, this itty-bitty cabin where the pilots would stay overnight." Linda responded.

"It's small," Felix verified. "I don't think Randy would leave them with that one."

After dishes and over tea Linda sighed. "You know, it's too bad we didn't know you before. We'd love to have someone stay here for the winter."

"Too bad we didn't know you, because we'd love to stay here," I replied, my mind whirring. *Could we change plans?*

Felix rose first the next morning, boiling a pot of coffee and starting the fires in the living room and the kitchen. "Linda won't get out of bed before the coffee is done," he said.

Linda came in, poured a cup of coffee, lit a cigarette, sat at the kitchen table, and started speaking as if in the middle of a conversation. "Randy's a nice enough guy, but not too organized," she said. "I'll bet he's left the pilot house open. You can't stay in the pilot house."

Felix offered to take us over to Minor Bay Lodge in his motorboat to check on the housing situation, then we could paddle over for good the next day. But the weather turned "snarkly," as Linda reported it, and we decided to stay another day.

Over blueberry crepes, Felix told us more about Wollaston Lake. He and Linda didn't lock the cabin in winter and left a coffee pot on the stove with a note that read "Help yourself to coffee and tea."

"We've learned over the years," Felix said. "It doesn't make sense to lock the cabin." Anyone who wanted to come in would break the door down anyway. One year a nurse took up residence in the cabin over the winter. Felix and Linda knew only because they found little clues, such as a moved woodstove, when they returned in the summer. One day Felix ran into this particular nurse, who casually said, "I used your cabin last winter," and that was it.

In the early years, Linda and Felix would return to find items missing. A clock, some blankets. Felix later spied his clock at a friend's house. "Nice clock," he commented.

"Thank you," this friend responded. Felix and Linda had learned their lesson and had eliminated everything of value.

"Usufructuary rights," Charly commented.

"They don't think of it as stealing," Felix agreed. "It's not being used"

He was midsentence when Linda shouted, "Squirrel!"

Felix bolted from his seat, hustled to the living room, grabbed a gun, and trotted outside. I could see a red squirrel looking in through a screened window in the next room. The noise of the gun broke our silence. I watched as the bullet blasted the squirrel out of the frame of the window.

"Got him," Felix said, obviously pleased. Linda clapped her hands and stood up to mark it on the calendar.

"Oh my god," I whispered to Charly, laughing. These people were madder than John Elander, Man of the North.

Charly laughed too.

Felix hated squirrels—they messed up his cabin in winter—and kept track of how many he killed. He and Linda also tracked fish caught, visitors to the island, and any other unusual occurrences each day.

The next morning Felix and Charly planned a fishing trip for lake trout and northern pike. "So, Linda, how many do you want? What size?"

"I'm going to can today, so three of each, and we should have one for dinner," she said.

Charly and I looked at one another. She was putting in her order for fish, and Felix fully expected to fill it. While the men were out fishing, Linda, who was feeling better, taught me to bake bread. Her secret ingredient was Red River cereal. She baked the bread in coffee containers so they came out round with the markings of a tin can.

She told me stories that women tell one another in kitchens everywhere. Stories of love, loss, and heartache. She kneaded bread; made blueberry jam; smoked cigarettes; and revealed how she and Felix had both been married before, had known each other a long time, and had found one another later in life. She had kids and he had kids—and some were happy for them and some weren't so happy. I couldn't imagine Felix and Linda with anyone else. They were like two pieces of a puzzle that neatly fit together.

I heard Charly yell, and Linda and I walked down the path toward the dock to find him holding up a fine looking trout in one hand and a northern pike in the other.

"Look, Hon, I caught some fish," he grinned. I loved Charly best after he had caught fish. Very few things in life made him happier or more childlike.

He and Felix lined all the fish out on the deck for a photo. I'm sure Felix had done it a thousand times with guests, but you'd never have known it. Felix showed Charly his system for filleting northern pike. Northern pike possess lots of bones—so many that some fisherman don't like to keep them. The most troublesome of the bones are Y-shaped, aptly called the Y-bones. Felix showed Charly how to easily remove them for bone-free eating.

For dinner we ate fresh trout and northern pike, salad, and fresh warm bread. I enjoyed nearly a loaf of warm bread, slathering on butter and fresh blueberry jam—and didn't think a thing about it. There was no talk of Atkins, South Beach, or low-carb dieting. For four months I hadn't thought about food intake except to make sure I was getting enough. I'd been working so hard that I had eaten everything I wanted and still lost twenty pounds.

After dinner Felix motored us over to Minor Bay Lodge to check out our winter accommodations. A bundle of letters addressed to Charly and me were hanging on the doorknob of the pilot's cabin, the only cabin left unlocked. Linda wasn't exaggerating: it was small. I could touch all four walls by standing in the middle. There was no cooking stove, and no wood heat. To say I felt disappointed would be an understatement. We walked around the entire camp, peering in locked larger cabins. Charly and I talked briefly of plans to set up our winter camping wall tent to store our stuff and create more space, but for the most part, the three of us rode home in silence.

Linda greeted us at the dock, "You want to stay here for the winter?" she asked.

"How did you know?" I asked.

"You can't stay *there*," she said, looping her arm in mine. "I have a third daughter."

That night all four of us bounced off the walls, drinking precious beer and laughing. Linda acted almost drunk. She wanted to return for part of the winter. "Felix, don't you think we could?" she asked. "I want to come back for winter."

Felix hesitated. He understood himself too well. He was an extrovert who needed social contact. He also didn't want to have to deal with snowmobiles. "We'll see, Linda."

Felix wanted to clarify details. "Charly, you've got a wood problem," he said. "We don't want any wood cut around the house. How will you get wood?"

"We can get wood from the islands around here and haul it by canoe," Charly suggested.

Felix and Linda planned to take the motorboat, the mobile phone, and almost everything in the cabin. We planned to leave the first of April. If they didn't return until June there would be a two-month lag with no one watching the cabin, so they needed to close up as if the cabin were empty for the winter. In fact, our staying there helped them little. Several fishing camps had told us they'd rather not have anyone for the winter. Our tracks would only attract people, not keep them away. We were a risk. We would be starting fires every day and creating a trail right to the cabin.

It was September first. Felix and Linda planned to leave on September eighth.

"Don't leave early because we're here," I said. "We can go camp somewhere for the next week or so until you leave."

"No, we need to get back for goose hunting season," Felix said.

Charly started to mention fix-up projects we could do over winter, and Felix put a stop to it.

"Linda and I have a certain way we like things," Felix said. "I have a list of projects; that's what I like to do in the summer. We like the cabin the way it is."

The next eight days were a blur of helping Linda and Felix close camp, fishing, picking berries, and making logistical arrangements for our stay. One afternoon I caught a thirty-eight-inch northern pike. Northern pike have a prehistoric look—long snouts with big mouths full of teeth. I thought I had caught a log, and so pulled and pulled, not enthusiastic until I saw what was at the other end. Charly stuck an oar in the pike's mouth, while Felix loosened the hook. Felix worked expertly so the fish could live, held it up next to me for a photo, then let it go. The fish paused in the water, stunned, then suddenly and quickly swam away. Felix told me about a fishing contest he and his family held each year for visitors. The minimum entry was forty inches. My monster didn't even make the minimum cut.

Charly and I began to haul wood for winter. Felix told us to take his motorboat to other islands, cut wood and load the boat, then return and stack it near the house.

John, Man of the North, motored out from Wollaston Post to say goodbye to Felix and Linda. If he was surprised that we were still at Estevan and that we were staying for the winter, he didn't show it. He looked at the stack of wood that we'd been working on. "That will last a week," he said, only increasing Felix's worries. I rolled my eyes. Charly and I had been living outside for the last four months. We'd been living with wood heat for seven years. I was not worried. We had no commitments for the next eight months. Cutting wood was all we had to do.

We puzzled over one real logistical conundrum—how to get our supplies and food for winter to the island. Estevan was located twelve miles from town, seventeen miles from the road, and twenty-eight miles from the nearest boat launch. Five months earlier we had sent our winter gear—snowshoes, wall tent, winter clothing, and food supply for the winter—in an empty Camp Manitowish Suburban that was driving north to shuttle canoes to Churchill Outfitters, located north of LaRonge.

In two weeks, Charly's dad planned to pick up our gear and food from the outfitters and deliver it to us on Wollaston Lake. That plan was hatched when we intended to be at Minor Bay Lodge, next to the road. A simple plan. Now we had to figure out how to get Herb, the gear, and all that food to the island.

After endless discussions with Felix and Linda and between ourselves, we decided that Charly would motorboat out with Felix and Linda and ride with them south to meet Herb. Charly, Herb, and the gear would drive north in Herb's rented car to Points North Landing, a permanent camp on the mainland that acted as a plane hub for the region. The landing stayed busy supporting uranium mine exploration and running supplies to fishing lodges, trappers, and northern towns. Charly, Herb, and the gear would then fly from Points North to the island.

We needed more information. Felix turned on the generator, dug out his mobile phone, called Points North, and handed the phone to Charly. Charly talked fast in an effort to find out everything he wanted to know before Felix became nervous about using the generator for too long. Charly asked what size float plane would be needed, how much it would cost, and how the system worked. He finished the call and everyone kept talking logistics.

In the middle of all the chatter, I felt hot tears forming. I stood up from the kitchen table and walked to the bedroom and started to cry. I realized that our canoe trip was over. Premenstrual? Probably. But still, I had anticipated arriving at Minor Bay Lodge and just the two of us working hard to get ready for winter. Now everything was ready and we wouldn't have any time alone until after Herb left. And the Fischers were so damn nice, it made me cry more. Charly walked into the bedroom and sat next to me on the bed, putting his arm around me.

"You okay?"

"I'm not ready for our trip to be over."

"I know what you mean. Who knew Compulsion Bay would be our last night alone for a while?" Charly said, nuzzling my neck.

"I just want you to myself again. You, me, and the canoe."

"Don't worry. You'll get plenty of that this winter."

That evening a moose hunter named J.B. stopped by. Felix invited him to stay for a dinner of grilled stuffed trout. Felix told J.B. how we had built our own canoe and paddled to Wollaston and were now staying the winter.

"What do you think of that?" Felix asked.

J.B., burly and deep-voiced, responded, "I think you're going to die."

I half-smiled, ready to laugh, but stopped myself when I saw he wasn't laughing. I wasn't sure if his statement was a threat or a prediction. Local people must have thought we were city-slick morons. Felix told us later that the moose hunters liked to use the Estevan cabin and were likely a bit put out that we would be staying there. J.B. had lived in the cabin as a little boy, but only nodded when Felix asked him about it, revealing nothing.

I called Mom and Dad later that evening using Felix and Linda's mobile phone. They had planned to visit at the end of October, but according to Felix, Linda, J.B., and John, the ice formed around that time and a floatplane couldn't land. I talked to them about coming earlier or later. I suddenly felt claustrophobic about island life. I had jumped on the idea of staying at Estevan without thinking about the added logistics. There were definitely challenges that went along with this cabin. I was tired of Felix's worries, J.B.'s prediction of death, and everyone's opinions about how we should prepare for winter.

Felix began the next morning's conversations with "Linda and I have some concerns . . ." Felix worried about the generator, the cabin, and the lack of available wood on the island. "You've really got a wood problem," Felix repeated, meaning we didn't have a chainsaw or a powerboat or snowmobile to haul the wood. They were adamant that we not make any changes or any improvements on the place. They wanted to return and find everything as it was.

"Linda and I retired on a limited income. This is all we have," he said.

I felt sick to my stomach. "We respect that. We don't need the generator, don't expect it," I explained.

Charly and I set out in Felix's motorboat to haul wood in the afternoon.

"I think they want to back out, but feel obligated," I said.

"I don't think they want to back out. They're nervous."

"Right. And I don't want to be responsible for burning down their dream cabin," I said.

"I'm with you. I don't want to burn down their dream cabin either. But I think everything will work out fine."

We should give them an out if they want it," I said, tossing logs into the boat.

"I agree."

"You talk to Felix."

"Hear that?" Charly asked, pointing toward the sky.

I strained to hear something and then did.

"Sandhill cranes," I said.

"Heading south."

When we got back to the cabin, Charly and Felix took a walk. To Charly's offer of backing out Felix responded, "No, we feel fine about this decision." Felix and Linda decided to take the generator with them.

The tension dissipated, and we all enjoyed Felix and Linda's last day on the island—picking cranberries, making jam, napping, and preparing meals. We lingered longer at coffee in the morning and ate fish for lunch and dinner.

"Me and Linda always have a tough time leaving the cabin each year," Felix said. "This year is even harder. We have mixed feelings because you two are here, and we've always thought about staying for winter."

We heated water for baths, and the four of us went fishing for the last time. It became a spirited game of men versus women. The men won eleven to five.

The next morning Felix, Linda, Charly, and I rose in darkness at four and loaded the motorboat with all the essentials. At five thirty, I hugged Linda tightly and said nothing for fear of crying. I stood on the dock waving goodbye as Charly and the two gnomes disappeared in the motorboat. For the first time in four months, I was alone.

18

Island Life

Silence. A new kind of silence. The silence of being alone on an island. For two days I could eat, read, and hike whenever I wanted. I returned to the cabin high on the idea of not being responsible for half of all conversations. I pulled *Lonesome Dove* from Felix's bookshelf and looked it over. It was 975 pages, had won a Pulitzer Prize, and began with the sentence "When Augustus came out on the porch the blue pigs were eating a rattlesnake—not a very big one." Perfect.

I lay in the living room on the stiff couch with the satin peach cover, turning page after page and learning about Call, Gus, Pea Eye, Newt, and Deet. The novel was about the first cattle drive from Texas to Montana and two men's reasons for doing such an insane journey. If not in the name of war or commerce, why take on the adventure? For Call it was inertia; for Gus, a desire to see unsettled wilderness for the last time. What was our excuse? Probably a bit Call and Gus in both of us.

I baked cookies and made Linda's fish haddie for dinner. A pine marten, a member of the weasel family, half hissed, half barked at me as I walked to the outhouse. It sat in a spruce tree, brown and small, eyeing me up, poking its nose closer to get a good look. It was still there when I returned. We stared at one another until I gave in, walking back to the cabin. I watched from the window as the pine marten scurried awkwardly down the tree and ran off.

Two days later, not long after finishing *Lonesome Dove*, the sound of a small engine broke the silence. I ran to the dock, waving to the sky and jumping up and down at the sight of a plane circling overhead. Water sprayed from the floats as the blue-and-white seaplane landed and motored toward the dock. The pilot, who didn't look old enough to drive a car, got out first. Charly jumped out next, smiling, looking like the poster child for health. Herb smiled too, but he looked older, thinner— and I tried not to notice. Just a year before, Herb could have been the month of June in a men-of-retirement-age calendar. He had played tennis three times a week, worked in the yard, and sailed often. He had kayaked with Charly in Alaska and Georgian Bay in Ontario, hiked with Charly's sister, Kati, in Kenya and alone in New Zealand, and sailed with his two best buddies through the Greek Islands. He had worn a tuxedo the night before our wedding and looked absolutely stunning. My older friends joked that he was the ultimate catch: handsome, retired, single, active, and financially fit.

"You wouldn't believe the view from the air," Charly said, turning to unload boxes of winter gear and food. "Wollaston Lake sprawls forever."

We stood on the dock and watched the young pilot take off, using the lake as his runway.

Herb grinned, laughing as Charly began recounting his tales of the "outside" and we hauled boxes back and forth. Charly had stopped at Robertson's Trading Post in LaRonge—a commercial institution that buys and sells, outfitting trappers and prospectors with everything: groceries, toboggans, clothing, and kerosene lamps. Charly had talked to the owner, Alex T. Robertson, a small man with silver hair and quick eyes, and told him about our trip. Alex replied that he had a son who "worked well below his capabilities" so he could find time for canoeing. Charly, Herb, and I hooted at that—Herb maybe a little more than the rest of us.

Alex had called his son and handed the phone to Charly. "It wasn't until I was nearly done talking to him that I remembered that I had called him last spring tracking down information for our trip."

Herb and Charly had stopped at Johnson River Camp on the road back to Wollaston Lake. The owner, Jean, had given Charly a quick lesson on kerosene lamp wicks and hints on where to get bulk fuel. She loaded him up with dried hashbrowns and jars of minced garlic. "I knew you were staying on Estevan before you knew," she told him.

Herb brought his own brand of silence to the island. It wasn't an angry, despondent, contemplative, or spiteful silence. His was the silence of someone who'd grown accustomed to living alone, to sitting at his kitchen table reading *The Economist* and fully expecting to finish it without interruption. For me it was an uneasy silence. I didn't know how to respond. He and I sat around a small bonfire, baking a trout that he had caught earlier, while Charly picked greens for a salad from the garden.

Herb didn't like small talk and so rarely asked the most basic questions for making polite conversation, such as "How are you?" or "What have you been doing?" He never offered unsolicited information about himself. For me, conversing with him was like playing racquetball with someone who never lifts his racquet. After a while it became exhausting. I told stories of solo island life—reading *Lonesome Dove* and staring down a pine marten—and asked him how Kati was doing and about a recent trip he had taken. He answered in brief, and we returned to staring at the fire and the sizzling trout. Herb's brother, Phil, had told Charly and me a story that helped explain Herb. Phil told us that Herb and his siblings had grown up in a house where "children are seen, not heard." Their dad, Charles—the one who had stopped a horse midgallop with his voice—was an intellectual without the credentials, so he was bitter. He really had little patience for chitchat, so he had created a house shrouded in silence. Herb was able to break through, Phil said, because he developed a mind for economics and politics. Charles appreciated Herb's intellect and liked to debate.

Knowing about Charles's oppressive silence helped me understand Herb. And in fact, I thought he had done pretty well, considering. He was a devoted, interested father, and he knew how to have a good time. I had seen fraternity pictures of him laughing, his arms around friends. Charly walked over to check the fish and take it off the fire.

"Dinner's ready," he said.

Around the table, Charly told another "outside" tale. He and Herb had arrived in time for lunch at Points North, the airport of the north. There was a sign on the door that read "Remove shoes before entering the hall." "So we did," Charly laughed.

Herb nodded. "We'd never been in a socks-only diner. A handsome woman took mercy and showed us the ropes for the self-serve cafeteria. Great food, lots of drinks and desserts. Fresh vegetables."

"So why no shoes?"

Herb and Charly shrugged. "I don't know. I guess all the mud from the road," Charly said.

The next morning Charly and Herb strung out the antenna for the SBX trapper radio—a shortwave radio that worked like a CB. Charly had picked it up in LaRonge from the government-run phone company so we would have some form of communication during the long winter. With the SBX we could converse with other radios hundreds of miles away, or we could radio the operators at the key station in LaRonge to be patched through to a phone line. Charly had filled out the paperwork necessary to get licensed as a shortwave radio operator and be assigned our call sign, "VEE864."

"Call anytime," one of the operators had told him. "It's free and we need the business." The only other key station in the world at that time was in Australia. The SBX has since been replaced by satellite phones. The SBX technology worked off a minimal power source whereas cell phones of that time and mobile phones needed to be recharged after an hour or so. The SBX could run for a month or so powered by nine D-cell batteries, and the phone company mailed unlimited batteries with the eighteen-dollars-per-month base service.

We called Mike and Phyllis right away. The way it worked was this: we contacted the LaRonge key station by pressing the CB trigger and saying, "XLB51 LaRonge this is VEE864. Do you copy? Over."

Then we hoped for this response: "This is XLB51. Go ahead VEE864."

Shortwave radios use the ever-changing ionosphere to reflect radio signals, so sometimes the signal was crystal clear, sometimes it sounded like everyone was underwater and breathing helium, and often it was just static. When we expected a call we would leave the radio on, listening to the bush banter in English, Cree, and Dene hissing and humming in the kitchen, waiting for the crackle of "VEE864, VEE864, this is XLB51. Do you copy?"

To have a conversation with someone on a landline we needed to say "over" each time we were finished with our piece of the conversation. When the operators in LaRonge heard the word "over," they flipped a switch so we could hear the people at the other end of the conversation. When those people finished their bit, they had to say "over," and the operators flipped the switch back. All conversations were public—aired so anyone with a radio could listen.

"Sounds like you're in the Arctic. Over," Mike said.

"Not far from it. Over." Charly responded.

"Tell Julie that Knock-Knock has taken over our couch. Over."

"I'm not surprised. Over."

It was good to hear their voices, but the call made me homesick. Charly hung up the microphone and, like a hound dog, pricked his ears toward the dock.

"Motorboat," he said. And here came our first visitors.

Charly charged out the door, greeting the three men at the dock. I walked behind him; Herb walked behind me. "I'm Charly Ray," Charly announced, holding out his hand.

"I know," replied a man who introduced himself as Jonas. Jonas had overgrown black hair and wore a baseball cap. He pulled a small bundle of letters from his pocket and handed them to Charly. Somehow our mail, sent to Points North, had ended up on the truck windshield of the owner of Pike's Island fishing camp. He passed them on to his guide, who brought the letters to us. Confused? So were we.

The next man was Baptiste. At sixty-one, he had a twinkle in his eye, chain smoked cigarettes, and had cheeks that showed signs of former frostbite at the peaks.

Third came J.B., the man who'd grown up in "our" cabin and who'd said we were going to die.

"J.B., did you bring us a snowmobile?" Charly asked.

"No," said J.B., shaking his round head.

"I think we're going to die!"

J.B. broke into infectious laughter.

J.B., Jonas, and Baptiste conversed in English and Dene, laughing easily among themselves. The Dene language sounded like a clash of clicks and hisses that I never did figure out. One word that came clearly through the mix of English and Dene on our deck that sunny afternoon was "chicken!" The three men looked at the two spruce grouse pecking at seed in the grass.

"Kill them," Jonas said, nearly bolting from his chair.

"We need a few friends around," Charly said.

"Kill them now before they go away!"

Jonas relaxed until I said, "There's a third one."

His eyes followed those three grouse. I think it took all his restraint not to clobber them.

Herb stood to take a picture of the group. Jonas tipped his hat back so his face wouldn't be shaded and released a huge grin. "Thanks for the tea," said Baptiste. Then the three men left as quickly as they had come. They had delivered our mail and, more importantly, checked us out. I wondered if we had passed muster.

That night the northern lights flared all around us. Charly set up a tripod to take photographs while Herb and I stood and watched. "You know you're north when you're looking south at the northern lights," Herb commented.

In bed that night, Charly and I whispered back and forth. "I'm glad the guys came to visit while your dad was here. He obviously got a kick out of it," I said.

"Then the northern lights, and catching a fish this morning—it all made him so happy," he said, then switched the subject. "I met this guy who worked behind the desk at Missinipe. Real funny, bullshitter type. Said a client had just flown back from Ohara Lake, northwest of Wollaston, with footage of a polar bear."

"No," I said disbelieving.

"Polar bears in northern Saskatchewan," Charly nodded, taken with the possibility.

The next day was our last with Herb on the island. Charly and I wrote our third installment for the *Ashland Daily Press* series of articles and made a list for my parents of things to bring. We planned to send both items with Herb, who would deliver the handwritten article to the newspaper in person and call Mom and Dad to recite the list. Charly developed a to-do list for Herb, since he was planning to stop by our house. We picked a bag of vegetables for Herb to drop off at Jean's, the woman who knew we were staying at Estevan before we did, on his drive to LaRonge. In the afternoon, the three of us cut wood and picked berries. Herb was gung ho to work—he always liked projects, even at our cabin at home. He told us about how he had just helped Charly's sister build a front porch.

In the woods, Herb looked even frailer, thinner, paler. We had only briefly talked about his heart condition and colon cancer, but the endless trips he took to the outhouse were a constant reminder. The year before, when Charly and I had begun making wedding plans, Herb had come to me and said, "I have no idea what I'm supposed to do but will do whatever you tell me to." I thought it had taken great courage to admit he was out of his element but willing to learn. I wished I had the grace to ask him the same about his heart condition and cancer. I didn't know what to do and didn't know what he needed. But I never asked. We picked a pail of cranberries and a pail of blueberries and loaded a wheelbarrow with kindling. We all looked toward the sky as a hundred or more Canada geese flew southward in V-formation.

Dinner that night was a celebration of autumn in the north: baked grouse with rosemary and California bay laurel, sent by Charly's California friend Keith; wild rice with carrots, peas, and onions; cranberry sauce; lettuce and tomato salad; warm homemade bread with butter; a bottle of Cabernet Sauvignon; and for dessert, cranberry pie. What a feast! A celebration of the abundance of food. Herb smiled. Charly looked so much like him it made me want to cry. I had always assumed Charly's smile was that of his mother, but now I could see it belonged to his father—handsome, open, and engaging. I smiled. Charly smiled. I loved them both. We toasted the splendor of the meal and quietly chewed our food in the glow of the candlelight.

Our resupply arrived along with Herb and Charly.

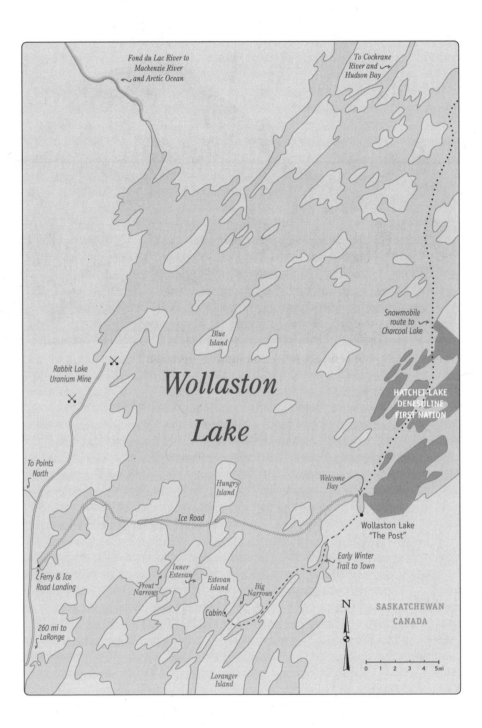

Fond du Lac River to
Mackenzie River
and Arctic Ocean

To Cochrane
River and
Hudson Bay

Snowmobile
route to
Charcoal Lake

Blue
Island

Rabbit Lake
Uranium Mine

Wollaston

Lake

HATCHET LAKE
DENESULINE
FIRST NATION

To Points
North

Hungry
Island

Welcome
Bay

Ice Road

Wollaston Lake
"The Post"

Ferry & Ice
Road Landing

Inner
Estevan

Prout
Narrows

Estevan
Island

Big
Narrows

Early Winter
Trail to Town

Cabin

260 mi to
LaRonge

N

SASKATCHEWAN
CANADA

Loranger
Island

0 1 2 3 4 5mi

Part II
Winter

19

Anniversary

September 19, 1999. Our first anniversary. Charly and I sat on a smooth granite knob looking out at Wollaston Lake, a shimmering panorama that seemed to extend forever. We were seventeen hundred paddling miles from our home and more than a thousand from our arctic destination. With yellow birch leaves ablaze against black-green spruce, we had put down our paddles for the most part and settled in for winter.

We picnicked on tomato sandwiches, Yukon gold potato salad, and blueberries—the garden bounty we had inherited from the Fischers.

"We'll probably spend our next anniversary at Gjoa Haven," Charly commented.

How strange to think our journey was really only beginning. The start seemed so long ago and the end so far away.

I poured wine into stainless steel mugs and raised mine in a toast. "To Wollaston, to Gjoa Haven, and to us."

20

The Last Outside Guests

D o you have any idea where you are?" exclaimed Mom as she descended from the floatplane on September twenty-sixth. "Three days we've been driving. Three days! And I'm thinking the entire time, *they paddled this whole way.*"

"Welcome to the end of the earth," Charly laughed, pleased by Mom's comment.

Mom and Dad had flown with the same cherubic pilot who'd brought Herb just two weeks before. The pilot handed me a bundle of letters that had been delivered to Points North. So far we had found a packet of mail on the door of the pilots' cabin at Minor Bay Lodge, had another bundle delivered by motorboat, and now received a bunch by plane. Mom insisted on taking the pilot's picture to prove to her friends just how young the pilots are in northern Saskatchewan.

We stood on the dock watching the Beaver plane scoot along the water and take off. Dad had ridden in floatplanes when he and Mom lived in Alaska, but Mom had never been in one before today.

"I've always wanted to ride in one of those planes. I can't believe I just got to," Mom said, looking toward the sky.

"It really is an amazing view," Charly agreed.

"Water and trees for as far as you can see," Mom said. "No one would believe how far you've come—I wouldn't believe it if I hadn't just traveled it."

"What'd you think of your pilot?" I asked.

"I thought it was take-your-kid-to-work day when I first saw him. I was waiting for his dad to take control of the plane, but he was it," she laughed. "When I commented on his youthful appearance, he replied, 'I'm not young; I'm twenty-two.'"

"It's a school-to-work program. It *is* hard to find pilots up here," Charly joked.

We carried the boxes to the cabin, gave the grand tour, and settled in for tea and hot chocolate.

Mom and Dad had driven 1,836 miles in a white Voyager minivan purchased for three hundred dollars. "The alternator went out in the Dakotas," Dad told us.

"A tire went flat north of LaRonge," Mom continued.

"And the jack busted through the floorboard," Dad said, laughing through his sentence.

"And everyone we talked to looked at the vehicle, squinted their eyes, and said, 'You're not taking *that* to Saskatchewan!'" Mom said.

"How was the road?" Charly asked, referring to the gravel road that started in LaRonge and continued roughly 280 slow miles to Points North.

"Well . . .," Dad started.

"Hell!" Mom said.

"The road was fine when Dad and I drove it," Charly said.

"It would have been fine, but a road crew had graded the road to one lane," Dad explained.

"These huge trucks would come barreling down the road, and we had to get out of the way—and fast—or they'd run us over," Mom said.

"And we couldn't get through in some parts, not with our van," Dad added.

"Garry had to push boulders out of the way while I rolled the van forward."

Charly laughed. "Garry, you might want to get an official position with the road crew. I hear they pay pretty well."

I boiled more water for another round of hot chocolate and tea and served a plate of peanut butter cookies I had baked that morning.

"Any trouble at customs?" Charly asked.

Mom and Dad looked at one another and started laughing.

"What happened?" I asked.

"Border crossing had asked if we had a gun, and Garry told them he was transporting one 'for protection,'" Mom started.

Dad continued, "The guard asked, 'Wildlife?' So I said, 'Yup.' He asked, 'How much ammunition?' and I told him, 'A box of shells.'"

"And the guard turned to his coworker and said, 'This guy says he's got a gun for protection, and he's carrying enough ammo to start a war,'" Mom shrieked.

"He said, 'Pull over,'" Dad said, laughing.

The guards inspected the van filled with our supplies—two pairs of cross-country skis, an extra wall tent, an extra winter camping wood-stove, and a gun—as well as Mom and Dad's stuff. They were particularly interested in what Charly and I were doing for the winter. Where did we cross the border? Where were we working? Not working? What did we do for a living?

Laughing, Mom said, "I told them that you were a writer and Charly an environmentalist. The guy nodded as if everything had suddenly come clear and said, 'That figures. Now this is beginning to make sense.'"

This comment made us all laugh even harder. Tears rolled down our cheeks and my stomach muscles hurt. If laughter is the best medicine, I should have bottled that afternoon.

"And through the whole ordeal, Laraine kept mouthing, 'We're. In. Trouble.'" Dad said, barely able to speak through his laughter, but able to demonstrate how she had silently over-enunciated.

"Finally they looked up your names on a computer and saw you had gotten a remote area border crossing permit and then let us go," Mom said.

In the tennis match of this conversation, it was Charly's turn.

I knew the story that would come next because I had heard it several times over the years. In fact, the last time had been the night after our wedding, at dinner in Bayfield with our friends who had remained for a weekend kayaking trip. Charly's childhood friends are animated story-tellers and told one story after another, including this one, keeping everyone at Maggie's restaurant laughing until the waitstaff turned the lights out.

It was the 1988 border crossing story. One of my favorites, right after the musk-ox story. Charly and his childhood buddies, Chris Lunn, Jim Eberhard, and Jim Young, were returning from seven weeks on the trail where they had encountered the mating musk-ox. These twenty-year-olds, who had paddled for eight hundred miles from Wollaston to Baker Lake in the Northwest Territories, had not taken along clean clothes for the ride home. They looked like drug runners.

At the border, the US customs agent asked Jim Eberhard, who was driving, for identification. Jim started to pull out his license then said, "Oh, not that one," and retracted the license, looking for his real one.

"I knew we were in trouble then," Charly said.

"Pull over and come into the station," the agent said.

Charly continued the story. "Into the customs station we went. We took a seat and were taken one at a time into an investigation room for a 'pocket search' by a customs agent wearing rubber gloves and looking the part of the mother from Pink Floyd's, *The Wall*."

My parents didn't get the reference, but Charly continued on.

"The customs agent stood behind a stainless steel table and placed a Frisbee-shaped plate on the table. When it came Chris's turn she asked him, 'Does your mother know you dress like this?' Lunner was speechless. But he had the last word.

"We were still wearing our trail clothes, down to our heavy wool German Army surplus cargo pants with massive pockets we used as surrogate backpacks on the trail. 'Empty your pockets into the tray,' she said.

"Lunner filled the tray. She brought out another tray and he filled that one too. 'Just empty it onto the counter,' she said. And he spilled out the rest of his pockets," Charly told us, mimicking Chris Lunn's actions.

"Our pockets had our collections accumulated along the trail of rocks, bones, plants, and our utilities—bug net, spoon, toothbrush, snacks, bug dope, slingshot, and whatever we could fit. Lunner was a naturalist pack rat.

"She poked through the heaps with a ball-point pen for the incriminating evidence. She picked out a baggie of white powder, 'And what is this?' she asked, sure that she had us.

"'Milk powder,' Chris answered. She held it up and examined it in the light, feeling the texture of the powder through the bag, then set it down and grabbed another item.

"'And what is this?' she asked, poking at a hollow bone about the size for making a pot pipe. Chris picked it up saying, 'Oh, that's my arctic fox leg bone I use to store my ptarmigan foot in,' and he proceeded to shake the leg bone until a little furry ptarmigan claw foot fell out, blood crusted on the feathers. She jumped back and ordered him to pack up his stuff.

"That was the end of the investigation, and we were on our way," he finished to great laughter.

Charly and Dad took the canoe to fish for trout. Mom and I sat in the kitchen chopping vegetables and talking. She had just returned from a nursing administration conference in New Orleans. As she talked, her enthusiasm for a nursing career that was about to take off was palpable. I reveled in the easy chatter and gossip about work, family, and friends. Mom and I were so close in age that we both belonged to the same generation of baby boomers. She was one of the first, born in 1947. I was one of the last, born at the tail end of 1964. I was about to turn thirty-five; Mom was nearing fifty-two.

Mom had met Dad in high school. He had slicked-back hair then, wore black clothes, and was as thin as Elvis in his early days. She got pregnant, married Dad in May, and had me in December—two weeks after her seventeenth birthday. She and Dad beat the odds and stayed married. They had broken all records, because they actually liked one another and urged one another to be the best they could be. To say they were role models sounds corny, but they set a high standard for me and my siblings and our spouses. I watched and observed and hoped to do as well.

Mom and I walked outside for the red-splattered sunset.

"I think that's the prettiest sunset I've ever seen," Dad said from the bow of the canoe as he pulled up to the dock.

"Isn't this place just like Alaska, Garry?" Mom asked.

"Mmm hmmm," Dad replied, staring out at the lake. "It's good to know there's places like this left," Dad said.

"You two should think about coming up in March and hauling our extra gear home," Charly said.

"Yeah, well, I might be up for that," Dad said.

"You might as well leave me for dead if I have to walk in snow," Mom joked, referring to her polio leg.

"We'd take care of you, Laraine," Charly said.

The next morning the four of us cut and stacked wood. First we scoured the woods, paddling away from the cabin, searching for the best trees—dead, dry, solid, and tall. Those that were just right made a certain clinking sound when thrown into a pile. We cut some trees down; others had already fallen. One of us would knock off the limbs with an axe or boot while another began sawing. We had two saws: a collapsible wooden one we had used on the trail and a metal bow saw that had arrived with Herb in our winter gear.

On this day Charly and Dad sawed the trees into five- to eight-foot lengths and piled them near the shore. Mom and I loaded the canoe, hauled the log lengths home, and unloaded them at the dock. Later we carried the logs up to the house where we sawed them to stove length. The wood cook stove required logs less than fifteen inches, the heat stove less than twenty-three inches. For our final step, we stacked the wood into neat rows, where it waited to be carried into the cabin when we needed it.

The next morning we woke to snow on the ground. First lasting snow as it would turn out, and it was only September thirtieth. Charly and Mom hustled out the door to take photos of spruce grouse tracks in the snow and blueberries dusted in snow while I made lemon-ricotta pancakes. Later, the four of us cut and stacked wood. For the next two days we fished, picked berries, baked bread, hauled more wood, and took more photos. Snow fell again, and the wind blew most of the remaining leaves off the trees. The blueberries were left naked on twigs with no leaves to cover them.

"Let's make bets on when the lake will freeze," Mom suggested.

"What are we betting?" I asked.

"*Guimauves*," Charly piped in.

"Alright, marshmallows. A kilo of them," I said. We had seen a bag of marshmallows in town and had loved the French version of the word.

"October thirtieth," Dad said.

"Let me get the calendar and write it down," I said. "Mom?"

"Hmmm. I need to think a bit," Mom said.

"November tenth," Charly said.

"I'll take November eighth," I said.

"Put me down for November twelfth," Mom concluded.

"They have us sandwiched in, Charly," I said.

Charly radioed Points North the next morning to see if they could send a plane later than scheduled to pick up Mom and Dad. Over. They could. Over. We had a last photo shoot, played a few rounds of horseshoes, walked the hill, ate lunch, and played canasta. And again Charly and I sent our visitors off with a long list of things to do for us back in Wisconsin. Dad said he would drive up to our place and make sure everything was winterized and working. Mom had orders to get Christmas and birthday presents on my behalf, including a kayak paddle for Dad. At the sound of the plane, Dad darted out the door first, and the rest of us followed to watch the pilot land the blue-and-white Beaver. They loaded their two packs. I hugged Dad first, and he hopped in. I turned to Mom, who was already crying. Charly helped her into the plane.

"I'll take good care of her," he told Mom and Dad.

"You take care of each other," she said, leaning out of the plane.

"We know you will," Dad said.

I stood on the dock waving, tears dripping onto my winter jacket. The pilot started the engine and motored away. Charly walked back and put his arm around me. We waved at the plane until it flew out of sight and then stood there in silence watching the gray sky. Charly reached in his pocket and handed over a Kit Kat chocolate bar. "Times of crisis call for chocolate," he said, and I had to laugh.

That afternoon we hauled two more loads of wood before the sky turned black and everything disappeared behind a layer of gray snowfall. Snow was pelting our faces as we carried the last logs. Everything was soon coated white—trees, birdfeeders, deck, and garden. We picked the last of the tomatoes, potatoes, kohlrabi, beets, dill, and onions, then scurried inside. As I walked into the cabin, my hands and feet chilled, I thought, *I am going to be cold for a very long time.*

Mom and Dad in their beaver fur hats

21

Thanksgiving in October

October twelfth. Charly rose before the seven o'clock sunrise, lit a fire, and boiled water for oatmeal. He experimented with his Grundig radio by kerosene lamplight, locating the BBC, Voice of America, Radio Havana, Radio Deutschland, Radio Netherlands, and a Russian-English station. The news reported Muhammad Ali's daughter had fought in her first boxing match and knocked out her opponent in thirty-one seconds. Pinochet was to be extradited to Spain. I lay in bed and listened to the clink of dishes and the sound of the radio, then rose with the sun.

Outside the window the sky started to lighten and the thermometer read twenty degrees. Common redpolls—brown-and-white birds with red caps—landed in flocks on the birch tree branches, hanging like Christmas tree ornaments, eating the catkins. They twisted, turned, and even hung from one foot to get a nibble. A black-backed woodpecker with a yellow crown pecked at the trunk. Charly and I had become bird-feeder people, filling Felix and Linda's flat wooden boxes with birdseed they had left behind. Plump slate-blue dark-eyed juncos jostled for space next to grosbeaks and sparrows, flitting feeder to feeder.

I turned on the trapper radio for the eight o'clock weather report. Calm and clear.

"Let's go," I said.

Charly loaded the canoe with a wall tent, woodstove, tarp, two sleeping bags, axe, emergency radio system, headlamps, kettle, rain gear, survival gear, two days of food, and reading and writing material, just in case we got stuck somewhere. For three days we had considered paddling to town for no other reason than it was something to do. But the wind had kept us close to home. We followed Estevan Island's shoreline up Big Narrows, past a cliff-like stretch where people had scratched their names in the lichen. The sky and water were so gray and foggy that we could only see the shoreline when we were a few feet away. Visibility was one hundred feet, enough that we spotted a whiskey bottle threaded on a birch limb near shore—likely to mark the narrows for snowmobile travelers.

Charly lobbied to stop at a nearby island to pick cranberries. The frost had turned them a dark burgundy, contrasting with the rich greens of sphagnum and reindeer moss. Uninspired by the late season pickings, I wandered among the sweet-smelling Labrador tea and spruce trees, finally choosing a sunny spot to drink hot chocolate and sit and think.

There were two ways of looking at our time on Estevan Island—and my mind went both ways depending on the day, the hour, the minute. On the one hand, we were lazily waiting for winter to come and go so we could continue with the next leg of our journey. This seemed to me a limited, somewhat destructive perspective. I hadn't realized what a goal-oriented person I was. After dreaming of doing nothing, doing nothing was driving me crazy. I was surprised at how quickly I grew restless. Without the satisfaction of making miles, I felt listless and useless. I couldn't figure out what to do with myself. The cabin was ready for winter, the berry picking done, and the fishing nearly done for the season. All that was left to do was stack the woodpile even higher and prepare for the next portion of our trip.

On the other hand, there was a more upbeat perspective: We had created an incredible space in time and place and had the opportunity to write, sketch, read, create, talk, think, and dream. No distractions, no real worries. No driving to work or joining committees. Just endless time. I just had to remind myself of this. We had discussed ad nauseam the possibility of returning home for the winter, but staying seemed the most logical. Things back home had been set up for the year, and our house was rented. Plus it seemed like cheating to go south for the winter and lose the momentum. The voyageurs had toughened winters out. Charly's life dream had been to spend a winter in the far north, and we were here. I didn't really want to leave. I just needed more tasks to accomplish and people to talk to.

Charly joined me with his bucket of cranberries.

"Where are your cranberries?" he teased.

"Couldn't find any," I said.

"Give me some hot chocolate."

We paddled close to shore, which added miles to the trip, but it was cold and we wanted to play it safe. The fog lifted a bit as we came closer to town.

"I bet we only have a few weeks left of paddling," Charly predicted from the back of the canoe. "Reminds me of the story Felix told us about Jimmy Kkaika."

"I don't think I heard it," I said.

"Jimmy Kkaika and his wife were out late in the year, pinned down by a storm miles from town, and woke up to a sheet of ice. They waited a day and got more ice. So Jimmy sent his wife out ahead to check the ice, and they walked home on one inch of new ice. It's said the women have an instinct for ice, so they go first."

"Sounds like a bullshit excuse to get his wife to go first."

As we pulled up to John's dock just before lunch, we saw that he was busy with his motorboat. As usual he took our surprise arrival in stride.

"I was just on my way to visit you," he said. "You here for Thanksgiving?"

"Thanksgiving?" I asked, wondering what I was missing—a month perhaps?

"No mail today," he replied as way of an answer. "I just sent off the last barge of the season."

No barge equaled no regular travel. Until freeze up, the way in or out for people or supplies would be by airplane or a long motorboat ride.

"I tried coming out last week with one of the elders, but it was too rough," John continued. "So rough, he broke a couple of ribs."

"Who did?" I asked.

"The elder."

"He broke his ribs riding in the boat?" I asked.

Charly nodded his head, impressed. "That's rough," he said.

John invited us in for tea and put a kettle of water on his stove. The television, as always, was on, and Charly started clicking the remote to find the weather channel.

"How'd you like the caribou ribs?" John asked, referring to his latest gift.

"They were great," I lied. They had been tough and tasteless, and we had gnawed on them awhile then thrown them out.

"Be sure and grab some more before you leave," he said.

"So how do you fix your ribs?" I asked

"I boil them in water and ketchup and spices," he said.

The post office was closed, but John had picked up our mail the Friday before. I looked it over quickly—packages from friends and family and a Prince Edward Island postcard from the canoeists we'd met on the Rainy River.

Hi Guys, We made it! Arrived at PEI Aug. 14 well ahead of schedule. Grand Portage took us 12 hrs mosquitoes worst there. Superior awesome had good weather met Gary McGuffin, author of Where Rivers Run *. . . Unexplainable emotions as we crossed the CanFederation Bridge 9 miles [from] home. We had a few arguments and eruptions along the way and found we were two very different people. I hope you two held your goals together and make it to your finish. I found that was perhaps the hardest part of our journey—making the goal and staying friends. Dana*

I smiled and handed it to Charly.

John showed us a woodstove he had scavenged from the dump, thinking we could use it. "That stove you have won't keep you warm this winter," he said, sitting down for a dinner of caribou and potatoes. He had plans to play basketball. "I need to eat two hours before playing basketball. One hour for volleyball."

"Take my four-wheeler over to Welcome Bay, if you'd like."

"I don't think we need to," Charly said.

"Go ahead. I don't need it."

The phone rang and John answered, waving as we walked out the door.

Charly drove and I rode along on the four-wheeler to Welcome Bay Store, where we took a closer look at the complex of buildings, chain link fences, and a mud driveway. A dozen or so trucks sat scattered in various stages of disrepair. A warehouse was large enough to fit two semis. It smelled of chicken. I bought a few supplies: ketchup, four cans of evaporated milk, two cans of tomato soup, two cans of diet Pepsi, a bag of marshmallows, Earl Grey tea bags, toilet paper, and a bag of screws. The bill: sixty-four dollars.

Capitalist Jim was in his office on the phone but paused to invite us to stay for Thanksgiving dinner. It was indeed Thanksgiving in Canada. Jim lived next to the store in a small house with running water, a modern kitchen, and a bathtub. It had the look of a place where people slept, ate quickly, but rarely spent time. The books scattered around the house reflected Jim's divergent personalities. There were self-help books for the burgeoning businessman in the bathroom and books on wilderness travel in the living room.

Sitting around his kitchen table, eating a most un-Thanksgiving-like Thanksgiving dinner of leftover Chester Fried Chicken—bachelor!—Jim listed one bad business decision after another. He had opened a Chester Fried Chicken franchise for fifty thousand dollars but soon realized that it only paid (kind-of) to have it open on weekends. The franchise needed to serve a population of at least three thousand people to make it viable. Wollaston had twelve hundred. Small shops, like Welcome Bay Store, favored Chester Fried Chicken because the equipment was cheaper than other franchises and took less space. However, Jim was required to buy

Chester Fried Chicken's "special spices," which were expensive.

He opened a toy section in the store for the Christmas season, and shortly after, the tribe organized bus trips to the city for Christmas shopping. He rented out cabins, but the tribe built a motel and required contractors to stay at that motel. He started a credit union so locals could get loans for their snowmobiles. He required half down for snowmobiles and large payments, so debtors could pay off their machines before they ran them into the ground. For the first time everyone had established credit.

"So when dealers in Prince Albert offered zero dollars down and four years to pay, the town picked up and went south to buy snow machines," Jim told us. "Now everyone is armpit deep in debt. They have a string of credit cards and debts, all because I gave them credit in the first place. Not the outcome I intended."

I didn't understand why Jim had chosen such a harsh place to make a living. Charly theorized that it had to do with the pissing match between him and John. They had split not only as business partners but as friends as well. Neither would be the first to leave town. In fact, they rarely spoke even though they were two of a handful of nonnative people in a native town.

We slept at Social Director Doug's, trailer, located next to the store and Jim's house. Doug filled us in on the background of the Capitalist Jim and John saga the next morning while he prepared for the day's carpentry, dabbing iodine tincture on the little cuts on his hands from the day before. Doug and John had gone to high school together, but it was Capitalist Jim and John who had become best friends. The two decided to go into business selling and fixing snowmobiles. John had wanted to stick with snowmobiles; Jim expanded into groceries and just about everything else.

"It's tough. It's like a divorce, and I'm in the middle," he said.

"So why did they split?" I asked.

"John couldn't stand people taking credit. He'd see people and think about how much they owed the store," Doug explained.

"That's too bad," I said, immediately thinking of Disney-movie-like ways that I could be the one to reunite them.

"How do you keep warm on the trail?" Doug asked, looking at our bags. "I'm always cold. Can't stay warm."

"It wasn't a problem during the summer," I said.

"In the winter, we take three bags and sleep inside a wall tent with a woodstove," Charly said. "Funny question from a guy who lived in the Arctic and hunted polar bears and caribou."

Doug laughed. "I wore polar bear pants—the only thing that could keep me warm."

Doug slipped easily into telling us a hunting story. "When a native guy thinks about caribou hunting he says, 'Snow machine, gas, gun, kettle, tea. Go!' If he's got no matches, someone else will have them. I went out with a group once and no one brought ammo except one guy. He had enough for one shell for all ten of us, except for me. He knew I'd miss. Ten shells. Ten caribou."

Charly and I packed to leave and walked to the store to say goodbye to Capitalist Jim, who offered us one of his puppies for the winter, a short-haired black dog with brown eyes and floppy cocked ears.

"You'll need the company," he joked. "I'll throw in some dog food."

She had a tail shaped like a question mark, white tips on her paws, and a sweet personality. Jim named her Heike for the German woman who had saved the dog from a bullet. Wollaston Post was not kind to dogs. Without a town vet, dogs—many of them running loose—had lots and lots of puppies. Dogs were not neutered, adopted, or housed. There was no shelter. Instead, dogs were shot. In fact, the town had official days where all loose dogs were shot. People knew if they wanted to keep them, they had to keep their pets inside on that day. If dogs survived the bullets and the elements, there was also the risk of wolves. Capitalist Jim told us the story of a wolf that lured two of his dogs to the outskirts of town where the rest of the pack made a meal of his female dog. The male got away.

Jim wanted to keep Heike alive and was confident he could eventually find an owner, if she turned out all right. A winter with us might do the trick. We paddled out of town in late afternoon with gray skies and a rising south wind. Heike sat between my legs, shaking. At sunset the gray clouds slid away like a lid off a kettle, revealing beautiful orange light. Stars came out as we started down Loranger Island, and it turned dark at Big Narrows until the moon broke. We followed the shore, arriving home in less than five hours, and never had to break out the wall tent. We stiffly, coldly unloaded the boat, happy to be home.

A few days later we had just unloaded a canoeful of firewood when we heard a motorboat. I squealed with happiness, and we both ran down to the dock. John Elander, Social Director Doug, and Doug's dad, Norm, pulled up. John wore a blue snowmobile suit, and the other two were bundled in orange insulated survival suits, red life jackets, and fur-lined caps with earflaps.

"We can't stay long, the weather is changing," John said. "Just bringing out mail."

"Well come in for tea and warm up," I invited.

Doug and Norm took off their survival suits and placed their chairs directly in front of our new fireplace. We had installed the Four Dog stove we had brought for winter living in the wall tent.

"Nice little stove," John commented, walking around it. "I'll bring the one from the dump as soon as we're traveling by snowmobile."

John handed me a stack of mail and some caribou steaks. I started heating tea water and brewing coffee next to the ribs, already simmering on the stove, and brought out cinnamon rolls and peanut butter cookies.

Doug leaned back in the blue vinyl chair, his feet on the yellow footstool, reading the Duluth Pack catalog that had arrived earlier in the mail. The only thing those guys—and I'm including Charly here—found more fun than scrutinizing, evaluating, and discussing real gear was reading the gear catalogs front to back and over again. With glasses resting at the edge of his nose, Doug looked like a professor settled in for hours of study. The more comfortable Doug became, the more nervous John grew. Norm remained in neutral territory sitting on the satin peach couch at the edge of the room, telling a string of "true stories"—that's what he called them.

John paced, moving from the couch to one window and to the next window and back to the kitchen.

"Weather's changing. We gotta go," he said, poking Doug.

Doug didn't move, taking a sip of his tea.

"It's getting worse," John said.

Norm rose and Doug followed, putting on their survival gear until John nearly pushed them out the door. We trotted behind them down to the dock, watching as they motored off into growing waves.

"We'll see you after freeze-up," John yelled.

Invigorated by the hour-long distraction, Charly looked at maps while I opened some of the mail: a book from one friend and a postcard from Mom.

"Dear Julie and Charly," I started reading aloud. "Did some research on the winter roads and it looks like we'll see you in March. Your dad is determined to get back up there, and Link says he's in. So, why not?"

"We got her," Charly said. "Hey, I hear a motor."

We ran down to the dock.

"Wind stayed," John said, getting out and tying his boat to the dock.

"Stayed, as in you're staying here?" I asked.

John nodded.

"Oh, goodie," I said, jumping up and down and clapping.

"Let's get the maps out," Charly said, and John smiled.

Charly baked a kuri squash that Mom and Dad had brought; John, Norm, Doug, and I sat around the kitchen table exchanging stories. John told us about working as a Ministry of Natural Resources officer in Wollaston.

"When I was a kid in Saskatoon, we thought Martensville was north," he said.

Norm nodded in agreement.

"Then I thought Waskesiu Lake was north. I worked a summer in LaRonge for Natural Resources and I thought *that* was north—the map showed the road ending there. When I got assigned to Wollaston Lake, I had to look it up on the map. I thought *Holy Shit!* When the Resources guys picked me up in LaRonge to bring me to Wollaston we drove north on the gravel road and kept driving and driving," he laughed.

"Why did you quit the MNR?" I asked.

"The Natural Resources guy that worked before me had to be flown out after he busted a nontreaty guy for shooting a moose and then confiscated it. His tires had been slashed. They had to get him the hell out of here and fast," John said. "Natural Resource officers north of LaRonge are here to monitor, not enforce. It drove me crazy."

"What are the rules up here for taking game?" Charly asked.

"If you're treaty you can take all you want. If you're nontreaty you abide by Saskatchewan rules," John said. "My second winter here a caribou herd came right into town. They'd never come that far south before. People went nuts, and the caribou got slaughtered. There was blood everywhere."

"I bet it all got eaten," Doug said, looking up from reading our book about Nunavut, the newest province in Canada, where we would be paddling the next summer. John rolled his eyes.

"I lived in the Northwest Territories for two years and Baffin Island in the early 1970s. I was there before Pepsi or Coke," Doug told us, nodding toward the Nunavut book, meaning he was there before everything changed.

Charly and John pored over maps, an ongoing conversation between them that never ended. Charly could spend a lifetime looking at maps. To him, they are a great novel and picture book combined. Where I see a bunch of squiggly lines, he sees the landscape and can imagine where people before have traveled. John noted landmarks, such as old settlements, icehouses, cabins, the Cochrane River camp, and old churches, then marked snowmobile routes going north and east and southeast to Brochet. He told us about an old dogsled route to Black Lake along the Fond du Lac.

"No one uses it anymore because there's a road and power line all the way up there now," John said. "It's been eight years since anyone broke it out."

"So, how hard would it be to break it out?" Charly asked, thinking about the snowshoe part of our trip. We planned to snowshoe two hundred miles north for a few weeks in March, reunite with our canoe and food, which would be flown north, and paddle from there at ice-out, sometime in June. Charly was exploring our options.

John shrugged. "Depends on the conditions. You have a thick crust—no problem. Turns warm—you have a problem."

Doug, Norm, and John impressed me with their calm demeanor. They did not care that they were delayed on an island with no electricity or running water and a winter storm brewing that could potentially leave them stranded for days or weeks. I thought about how people, including myself, freak if a plane is postponed for an hour. Using the trapper radio, John radioed someone in town and told him to tell people they were safe so no one would go looking for them. Over. Then he radioed the operator in LaRonge and told her to call someone at the airlines and tell them to go in to work for him the next day. Over. Doug and Norm never mentioned work or pressing projects and didn't contact anyone.

That's the way the North worked, I was learning. There was a respect for weather. If it turned bad, people sat it out. Travel meant taking chances. Work mattered less than being alive, warm, fed, and comfortable. I was able to offer everyone sleeping bags and even toothbrushes, since my Aunt Donna had just sent a bunch.

"This might be it for the season," John said, laying out his sleeping bag.

"What do you mean?" Charly asked.

"This could be winter. We might be waiting here until there's enough ice to Ski-Doo out of here. Wake me up when it blows over," John said, pulling the sleeping bag over his head.

The five of us slept in the living room while the wind howled, the temperatures dropped to twenty degrees, and the sky let loose some snow. The next morning we ate breakfast, watching the white-capped waves, then played horseshoes until the wind died and the waves flattened enough for them to make a run for town.

"We lucked out," John said. "We'll see you in three weeks." That's when he predicted freeze-up. They motored off into big rolling waves.

We returned to our mail. Charly read a letter aloud from his dad.

Dear Charly,

Your old man is losing it. All sorts of things I should have done since getting back but my progress is very halting. I always was better working against deadlines and with retirement I don't seem to get anything done. Anyway I tried the key station a few times and got a busy signal. But got through today and they said your radio was now working.

Did stop by at Jean's on the way out and delivered the produce. She seemed to be most appreciative. Mailed most of the letters from LaRonge since I thought that postmark would sound more remote than Saskatoon. Sent the newspaper story from here as soon as I got home . . .

I saw your grandmother the day before yesterday. In contrast to my previous several visits, she seemed to know who I was, and was quite responsive. When I talked about you she seemed to track it and was quite animated in her reaction. Of course, she didn't remember what I had said a few minutes before, but that didn't diminish her pleasure.

Love to both of you. Dad

Two days later, Charly and I walked to the hill for the sunrise, our feet crunching in the fresh snow. No wind, and the sun warmed my cheeks. Wildlife had become scarce, but animal activity was now visible in the snow. I spied the chicken-like tracks of spruce grouse. Charly pointed out the tracks of my friend the pine marten—larger than a mink and smaller than a fisher. And there were numerous tracks of Felix's enemy *Tamiasciurus hudsonicus*, the red squirrel—though none near the cabin.

We decided to wash laundry. Charly rigged a ringer using poles like he does for tanning hides. I heated water on the cookstove and filled one tub for washing and another for rinsing. A slight breeze blew off the lake, causing goose bumps on the back of my neck. The sunshine made me forget that it was fall. I instead felt the butterflies of spring in my stomach. Smiling, happy, still high on having overnight visitors a few days before, I scrubbed laundry on a washboard and then set it in the rinse bucket.

"Laura Fuckin' Ingalls," I said to Charly, who wrung out the laundry.

"My fantasy girl," he replied.

"Strong and cheerful," I said, referring to a letter Charly had just written to his grandmother reporting that I was "strong and cheerful and so made a good paddling partner." It was accurate, but made me sound like a pioneer woman.

"Who knew there was more to life than iceberg lettuce," Charly said. This joke had started years before when I was a reporter at the *Ashland Daily Press*. I had written a story about a farmer's market and started the article with "There's more to life than iceberg lettuce." Doug and John had brought iceberg lettuce with them for their visit, so the line had been revived. My brother, Link, loved to tease, "What's wrong with iceberg lettuce?"

"I think it should be my epitaph," I said.

"Mental note: Your tombstone will read, *She was strong and cheerful and knew there was more to life than iceberg lettuce.* Except, of course, you'll long outlive me."

"Yes I will," I said with a smile.

Charly ran lines from tree to tree, and I hung the laundry out to dry.

"Let's paddle over to the cliffs," Charly suggested.

As the season faded into winter, each calm day with open water could be our last, and so we tried to grab each one—particularly days like these. We paddled down the shore and across a bay to explore more of Estevan Island. Charly tied off *Le Strubel* and we hiked to the top of the hill. Wow! Estevan Island sprawled across thousands of acres with its own lakes and an interior bay we would come to refer to as "Inner Estevan." Another world to explore had opened up. I could see two of the inland lakes, one frozen and one partially frozen. The point where we lived seemed so skinny from the cliffs, the cabin barely visible. We scrambled down the hill and paddled the canoe down the shore where Charly and I each cast a few times, then we set out for home, trolling. Charly caught a nice trout in the deep water. For dinner, with the full moon providing mood lighting, we ate fresh fish, fresh garden salad, mashed potatoes, and sautéed onions on the side.

October twenty-fifth. Snow, glorious snow. "It's beautiful outside," Charly mumbled, as he crawled back into bed in the middle of the night. When it was light, I peeked out the window to Heike running through snow. A few inches coated the branches, bird feeders, and upside-down canoe. I could not stop humming "Walking in a Winter Wonderland."

"Should we try it one last time?" I asked of our idea to paddle to town. The lake looked cold and gray, but a silky, calm gray. And we needed some adventure.

"Well, we can go to town or sit around here bored," Charly responded.

"Hmmm. Let's go."

And again we packed enough gear to survive a week.

Three hours later, we glided through gelatinous water toward John's dock. He wasn't around, so we continued toward Welcome Bay Store. Suddenly *Le Strubel* started breaking ice, and sure enough, I looked around and could see ice farther out in the bay, holding a dusting of snow. We pushed our way through to the Welcome Bay Store dock. I swear I could see the water thickening as I stood onshore. We had just paddled to town for the last time.

22

$\mathcal{H}eart's$ $\mathcal{D}esire$

There are two tragedies in life. One is to lose your heart's desire.
The other is to get it. — George Bernard Shaw

The lake turned gelatinous, pans of ice floating alongshore. A thin sheet of ice laid itself across the bay, new crystals forming patterns like fanning feathers. We should have reveled in the beauty of it, but instead we both grew ornery and despondent. It had been weeks since John, Doug, and Norm spent the night. And there was no sign of freeze-up. On the first of November, Charly worked on varnishing the canoe. I built a doghouse for Heike. We bickered over my choice of rags for sealing the doghouse and didn't speak for the rest of the day. Heike had the last word, dragging her dog dish to the cabin and choosing to sleep beneath the house.

The days were short and grainy gray, the color of granite tombstones. This was purgatory. The sun, if it appeared at all, didn't rise until nine and then disappeared by four. Charly and I talked about the great pressure that goes along with the gift of time.

"I hate myself for not being inspired and productive with so much time at hand," he said one morning after a round of push-ups and sit-ups.

"Hmmm," I said, still half sleeping. I rolled over and propped my upper body on my elbow. "I know. I feel like I have this great privilege of having this much time, and what have I done except mope?"

"Like if we don't produce something great with so much time . . .," he continued, standing to put wood on the fire.

"We're total losers," I said.

"I've always said the toughest thing about getting older is coming to terms with mediocrity."

We sat in gray silence, the sounds of a crackling fire filling the space. I thought about my dream from moments before: Charly worked as a pilot, hired to take burn victims to Southend on Reindeer Lake.

"What I really love is the learning experience, how to live simply, cheaply, using the old ways. You need a tribe for that and . . .," Charly continued, poking a stick at the fire.

"Two don't make a tribe."

"Maybe with kids it would come close. I'd like to think if I had some of my buddies here, I'd be fired up to do stuff, but who knows? Maybe we'd all succumb to the weather and sit in the corner drooling on ourselves."

"Yep, it's hard without that energy around . . ."

To shake us from our funk, Charly declared a no-more-moping day. We sat at the kitchen table and scratched out a list of weekly rituals, meant to give us something to anticipate. Goals. A sense of purpose.

Monday: Laundry Day, sauna

Tuesday: Charly gets massage, poetry

Wednesday: Bread Day, Julie makes special dinner

Thursday: Mop floor, reading, Julie gets massage, poetry

Friday: Trip writing morning, sauna

Saturday: Charly makes special dinner

Sunday: Free Day! Pizza for dinner

That was it. An entire day for mopping a floor that even if mopped with a toothbrush wouldn't take much longer than an hour or two. Laundry? We each still only had two pairs of pants, a few shirts and underclothes. The list should have depressed us even further, but oddly enough, it worked—for a bit. We began immediately.

Saturday: I worked on a watercolor that I had started for Mom's birthday. It was called *Barge Girls* and was a painting of her and me paddling a load of wood by canoe. I could sketch the canoe and the outline of our bodies, and the background was easy, but I struggled with the faces for most of the day. It was my fourth attempt. I planned to send it to Dad as soon as we could get mail out. Having long finished *Memoirs of a Geisha*, I started *Seven Years in Tibet*. Not surprisingly, it was slower paced than the movie, but hey, I wasn't going anywhere. Charly wrote a letter to our tenants, who had written us about getting a break on their rent because the apartment wasn't finished before they moved in. He read an *Orion* magazine that Mike had sent and dreamed up environmental projects for back home. We walked to the top of the hill in the bleak afternoon light, discussing the ski trails we'd create once the snow came.

Estevan Island's terrain was so rugged—a combination of steep rocky hills, dense forests, Labrador tea thickets, soft sphagnum moss beds, spongy bogs, and lakes—that it was nearly impossible to hike beyond the hill behind the cabin. We needed frozen ground and ice in order to go anywhere else. I worked on one—and only one, I was pacing myself— crossword puzzle from the *New York Times* book of Tuesday puzzles that my brother had sent. For his special dinner, Charly fried venison medallions (left from Felix and Linda), baked squash, and boiled wild rice.

Sunday: Free Day. Charly started a photo-a-day project, modeling it after Jim Brandenburg's project, *Chased by the Light*, when he limited himself to one photo per day from the autumnal equinox to the winter solstice. Charly and I had seen his photo exhibit. Charly left the house after lunch to scout the best shot of the colorless day. By breakfast, I had solved my one puzzle for the day. By lunch, having finished *Seven Years in Tibet*, I started reading *The Poisonwood Bible*.

Monday: "Laundry Day!" Charly sang, waking me from slumber.

I repeated "Laundry Day," and started to cry.

"What's wrong?" Charly asked, rushing to sit next to me.

"That's all I have to look forward to?"

"You don't have to do laundry today."

I cried through breakfast, hot big tears that streamed one after another over my cheeks, past my lips, and onto my shirt. I once took a Myers-Briggs Type Indicator assessment that identified me as an ENTP: extrovert, intuitive, thinking, and perceptive. The noteworthy thing about the test is that I was a big E. An off-the-charts E. Charly had taken the same test somewhere along the way. His results: INTP. I for introvert. A backpacking trip to the Bob Marshall Wilderness during our first years together defined the difference between the E and the I. The trail turned out to be one with few visitors, and we didn't see anyone for days. My energy waned. Meanwhile, Charly grew manic, chattering about how we might not see anyone yet again and wouldn't that be great. I hoped beyond hope that we would run into someone, even a park ranger. We sat atop a mountain peak on the fifth day. Alone. I lay back and took a nap. Charly stripped and streaked across the top, as if he had just downed a gallon of coffee.

According to the Myers-Briggs assessment, people who are extroverted draw energy from action and people. Conversely, introverts rebuild energy through quiet time and being alone. I was in the midst of the longest time-out of my life. Estevan Island made Lake Winnipeg and the Bob Marshall Wilderness seem like tea socials. I was homesick, and it had been two weeks since we'd seen anyone and would likely be another two weeks before we saw anyone again. I sniffled as I stared out the window into something resembling light and watched Heike run around. She looked so stupidly happy that watching her improved my mood briefly.

"Wouldn't Heike and Knock-Knock have fun together?"   Charly innocently asked.

I started crying again and couldn't turn it off.

"I miss Knock-Knock. I miss home."

He didn't know what to do, except hold me in his arms.

"I've never seen you like this," he said. "Tell me what to do."

I returned to bed to read *The God of Small Things*.

Tuesday: We studied the cereal box at breakfast in dim light. The wind blew, and the overcast sky spit freezing rain. Thanks to Quebec, Canada is a bilingual country, so everything is written in English and French, hence our knowledge of guimauves—otherwise known as marshmallows. French made the cereal box a bit more interesting.

After breakfast, Charly pulled *Trinity* from Felix's bookshelf and lay down to read. I finished my crossword of the day and started reading the stack of large-print *Reader's Digest*s. I had read all the books that my friends had sent the month before and was getting desperate. Charly hiked around the island for a few hours looking for his shot of the day. In the afternoon we sawed wood. We cut and hauled wood any time the weather allowed. Since we couldn't cut into Felix and Linda's supply near the house, we needed to hike way back on the island and cut and pile near shore to haul by canoe when the weather allowed. We patched trail clothing, and we started building a toboggan from plastic sheeting and scrap wood for our winter travels.

Wednesday: Bread day. Thirty mile an hour winds blew out the little bit of ice that had formed. It was a gray, gray day that spat even more sleet. I decided to bake bread using Linda's handwritten recipe.

1/4 cup warm water
3/4 tsp sugar
1-1/2 tsp yeast
2 cups water
2 cups milk
4-6 T honey
4 tsp salt
4 T butter
10 cups whole wheat flour
Mix warm water, sugar, and yeast. Set aside until bubbly. Heat the water, milk, honey, salt and butter until the butter melts. Cool and stir into yeast mixture. Add flour. Knead. Let rise for two hours. Punch down and knead. Divide and drop into greased coffee tins. Let rise. Bake at 350 degrees, 40 minutes.

I started in. The smell of the yeast warming took some of the gray out of the day. I tested the temperature of the milk and honey mixture using Linda's method of dropping it on your wrist like baby's milk. Then I mixed it into the yeast. Linda used Red River cereal mix in place of half the flour, and she had left some behind so I did the same. The cereal provided texture. As I kneaded the dough I started to hum.

While the bread was rising I turned to baking brownies and making tortillas for dinner. Charly ambled in and out on walks in between working on his sauna and looking for his photo of the day. He was circling the kitchen like a hungry wolf. "How's the bread?" he asked often.

After two hours I punched the dough down and kneaded it some more, still humming. I greased the coffee cans and put the dough in. Then I went for a brisk walk up the hill behind the cabin and came back with the last fragments of light. When I returned to the cabin, I lit the lantern to finish a crossword and write in the journal. The bread was ready to go into the oven. Forty minutes later, Charly stood behind me as I pulled the golden brown bread out of the oven by lantern light. Ripping warm chunks of fresh bread from the can-shaped loaves, we devoured an entire loaf. Mmmmmmm. Now there was a morale booster.

Thursday: Charly finished writing his first ever article. Called "Confessions of a Tarpist," it was about why he loves tarps and prefers them to tents. He planned to send it to his sister to have her type it and send it to *Canoe and Kayak* magazine. (It was published later that winter.)

The weather drizzled rain, and the wind blew out all the ice that had formed so far, further depressing my mood since we needed ice to travel. We listened to chatter on the trapper radio as we swept and cleared the floor and heated water for mopping. The trapper radio was our link to the outside, but it was an inconsistent link. We would go for days hearing only static, or we'd try to call someone only to frustrate them and ourselves with muddled reception. I had one hilarious conversation with my mother in which I mentioned onions. Ten tries at pronouncing onion slowly, then spelling it out, then pronouncing it slowly again, and I finally gave up. Days and weeks could pass without even being able to reach the operators at the LaRonge key station, so chatter on the trapper radio made for a good day.

We didn't understand most of the radio talk—a mixture of Cree, Dene, and sometimes English—but we liked the background noise and the laughter even if we missed the details. There were some words that were English-specific and stood out, like *Ski-Doo* or *spark plug*. The trapper radio conversations let us know that locals awaited freeze-up as eagerly as we did. "I'll come once it freezes. Over," was a common end to conversations.

Hazel was an older bush woman who lived a two-hour snowmobile ride from the road. Her mother was in the hospital. Hazel was convinced her mother had had a stroke, though the doctors had diagnosed arthritis. "Those doctors don't know a damn thing," she told someone. "They fed her an egg sandwich for dinner. She hates eggs. Over."

"Take her some whitefish. Over."

This conversation was repeated several times to several people. Each time she retold the story, Hazel's conviction that her mother had had a stroke strengthened. By the last conversation, she stopped mentioning the original diagnosis of arthritis altogether.

Or this one between a husband and wife that highlighted the awkwardness of the trapper radio. It went something like this:

She: I'm moving out. Over.

He: Oh. Over.

She: Is that all you have to say? Over.

He: Uh huh. Over.

She: I'm coming to get my stuff. Over.

He: Okay. Over.

"That's harsh," Charly said.

"Brutal," I laughed.

Friday: Charly finished building a sauna, using a white canvas tent and small woodstove. Carpeted with spruce boughs, it smelled sweet in the heat. In candlelight we undressed, cracked a beer, and sweated.

"Have you ever experienced hunger, real hunger?" Charly asked.

I shook my head no.

"I remember Debbie telling me she ate only carrots for a few days when she was in France because she ran out of money." Debbie was Charly's college girlfriend.

That reminded me of my own out-of-money story. "The first time I traveled to Europe, I totally ran out of money and for four days ate bananas that you could buy from street vendors. Lost a lot of weight. Ate peanut butter for weeks when I got back. I was in London. I remember the last day I was there. I didn't have enough money for a hostel, so I planned to spend the night at the airport. I was at a small restaurant, like a McDonald's but not a McDonald's, eating beans and rice. My last meal, and I was totally out of money. I can't remember how I started talking to this guy, a taxicab driver, but he found out it was my last day in London and insisted on showing me the sights. He said he'd been in Texas once, got a flat tire, and someone helped him out, fed him, and put him up for the night. He'd been waiting to repay the act of kindness to an American, and I was it."

Charly sat, attentive. "I can't believe you've never told me this before."

"I forgot about it until now." Somehow, after six months of being together every single minute of every single day but three, we had found new territory for conversation.

"So what happened?"

"He was a great guy. Drove me all around London in his taxicab. We went for beers at a pub, then for pizza, and just saw some sites. Then he dropped me off at the train station. I had a voucher that came with my plane ticket, so I could get to Manchester to catch my plane. He even handed me twenty dollars to last me until I got home. I still spent the night at the airport, but I was a lot more comfortable with food in my belly and a magazine to read. The part that bums me out is that he asked me to stay in touch, and I lost his address. I planned to send him a sweatshirt from Wisconsin."

Charly and I were suddenly energized and talked about my travels through Europe and Cuba. When we walked out of the sauna three hours later, northern lights shot across the sky. We stood in freezing temperatures, steam rising from our naked refreshed bodies, looking up at the sky. We were residing in the northern-lights hot spot. On a clear night, there was a 90 to 95 percent chance that we would see northern lights. That night, sparkling fluorescent green streaks danced up and down and across the sky.

The weekly schedule helped our state of mind, and on November fourteenth we got ice—sort of—making Mom the official winner of when-the-lake-will-freeze contest. The whole lake didn't freeze, but the bay that we'd been paddling to reach the rest of the island did. Ice formed around the dock, so thin and clear I could see the rocks beneath it, a window to the world beneath the water. Charly set out immediately to explore the bay, inching his way across and around, chopping holes in the ice every twenty yards or so. I watched from shore and Heike ran loyally behind. He carried a long pole in one hand to test the ice and an axe in the other hand, unsheathed and ready to dig into the ice if he went through. Once I knew he'd be okay, I hiked up the hill behind the cabin. I looked across the bay and saw a human on the ice and grew abnormally excited. Then I realized it was Charly.

"I can't wait to take you out tomorrow," Charly said of the newfound frozen territory. "It's like a new wing has opened up in the monkey house."

The next day, I kicked up two ptarmigan decked out in full winter plumage—fully white except for their eyes and the black triangles on their tails—on my morning walk up the hill behind the cabin. Heike spooked another half dozen, six tufts of snowy heaven floating upward. I could see ice to the horizon in all directions, steam rising where open water remained.

Skiing changed everything. The ice changed everything. No more crying. No more moping. That morning I followed Charly on the trail he had tested the day before. More ice than snow for skiing, but we didn't care. A few days later, three inches of snow fell, and we skied even farther into new territory, sunshine on our shoulders. Sunshine! After two weeks of solid gray, the sun had returned. The combination of ski trails and sun rays brightened our moods. The island and bays were ours for the exploring.

On November twentieth, Charly and I walked all the way across Big Narrows to Loranger Island, checking the ice every few feet. The ice was about three inches thick. We crossed the narrows one step at a time, heading to an abandoned icehouse once used by commercial fishermen. Safely on land, I looked back at the cabin before crossing up and over the hill to inner Loranger Island.

"Let's ski to town tomorrow," I said.

"Time to get off the island," Charly agreed.

Charly called John Elander. "We're coming to town tomorrow. Over."

"I'm coming out there tomorrow. Over," John replied

"There's only three inches of ice. Over," Charly said.

"That's enough. I have your mail. Over."

I could barely sleep that night. The moon shone bright, and I was so excited by the possibility of visitors and mail. I woke up early and finished *Barge Girls*, improving the faces and the canoe. I began preparing—sweeping and making soup and coffee. Starting about noon we began scanning the overcast horizon, looking for a snowmobile. At last we could hear the machines but still couldn't catch sight of them. Thirty minutes later I spied a headlight in the afternoon dusk. "They're coming!"

Charly hustled to the dock carrying two chairs. He set up the tripod for his Brandenburg photo of the day. We sat down, attempting a casual look, beaver-fur hats on our heads. Charly snapped a timed shot of us looking out into the gray haze as the snowmobilers headed toward us. Three of them were spread out across the thin ice, moving fast.

"When the ice is iffy, or you hit slush, you don't stop to check how thick it is. You just give 'er," John said.

Slush, which is water over ice but under snow, is the nightmare of the winter traveler. Often hidden under fresh snow, slush may first be detected by a sinking sensation indistinguishable from going through a patch of bad ice into the lake. A dogsled or snowmobile driver can get very wet and cold in the process of getting a sled out of the slush, and in very cold temperatures, the sled can become frozen in.

"I'm surprised you came out with just three inches," Charly said.

"You only need two."

Charly and I immediately adopted John's "you just give 'er" line. John carried a blue canvas bag filled with a month's worth of mail. Doug drove the second snowmobile, and someone I'd never met drove the third. James, who worked for Natural Resources, was a tall, quiet giant of a guy. The three disrobed from their snowmobile suits and made themselves comfortable in the living room. I served coffee. Charly brought out the cookies.

"How'd you two do out here?" John asked, his eyebrows raised.

"It was a long month," I said.

"Unusual winter. Freeze-up doesn't usually take that long," he said. "It's about two weeks late."

James sat silently while John and Doug told us about the Dene practice of grilling caribou heads over an open fire and then eating the insides.

"I'm all for caribou over an open fire, but I don't think I could eat the brains," I said.

"The eyes are the delicacy," John said.

Charly started nodding his head like he was ready for some eyeball soup.

"Have you tried it?" I asked John and Doug.

They shook their heads no, their attention diverted, like raccoons to foil, by a red-covered Tentsmiths catalog featuring authentic canvas historic period tents. Doug picked it up but needed reading glasses, so asked to borrow John's. He motioned to John to hand them over. John shook his head no.

"I want to read it," he said.

They stared at one another.

"Promise you'll read the passages aloud," Doug said, handing the catalog over.

"Tentsmiths' roots are in tipis. This is the structure that started us along the tentmaking path," John began, glasses resting midway down his nose.

Once the coffee pot emptied and the catalog had been read, the three got dressed in their snowmobile gear and roared away, fanning out across the ice. We stood at the dock watching them go until they made it safely across the narrows and to Loranger Island. Charly leaped and bounded for the cabin, singing "Mail, mail, mail." Letters, real handwritten gems, connected us to friends and family in ways not possible by phone, e-mail, or even personal contact. Letters felt intimate, trusting—written with the luxury of focus and time. Through references in letters we realized we had missed a boy wonder named Harry Potter. We knew the media continued to obsess on the millennium bug, but that was no concern here without a single electronic device beyond the watch I carried on a string. Letters also reflected the busy lives of our friends.

From Dawn: *Dear Julie, I've started a hundred letters to you in my head, but have not had the mental space to sit down and get a good letter out. The letters I've actually started are all so mundane that I don't want to send them. I fear for myself! I have no space for reflection or for introspection.*

And the letters just plain encouraged us.

From Felix and Linda: *Hi Charly and Julie, Your letter was greatly appreciated. To hear from you regarding the fish, birds and grouse, plus the garden and the scenery was heart warming and made us envious of you. It was also gratifying to know you are able to make use of the garden. . . . Say hello to our friends in Wollaston Post when you see them. Our questions may seem nosy, however we are keenly interested in your quest. We are not sorry in the slightest that we invited you to winter at our cabin. In fact as time passes we are getting more thrilled with your adventure and are just glad we can be a small part of it.*

"Hey, Jim wrote with an answer to our question," Charly said.

I looked up from my letter.

"What question?"

"From *Lonesome Dove*,"

"Oh, the Latin saying. What does it mean?" I asked.

Charly had read *Lonesome Dove* in two sittings. I'd walked in on him during the Deets death scene and discovered him crying. Charly had written his friend Jim, who taught high school Latin, about the sign at the ranch that read *uva uvam vivendo varia fit.*

"He writes, 'It's not very clear and doesn't make sense, but it translates as Eggs/Cluster vary by living.'"

"So Larry McMurtry was messing with us," I said.

The next day we set aside the letters and books and skied part way to town, following the snowmobile trail. We pulled our new toboggan filled with winter gear to see how well it would do on our spring trek north. It was a gray, gray day. We traveled about six miles, ate lunch in the snow, and then started back. A snowmobile pulled up beside us, turning off its engine.

"Where you going?" asked the man who introduced himself as Arnold.

"Estevan Island," Charly replied.

"Oh."

We must have looked like lost Scandinavians, skiing along in this land of fast machines.

"We're staying there for the winter," I told him.

"I just cleared a trail to the landing so people can get to town," he said. "Last year we were driving trucks on the ice this time of year. One of the latest freeze-ups I remember." That route acted as the early season ice road between town and the gravel road. As the ice thickened, the ice road would follow the barge route, which was more direct.

"There's not much ice," Charly said.

"About three inches out there. Just enough to get a Ski-Doo across."

Two more snowmobiles pulled up. A guy who introduced himself as William Hansen said he was the first to sled out. "I just picked up my nephew," he said, pointing his head toward the person riding with him.

John had told us about William Hansen. He was a Cree man who had married a Dene woman. The word was that Dene women never left Wollaston, so if you married one, you had to move to Wollaston. William was a trapper and fisherman in the area, and knew the backcountry well.

He handed three frozen whitefish to Charly. "I planned to cook them up, but I won't have time," he said.

"We don't need three," I protested.

"Feed it to your dog if you can't eat it all," he said.

Two days later, Thanksgiving in the United States, we packed two sleeping bags, two day packs with emergency kits, food for two or three meals, a thermos of hot chocolate, a pan for boiling water, mukluks, beaver hats, and down coats, then clicked on our skis and crossed Big Narrows to the snowmobile route to town.

We skied through sparkling hoarfrost, pulling the sled behind. Silver magic. It looked as if someone had gently lifted every shrub, blade of grass, limb, and twig and dipped it into a crystalline white substance. Snow weighed heavily on the spruce branches. "This is what heaven looks like," Charly exclaimed, cheeks pink from the cold. It took thirty minutes to ski from Estevan Island across Big Narrows to the icehouse. One of us pulled the sled while the other skied ahead—then we switched. Heike ran back and forth between us, diving and jumping in the snow.

As we climbed up and over the hill into inner Loranger Island, we spotted three snowmobiles coming our way. One directed its path as if it planned to run us over. John Elander. He and James and three others were headed for the road to pick up two new snowmobiles. John checked out our new toboggan, pushing it back and forth, and finally giving it his seal of approval.

"Take lots of pictures. This much moisture for so long is unusual," John told us, referring to the hoarfrost.

"It's pretty incredible," Charly agreed.

"Doug's warming a spot for you to stay at Welcome Bay. Dinner at my house," John reported, then rode away. We had not made plans to spend Thanksgiving with him and had not planned to run into him on the trail, but we had fully come to expect John would be somewhere taking care of us like a northern Canadian version of a fairy godparent.

"Okay. Personal goal. Get to town before John returns," I told Charly, remembering the raised eyebrow, the contained laughter when we had told him we would ski instead of snowmobile our way through winter. This was a contest of skis versus Ski-Doo.

"It will take him another hour to get to the road, then two hours back to town," Charly said.

"Plus time to eat lunch and get the new sleds," I added. "We should be able to do it."

Snowmobiles passed us by. One man stopped and turned off the engine, leaving the smell of exhaust hanging in the air. He was on his way to pick up Dene elders who were coming from Black Lake, located one hundred miles northwest of Wollaston. "Two elders died. The funeral is tomorrow," he told us.

We skied on through the hoarfrost, through blackened areas where forest fires had burned. The charred trees contrasted beautifully against the white backdrop. About three miles from town, we heard machines behind us. It was John. They had only one new snowmobile. James had driven his new machine only 9.2 miles before the engine blew. They left it on the ice to be rescued later.

"I already rung the dealer, and they're sending a replacement," John said, proud of his mobile phone. Then noting our slow progress, he smiled, "What? Are you on the five-year plan?"

"No, not the five-year plan, John. The five-hour plan," Charly said.

The last three miles were a sloping fun ride. A parade of snowmobiles passed us, hauling wood. We arrived at Wollaston Post at four in the afternoon, six hours after leaving Estevan. We had skied fifteen miles. Two-and-a-half miles per hour. Pitiful.

"The sled must have really slowed us down," I reasoned.

Capitalist Jim was out of town, so Social Director Doug told us to sleep at Jim's house. Charly took a hot bath and I called home, catching my family after their turkey meal. Dad had baked bread, using Linda's recipe, at his cabin during the opening weekend of deer hunting. "It turned out great," Dad said, pleased with himself.

Link expressed mock horror about it when I got him on the phone. "I told him, 'Wait 'til the guys find out about this. Can't get Dad outside to shoot a deer 'cause he's kneading bread.'"

"Did you tell the guys?" I asked.

"No, I was too embarrassed," he said, laughing.

The next day I sat in John's living room, the television broadcasting a curling match, and looked out at the bay, which acted as Main Street for Wollaston Post in the winter. People walked, rode snowmobiles, and ran teams of sled dogs along the icy corridor. Planes had not landed in Wollaston Post for over a week because of fog, so the town was wiped clean of groceries. Out of eggs, John called Doug to bring some over. Doug dropped by wearing caribou pants and coat, and so John pulled out his chopper mittens and mukluks. Charly and I oohed and ahhhed over the gorgeous display of outerwear.

A plane was scheduled to land after lunch.

"Ride along and take photos," Doug said, spooning eggs into his mouth. "This isn't just any plane. It's a DC-3."

Nicknamed the *Empress of Black Lake*, this DC-3 could carry eight thousand pounds. Pilots loved to fly her. We rode along with Doug and John and helped unload milk, cigarettes, eggs, and pizza pops. Doug climbed onto her wing. "Take my photo," he told Charly, embracing the large plane.

"Why don't you just make love to it?" one guy yelled from the ground.

The delivery of food and supplies created a carnival atmosphere around Wollaston Post the rest of the day. People piled into the Co-op Store to get mail, bananas, oranges, milk, and eggs. They crowded the aisles at Welcome Bay Store. I fought my way through for a box of Froot Loops and a gallon of milk. I met a woman named Martina during the craze. She was a fourth-grade teacher, and she'd heard about us from Doug. "Maybe I'll sled out with Doug to visit sometime," she said.

We finally left town in the fading light around three. Snowmobilers had blazed a new trail, one closer to our paddling route back to Estevan Island. This was good news, since it cut off three miles. We turned on our headlamps to stay on the trail, and together we pulled the sled, now heavier with our fresh supply of groceries. We could see the lights from the Rabbit Lake uranium mine, located across the lake on the gravel road. James passed us around seven o'clock. He was on his way to visit a friend at Wollaston Lake Lodge. William Hansen also passed us. He seemed amused and confused by our motorless plight.

Hours crept by.

Charly grew surly. "I hurt and I feel old," he said.

Nearing home, I changed out of my ski boots and into my mukluks. "I'll pull the sled home. You ski ahead to light a fire and haul water," I said.

"Are you sure?" Charly asked. "I don't like splitting up."

"Another mile and we'll be able to see the cabin. Really. A fire going at home would be great."

The last two miles dragged into infinity, though it felt good to rid myself of the ski boots. "I don't remember feeling worse," I said as I walked inside.

"Worse than the Bob Marshall?" Charly asked.

"Oh yeah," I said, remembering our second day backpacking in the Montana wilderness. Heavy packs, rough uncleared terrain, and shin-splinting downhill hiking. "Then there's the Quetico. I felt worse that day. Day five."

"I sure know how to show you a good time," he said with a laugh.

Charly boiled a dinner of mac and cheese at my request. As we sat eating by candlelight, he began listing ideas for improvements we could make for our next outing. He looked over at my tired face. "Maybe now isn't the best time to talk about it," he said. "It's a sickness, I know, this wilderness travel; but you're an enabler."

I blew out the candle. "Let's go to bed." Heike disappeared under the house, not even wanting to be fed. "It was a rough day for all of us."

23

The Social Season

See what we like to do in Canada is get a fire going, pack the stove, then damp it down so you've got some coals in the morning," John said, fiddling with our smaller stove. He had just delivered a Valley Comfort woodstove, an ugly but efficient heat source.

Charly and I looked at one another and grinned. "Really, John? You know, we do that in America too," Charly said.

"We just never knew the Canadians invented the method," I chimed in.

John turned around looking at me, then at Charly, saw our smiles and started to laugh. "Oh, we're going to be friends," he said.

Charly and I sat with a bowl of popcorn in front of us. Before John pulled up, we had been stringing kernels to decorate our miniature Christmas tree.

"So, John, we're thinking about getting a snowmobile," I said, poking a needle through a popped piece of corn.

"Really," he responded. Again, no surprise, but I think I saw a chuckle in his eyes.

"We need to socialize," Charly said.

John laughed, a knowing laugh. "Well, up here we have eight

months of great snowmobiling and four months of not-so-great snow-mobiling."

He stuck around for the morning, drinking coffee and telling us stories about his travels to Tijuana, Hong Kong, and Bangkok, then left for work. After days of not being able to transmit due to weather, we radioed and got through to Jim that afternoon.

"We're interested in a used machine. Over," Charly told him.

"I'll get back to you. Over," he replied.

December kicked off what I can only describe as the social season around Wollaston Lake. With the lake frozen, everyone became mobile. The gray endless days of November had passed, and even though it was getting darker and colder, the snow and ice made the days brighter. William Hansen, who had given us the whitefish, stopped by to say hello one afternoon. He had grown up in Pinehouse, Saskatchewan, but moved to Wollaston when he was younger. He worked at the mines for a while but hated it. He returned to trapping, commercial fishing, hunting caribou, and working for the fishing lodges. He had five children and nineteen grandkids. Charly invited him in for tea, and before the water boiled, John Elander snowmobiled to the front door, looking like a postal Santa Claus. He pulled a toboggan filled with Christmas packages and a blue mailbag.

"How many fur have you killed?" John asked William.

William shrugged, smiling.

"I'd like to get some caribou or moose hides for some projects," Charly said.

"I'll give some to you, but not selling them," William responded.

"The guys usually throw the caribou hides away because the sleds are full of meat. Go up north where the caribou are and you'll find piles of hides," John added.

William stood to leave. "I got to go to P.A. to get a tooth pulled," he said. P.A. stood for Prince Albert.

"How many do you have left?" Charly asked

"Three," he replied, grinning and showing them off.

It began to feel as if we would mentally survive the winter. We had access to mail and to the rest of the lake, and John visited often. We passed the time making Christmas presents, cutting wood, responding to mail, and refining the sauna. Charly had now added a larger stove and benches made of snow and had insulated with boughs and logs. I helped collect spruce boughs for the floor. And each night the northern lights came down like a curtain, shimmering greens, pinks, and reds across the sky.

Sunrise was now at 9:41, and temperatures dropped to twenty-five below zero. Cold and beautiful, the ice reflected all light, giving off a subtle soft glow—pinks, oranges, and yellows. Windblown mounds created shadows and relief. The wind blew snow into a sea of curves, fins, waves, prows, dunes, ripples, and smooth white drifts. I lay in the snow watching the sun go down while Charly set lines for ice fishing. Our days became a blur of snowshoeing, skiing, sewing gear, and preparing for the next leg of our journey.

At night I dreamed of family gatherings. In one dream my mom had arranged for all the Buckles women to come to the island for my birthday. They came by boatloads, wearing summer clothing. My cousin, Diane, had an Irish accent for some reason. I was surprised and confused and kept thinking, "What will we do with all these people?" They began baking cakes and making salads.

The trapper radio buzzed with families making holiday plans. We learned that *edza* is the Dene word for "cold." I talked to the LaRonge key station operator one morning, just to say hello. He told us that the operators had sent for an *Ashland Daily Press* subscription to receive our articles. Another operator had once mentioned that she was reading about us. I had let the comment pass at the time, but now I understood what she was reading. We had written four articles so far for our hometown paper. People could pay ten dollars and receive them in the mail if they so desired. Felix and Linda had also subscribed, hanging the latest articles at the Pilger library.

We called Jim again to check on the snowmobile. "I found one for you, but it's down in Saskatoon. Doug is down there now. He's coming back tomorrow afternoon. Over."

We talked to Kasba Lake Harold via the trapper radio. He lived at a lodge on Kasba Lake and took care of the place during the winter. Every Saturday night at six o'clock he would talk with the caretaker of a lodge on Obre Lake. Charly and I tuned in regularly like it was the *Ed Sullivan Show*. Kasba Lake was located about 150 miles north; we were headed that way in the spring.

Harold: "I saw some caribou the other night. Over."

Obre Lake: "I haven't seen any lately. I had a wolf come by though. Over."

Harold: "A wolf, eh? I haven't seen a wolf for a few weeks. Over."

Obre Lake: "How's your tooth doing? Over."

Harold: "I've been using some cream but it aches. Suppose I'll have to have someone look at it when I go out. Over."

Obre Lake: "I had a bad tooth once. Had it pulled. Over."

Charly jumped on the radio once they had finished talking.

"Kasba Lake Harold this is VEE864. Are you by?"

"This is Harold. Who's there? Over."

"Charly Ray. We're staying at Wollaston. Over."

"Say hello to John Elander next time you see him. Over."

"How long you been up at Kasba? Over." Charly asked.

"Since 1984. Over."

"You were probably there then when I came through with Camp Manitowish in 1986. Over."

"Yep, I would have been here. Over."

"You stay up there year round? Over."

"I stay at the fishing camp. I help run it in the summer and keep an eye on it the rest of the time. Over."

Life sped up as we worked through logistics for spring, answered mail, and created Christmas presents. Charly assembled a trail sewing kit for his sister, Kati, and I devised a challenging crossword puzzle with an Appalachian Trail theme, since she was making plans to hike the trail. I also worked on sewing a "tank" for my toboggan to keep our food and gear secure as we hauled it north. Laura F'ing Ingalls, I was. One late afternoon we set out for a snowshoe hike. The temperature rested at thirty below, with windchill at sixty-four below. Our snowshoes crunched on the snow as the ice boomed beneath us. A full moon rose in front of us as the sun set behind us. A snowmobile roared by—John Elander, wrapped in so many layers as to be unrecognizable, with a red scarf flying.

"So, you're practicing," he said, turning off his machine, looking at our snowshoes.

"Practicing?" I asked.

"For your spring hike to Kasba."

John had been out snowmobiling for three days, sleeping beneath the stars one night because he and his friends couldn't find their destination cabin.

"Come in for some tea," I said, getting chilled from standing still.

John didn't stay long. It was getting colder and darker and the wind was picking up.

"I'll come back tomorrow with your mail. Any word on your snowmobile?" he asked.

"We've called Jim a few times, but no snowmobile," Charly answered.

"You're learning," he said, rolling his eyes. "I'm learning over and over."

We called Jim to ask about the machine's status. He reported that it was in Wollaston but had a broken windshield, so he was awaiting a new one.

December continued without a snowmobile, heading toward my birthday and Christmas. I made a motion one night to open Christmas presents early. Charly seconded the motion, and we opened packages of homemade lefse and strawberry jam, writing paper, envelopes, candy bars, and from my parents, a pair of mittens made from Knock-Knock's fur. They were the most beautiful and the warmest soft gray-and-white mittens. Mom had found a woman who wove the fur into wool yarn, knitted the mittens, and washed them to partially felt them so there were no air holes. I pushed my nose into them hoping for some scent of Knock-Knock, but only smelled perfume. We were just about to open our first candy bar when we heard "VEE864 this is 5-1, do you copy?"

"A call!" I screamed and ran for the radio.

My friend Dawn. She called with the most animated conversation that may have ever hit those radio waves.

"I'm pregnant. Over." she reported.

"Congratulations. Over."

"My boobs are so big and my belly is swelling," she continued.

She told us about the pregnancy test, about telling her husband, Andy, about her anxieties—and the whole time I tried to tell her that this was all going live to the whole community of Wollaston Lake and beyond, but I couldn't because she never said "over."

"Why aren't you pregnant? Sounds like you've had enough opportunities. Over," she asked.

"I've got plenty of pills to last me another year. Over," I reported. Charly groaned and rested his head in his hands, thinking of all the trapper radios heating up across the north.

Later that same night, Herb called to talk.

"I'm all alone and feeling sorry for myself so thought I would call. Over." he said with a laugh.

"We can sympathize, Dad. Over."

"Chicago is headed for zero degrees. Expect packages of chocolate in the mail. Over."

He continued, talking about our finances, wanting to know whether he should reactivate our credit card, suggesting ideas about my student loan, telling us one renter was late, and so on. This time it was Charly who tried to cut in to remind him that he was live for all to hear, but Herb was not to be deterred either. The trapper radio was the original Facebook. Remote and insulated as we were, our lives that night were laid out for all of Wollaston and beyond, every bit as entertaining and foreign as Hazel and the married couple were to us, I'm sure.

On the twenty-first, Charly rose at five o'clock to bake a cake and prepare a greasy Wisconsin café–style birthday breakfast. I rose at nine, just before sunrise, and sat down for a plate of eggs, bacon, toast, and hashbrowns. "Extra crispy just like you like them," he said, setting a plate before me.

During one of our first dates—so early Charly and I weren't even calling them dates—Charly and I walked through the dark city streets of Washington, D.C. It was spring, and the air carried the scent of cherry blossoms. We stopped at a small coffee shop on P Street near Dupont, ordered a piece of Oreo cheesecake, and sat outside taking turns with bites. We walked the few blocks to Dupont Circle where the bike couriers hung out around a fountain and found a place in the trampled grass. Lying flat on our backs, looking up at the sky, Charly told me that his favorite day of the year was winter solstice.

"No kidding. That's my birthday," I told him. I knew then that he had potential. I mean no one particularly likes the darkest day of the year. And the fact that he did meant, well, he might be a keeper.

Charly treated my thirty-fifth birthday with particular care. I didn't know what he was planning, but I knew he had something going. It was extremely difficult for one of us to pull off anything without the other knowing. But for weeks he had been sneaking around, shuffling items away when I walked in the room.

"So, how does it feel to be so old?" he asked, smiling.

"I just read an article that said Naomi Wolf is thirty-seven; she's written three hot-topic books, is a total babe, and now earns fifteen thousand dollars a month consulting a presidential hopeful," I said, testing the crispiness of the hashbrowns. Perfect.

Heike slept on the floor, her feet twitching and teeth snapping.

"She's dreaming of chasing rabbits," I said, nodding toward Heike.

"I bet you could kick her ass."

"Naomi's? Maybe in a wood-sawing contest, if it were ten below," I said.

"Does turning thirty-five make you think about kids?" he asked, chewing his eggs.

"Don't you hear the big clock ticking even louder today?" I asked.

"When should we do it?" he asked.

"When we get back, don't you think? We can't wait much longer."

"Well, you can't," he said.

"Watch it. It's my birthday," I said.

Our bellies full, we pulled on all our layers, leaving only our eyes exposed. It was thirty below zero, and the sun was starting to peek over the spruce forest and through the clouds, brushing the lake snow pink. I inhaled the cold air deeply, burning my throat and lungs and sending me into a coughing fit. Heike jumped and twirled and snapped her teeth as Charly and I strapped on snowshoes. We set out across the ice and up and over the hill to Inner Estevan. Charly broke trail and cleared branches away.

We spied moose tracks and spotted a large bird, probably an owl, perched atop a spruce tree, with smaller birds circling to harass it. Our cheeks turned rosy, radiating good health as we trudged over the snow.

Later that afternoon, back at the cabin, Charly drank hot chocolate and I sipped tea. I opened presents: jasmine-scented lotion from my sister; pictures and thirty-five single dollar bills from my parents—a tradition that continues today, one dollar for every year along with a joke about the growing thickness of the card; and hand-crafted ornaments from Charly—a silver angel and a red canoe made from tomato paste cans. Charly prepared margaritas from mix leftover from Mom and Dad's visit in September. Mom and Dad called as we were taking our first sips. After receiving the bill for their first call to us—one hundred dollars!—they had found a phone plan for five cents a minute. When I told them about the moose tracks, Dad remembered that he had seen a moose and a calf on Loranger Island as they flew away. Our reception started to fade, and I signed off with them and looked outside for Charly. I couldn't see him, but I saw a flickering light, then another. I threw on my coat, hat, mittens, boots, and scarf and walked outside onto the ice as Charly lit the last of a string of candles inside ice luminaries.

"Oh, I wanted to surprise you," he said, turning around as if caught in the act of shoplifting a candy bar.

"You did. I saw them from the house," I said.

"Happy Birthday!" he said.

"What is this?"

"Thirty-five candles for your thirty-fifth birthday. Thirty-five paces apart."

Ice luminaries are big candle lanterns made of ice. First Charly had to haul water from the lake, which meant chipping through the ice (we kept a Styrofoam lid on the hole so he didn't have to chip every day). He filled five-gallon buckets and let the water sit for a few hours, and then at the correct moment, he punctured the top ice and turned the bucket upside down so the water in the middle poured out. If he waited too long, the entire bucket would freeze and he would have to start over. Tip too soon and the whole thing would fall apart. What remained if all went right was an ice lantern shaped like an empty bucket. A candle sitting inside, protected from the wind, twinkled off the ice for hours.

"How did you do this? When?" I asked, looking at ice candles spread down the lake and around the point.

"You didn't know? I thought for sure you knew when you saw me with a teapot of hot water outside."

The teapot with hot water had been used to urge a stuck luminary out of the bucket. I had seen Charly with the kettle a few days before, but didn't think much about it.

"It never occurred to me. You must have been working on this for weeks."

"I'd get close to thirty-five and then some would break. It took awhile."

"This is the best birthday present ever," I said and meant it, giving him a hug. I knew at that moment that I could count on Charly. I had known that he excelled at what interested him, but I never knew until that moment that he could excel at something that was specifically for me. I remembered a passage from *Corelli's Mandolin* where the father is talking to his daughter about love:

"Love is a temporary madness, it erupts like volcanoes and then subsides. And when it subsides you have to make a decision. You have to work out whether your roots have so entwined together that it is inconceivable that you should ever part because this is what love is. . . . Love itself is what is left over when being in love has burned away, and this is both an art and a fortunate accident. Your mother and I had it, we had roots that grew towards each other underground, and when all the pretty blossoms had fallen from our branches we were one tree and not two."

At that moment I, too, felt roots tangling and twisting, silently, forcefully.

"Here, each one represents a year of your life, so tell me a story from that year."

We walked to the first candle. I hesitated, embarrassed I guess, to have so much attention placed on my birthday.

"Come on. One year. One story," Charly encouraged.

"One. Hmmm. Well I know I got my dog Sparky for my first birthday. A black Labrador. Mom and Dad got her for me."

And so it went. I told a story for each year. "Twenty-seven. Isn't that when I met you?" I asked. We returned to the cabin for another round of margaritas, sitting at the table, playing canasta, talking as we watched the candles flicker in the distance.

Our winter routine continued. Now we couldn't find enough time to do everything we wanted: snowshoe, ski, ice fish, haul wood, photograph, sketch, read, and write. And then John delivered our mail and a loaner snowmobile from Capitalist Jim, as ours was not ready. The German woman for whom our dog was named drove the loaner. The welcome duo brought with them a bottle of rum. Heike was trained as a social worker, but worked as a secretary in Germany so she could work six months, then travel to Wollaston for six months. She first came to Wollaston in 1994 as an environmental activist to fight the expansion of the Rabbit Lake uranium mine, the mine whose lights we could see as we skied home from town. The mine grew anyway, but she kept coming back. Now she was working to develop an ecotourism business, incorporating Wollaston Post into the deal. She normally came during the summer, but this year she'd arrived for a month in winter.

Charly and John talked about old dogsled routes and looked at maps. I asked Heike something that I had always wondered about: the German obsession with North American Indians. She smiled, pausing to answer. "It's embarrassing," she started. "There are two branches, one that likes to 'play' Indian. They are the hobbyists. They have little interest in real Indians. They like to dress up and sleep in tipis. The other branch is looking for a culture to fill the void left after World War II. They want spiritual enlightenment. Since the Holocaust, people don't want to look back, to embrace their Germanness. It all began, in part, with a series of books by a man who had never met an Indian but wrote from his imagination of the 'noble savage.'"

"In the U.S., there are people who dress up and reenact the Civil War," I told her.

"People do that in Germany too," she said.

"What war?"

"The Civil War."

"You've adopted our wars as well," I laughed.

We sat up until one in the morning talking, then hiked to the top of the hill to watch the clear sky and northern lights. "We brought our sleeping bags," John informed us, and he and Heike rolled out their Therm-a-Rest mattresses in the living room.

On Christmas, Charly and I woke at one in the morning and couldn't fall back to sleep. It was thirty-eight degrees *above* zero. I tended the fire and lit a kerosene lamp. Heike the dog whined nervously outside. Charly got up to let her in. The sky was clear with a waning moon. A cloudbank threatened from a distance, and raindrops began to fall. Charly brought in our skis and snowshoes and covered the woodpile to keep the freezing rain off our dry wood. Then he looked outside, watching the stars disappear. "Here it comes, Jules," he said.

I walked over to the window to watch as wind-driven snow enveloped the cabin. The house shook and moaned from the stress. I thought the roof was going to blow off. Only about an inch of snow fell, but the wind drove whatever snow was out there into hard-packed drifts up to three feet high, and snow came into the kitchen through cracks in the wall. Charly measured wind speeds at fifty miles an hour. We climbed into bed, listening to the storm, and eventually drifted off to sleep.

"We're alive," I said, as I rolled over to look out the window.

"That was a doozy of a storm," Charly replied.

"Feels like the temperature has dropped," I said.

"I got up and looked about an hour ago; it's back in the teens. Christmas breakfast," Charly said, poking me to get out of bed.

I found a few inches of snow drifted behind the cocoa and tea tins on the counter. I made the Buckles traditional German apple pancake, using dried apples. Then we took turns opening presents: Herb sent a smoked turkey, pears, and his old manual typewriter. Mom and Dad sent books, socks, clothes, puzzles, and Scrabble. Gord Johnson, our friend we'd met at Point du Bois on the Winnipeg River, sent fishing lures, leather gloves, and safety-orange work jackets.

The wind continued to rage, but the sky cleared. Capitalist Jim had invited us to his Christmas party. We had a loaner snowmobile now, so we could go on the spur of the moment. But the wind had us debating whether to go. There was a party, after all, I urged. The sky cleared a bit and Charly agreed to try, figuring we could always turn back. This was our first real snowmobile run. Charly drove, gunning the gas, driving fast, and hitting the drifts too hard. The wind had carved the snow, leaving hard-packed dunes and patches of clear ice. It was rough. Too rough to go so fast.

"Let's turn back," I hollered. "It hurts back here."

"You have a white patch of frozen skin on your cheek ," he said, turning around in his seat. Charly pulled my hood tighter around my face, then turned the snowmobile around toward home. The slower pace felt okay.

"Let's try it," I hollered. "Just go slower." He turned the machine back toward town.

As we rounded the point into town, I could smell burning rubber and felt the snowmachine losing power. "I don't want to stop," Charly said and made a break for John's house.

"Just give 'er," I shouted.

"Is there a brain in there?" John asked, tapping my head. "I told Doug you were bush people, too smart to come in today."

"Oh, what, like you wouldn't go out today?" I asked, embarrassed to have been so stupid.

"No way, it's fifty below with the wind. I'm staying inside," John said, shaking his head as he stood by the fire.

"Is that Canadian degrees or American?" Charly asked, repeating an ongoing Fahrenheit versus Celsius joke between them.

"After forty below it doesn't matter. It's all cold," John said.

John walked outside to examine our snowmachine and determined that the rubber smell was from the track. It had overheated because there wasn't enough snow to lubricate where it slides along the bottom of the machine.

"No Christmas party. Jim's doing the grinch thing," John said. "The power was out for most of the day."

John, of course, was fully prepared for the power outage, and had spent the day lending this and that to everyone who stopped by. He had a generator, a box of batteries, fully charged flashlights, a woodstove, and a propane cooking stove.

Charly called Jim to check in. "He's doing the grinch thing," Charly agreed after a phone call. "Said, 'Maybe next year.'"

"Well maybe we should get going," I said.

"Sit down. You're not going anywhere. I'll make you the Danish traditional Second Christmas dinner," John said, pulling stuff from his refrigerator and cupboards. He assembled a plate of dark rye bread, Icelandic pickled herring and onions, creamed shrimp, goose, and dill cheese. Plus beer and wine and slices of oranges. Now this was a Christmas celebration. John explained the proper order to eat them—fish, meat, cheese—and we obliged, as he told us about other Danish customs. For one, the Danish Santa is called Yuleman, and his elves aren't helpers but rather tricksters who appear in unexpected places.

Charly used John's telephone to call Herb, who had to hang up after a coughing fit.

"He sounds really rough. I told him to go to the doctor," Charly said.

We pulled out our sleeping bags and slept on John's floor. I called home the next morning. The family was celebrating Christmas (we never celebrate it on the actual day), peeling apples, opening stocking stuffers, and having a lot of fun. Surprisingly, I wasn't depressed. Not much I could do about it; besides, I'd had a great birthday and Second Christmas dinner. Charly sledded over to Welcome Bay Store to talk to Jim about our snowmobile. The real one had a broken pin or something, so he was having it fixed and would call when it was ready. He said to continue using the loaner in the meantime.

Heike and Doug dropped by later. Welcome Bay Store had gotten a new supply of videos and they brought *Blair Witch Project* and *Swingers*, for a late night of pop culture. Finally, a bit of modern life my friends had referenced in their letters. Dawn had warned me not to watch *Blair Witch Project* because of its demonization of the wilderness as a scary place, but I was easy. I thought both films were a total hoot, made funnier by Heike trying to understand the American slang of *Swingers*.

The next morning John and Charly went out and dug up a toboggan that John wanted to loan us for hauling wood. So after John served up a breakfast special of fried eggs on toast, Charly and I sledded home on our loaner snowmobile with our loaner toboggan trailing behind, back to our loaner dog at the loaner cabin. It was a great ride. Charly drove slowly and avoided the bumps, until he hit a slush pocket. Then he gave 'er all she had.

24

The Oink Booth

"Welcome to Estevan Island," Charly said in his best Ricardo Montalban voice as he greeted our guests for a two-day New Year's Eve party and sleepover. He wore a shimmering blue bow tie that he had bought at a thrift store in Two Harbors and a pink "I Visited the Oink Booth" paper hat from the Minnesota State Fair sent by a friend. Heike the person and her fellow German friend Jutta, Doug and his Dene friend Ruby, and John stood bundled at the door.

For the last five days Charly and I had prepared for the party. We hauled wood and water, dug the sauna out from the snowdrifts, snow-shoed our trails, planned a dinner menu, prepared appetizers, and wrapped door prizes. Charly had made more luminaries, and they now stretched from the dock to the house and on to the outhouse. I cooked fudge, which our visitors had never heard of. Doug christened the candy pieces "chocolate orgasm cookies."

I set everyone to work preparing the meal. Heike made the rolls, Jutta the cranberry pies, Charly the potatoes. I made wild rice gumbo soup from a mix sent as a Christmas present and heated the smoked turkey sent by Herb. Ruby sat quietly to the side but seemed to enjoy herself, laughing out loud at some of Charly's jokes. She had long dark curly hair, dark eyes, and a round face. She worked behind the counter at Welcome Bay Store. John sipped rum, and Doug leafed through catalogs.

The seven of us squeezed around the table, passing plates of food by candlelight. A mediocre meal, really. The gumbo soup was too salty, the turkey too chilled, the rolls too hard, and the potatoes watery. But no one seemed to care. We laughed and told stories, interrupted by bursts of Danish, German, and American toasts—Skoal! Prost! Cheers! It seemed we had finally started to find our community. I handed out door prizes after dinner—soap for everyone, thanks to the many bars we had received in the gifts from back home. I also regifted a cloth shopping bag to John.

Heike concocted *feuerzangenbowle*, which roughly translates as "fire pliers punch." It consisted of warm wine sweetened with a large pyramid-shaped sugar clump, which hung over the pan by a sort of pliers—a German contraption. Heike dripped rum over the sugar then lit it on fire, creating a blue blaze. All this was done on our woodstove. It was a bit unnerving since the flame followed the ladle and occasionally shot upwards. The drink is supposed to be made with red wine, oranges, and spices, but Heike had to improvise with white wine, so didn't add the spices.

"You're wasting the alcohol by burning it off," John complained.

The drink tasted festive and fun, and it warmed my insides. Heike gave me the pliers to keep. At quarter to twelve everyone bundled up and walked to the dock, where we took a few group photos. At midnight John shot off Felix's gun. We all yelled "Happy New Year" beneath the faint green streaks of northern lights. Doug sledded home with Ruby, and the rest of us curled into sleeping bags in the living room.

The next day Doug returned. The weather was so cold that it kept everyone inside for most of the day. John prepared an elaborate New Year's Day lunch, another Danish tradition. He fussed about in the kitchen making open-faced sandwiches with the finest delicacies: herring, shrimp, and crab. The Danes eat this meal for New Year's, Boxing Day, "round" birthdays (twenty, thirty . . .), and anniversaries. The version he made for us was called *Dosemand* (with a silent *d*), which translates as "canned food" but with an emphasis on delicacies, not tomato soup and tuna fish. John orchestrated the pace and tempo of the meal. Herring and onions first and a swig of alcohol—"the higher the proof the better to help the herring swim." Then the other seafood—crab, shrimp, sardines, and eel—all on rye bread. Swig. Then the meat, which in this case was caribou sausage. Swig. Then finally the cheeses, both blue. More swigs. All the while shouts of *Skoal* rang out. In Denmark the meal lasts for hours, and the break between fish and meat might be marked with a cigarette, John told us.

"The conversation tends to be formal and upbeat," John said.

"In other words, no heavy dialogue on the subjugation of the native people," Charly said to Doug, with a smile.

We all ate until no one could eat any more, then moved into the living room closer to the stove. The guests were tired, but no one wanted to go outside in the dark and ride snowmobiles twelve miles home into the wind at thirty-two below.

Charly started to tell a story. I can't remember which one—the one about rounding Bark Point on Lake Superior or the musk ox or customs, but definitely a story I had heard often in the previous eight months. Whatever it was, I knew exactly what he was going to say by his first words. I had just spent more than twenty-four hours nonstop with our guests drinking, eating, and playing. And because I was tired and full, I couldn't stand to hear that story again at that moment. I put my hand firmly on Charly's knee and said, "Please, don't tell that story again."

He fell silent, not pissed but apologetic in a "Gosh, I'm sorry, have I told that story a million times?" way. Doug, Heike, Jutta, and John, who wore our "I Visited the Oink Booth" pink paper hat, fell silent as well, as if afraid to bring up a story that had been told before.

Time dragged forward, the sound of the crackling fire filling the room. I was immediately sorry. The people in the room had probably not heard Charly's story before. Just because I'd heard it a half-dozen times didn't mean he shouldn't tell it once more. By then, I was afraid to speak as well. What would I have to say that would be any better than Charly's story repeated seven times over?

Finally someone mumbled something about needing to go, and the tension was relieved as our guests prepared to head into the sub-zero night.

A few days later I decided to go winter camping alone. I needed some solo time away from the cabin. I wanted to prove to myself that I could set up camp and survive on my own, that in an emergency I could take care of Charly, the man I now needed to get away from. Besides, I didn't have the patience to wait for Charly to get ready. He wanted to finish the toboggan he was making. I told him to meet me the next day at a designated spot.

I had first camped in the snow during our first winter living together. We had packed a small plastic sled, a cheap one from the hardware store, and slept beneath a tarp on a bed of pine boughs. It was a simple system, but not highly effective for long-term camping. To keep warm we had to be either moving or sleeping. On our second trip we had burrowed into a snowdrift, creating a sort of cave. The cave had a small opening that required us to slide through like an otter. It was close quarters, only large enough to sit up. I barely slept, fully expecting to die of suffocation in the night. After that we discovered canvas tents and portable woodstoves—luxury camping. The tent and stove system was a lot more work, but well worth the effort for long-term travel and comfort. We had winter camped plenty of times, but it didn't hurt to work out the bugs for our spring journey—decide what was essential and what we could do without. I packed a seven-by-nine-foot canvas tent, a stove, food for three days, dog food, two sleeping bags, one change of underclothes, three books, a journal, notebook, emergency gear, and air mattress. John's dog Boola had followed us home the day before, and as I started off, he and Heike raced behind. They were wired for adventure. It was a warm sunny zero-degree day.

I snowshoed across the bay and into the woods, the toboggan floating on the snow behind. My destination: Inner Estevan Island. Boola revealed himself to be a bully for the first half hour. He barked in my face, bit at my gloves, and finally grew bored. I tugged the toboggan up a hill through a stand of trees. I reached the top of the hill and looked out at Inner Estevan, thinking about two bits of bad news delivered over the weekend.

Mike and Phyllis called to tell us that Knock-Knock was missing. She had been missing for three days. The radio did not allow for complicated stories. Mike talked to Charly, and the gist of the story seemed to be that Knock-Knock had taken off and not returned. They had dreaded calling and held off, hoping that they would find her. I knew it was unlikely that they would after three days. Huskies can run and run and run. And they look a lot like coyotes and wolves—and so are a target for those who don't care for wild canids.

The other miserable news was more immediate and definitive. New Year's morning, a toddler in town had frozen to death. Doug told us the news when he drove out New Year's Day. The boy had wandered away from his babysitter's house around seven in the morning because he wanted to go home. The boy's name was Dusty James Joseyounen, and he was just one month away from his third birthday. His babysitter was asleep. He wasn't properly dressed, of course, for weather so cold it had kept us inside most of the day. They found him in the snow about four hundred yards from the house. The news made me sick to my stomach and served as a reminder that the margin for error was very slim in the North.

My thoughts returned to the present as the sun dropped in the sky. I walked down the sloping hill onto the lake and set up camp at the first island—two hours to dig out a spot for the tent, set up the tent, cut wood, feed the dogs, and start a fire. I lit candles and made myself bacon, chili, and tea for dinner. I cut another tree into logs, saving a pile of small dry wood for a breakfast fire. Warm, full, and happy, I stayed up reading David Remnick's *Lenin's Tomb*. As the fire faded and my eyelids drooped, I strapped on my beaver-fur hat and slipped into my two sleeping bags.

My mukluks froze into an odd configuration during the night—a huge faux pas for winter camping. I should have removed the liners and slept with them in my bag, but the only witnesses to my blunder were the two dogs. I pulled on my down-filled booties and built a fire, then fried bacon and hashbrowns for breakfast. In the heat of the tent, the mukluks loosened and I pried them onto my feet. My first mission of the day was to retrieve a pair of leather gloves I had lost on the trail the day before. I gave the dogs a pep talk, telling them of our goal: find the gloves. We crossed the lake, the dogs racing ahead. Sure enough, they returned each carrying a glove. Disney couldn't have trained them any better. The miracle was that they handed the gloves to me instead of using them as a chew toy or making me play chase to recover them.

Charly appeared in late afternoon, and I was happy to see him. I'd found what I needed from our brief time apart—space, time, silence. We unloaded his sled, cut more wood, then settled in for the night, discussing our canoe route for next summer. Charly fried potatoes for dinner and talked about his renewed enthusiasm for paddling the Kazan River and for snowshoeing to Kasba Lake.

"I think we should snowmobile our canoe and food north instead of flying it," Charly said. "Now that we've seen how much can be done with a snowmobile."

"Keep the whole trip on the ground, skip the airplane," I said. "I think that's a great idea."

We hiked and hauled wood to replenish our campsite supply the next day. We talked politics, history, and language, spurred by *Lenin's Tomb* and *Anna Karenina*. The wind shifted to the north, then the east, and it snowed on and off. The dogs joined us inside the tent that night. The next morning it was too cold to play outside, so we decided to go home. We kept the fire burning while we packed, tearing down the tent at the last minute, leaving behind just a bed of spruce boughs and a small stack of firewood to mark our spot. The wind had blown snow over our trail, so we strapped on snowshoes and broke the trail again. It took us about two hours to climb up and over the hill and reach our snowmobile. Charly and I returned home at five-thirty to a frozen cabin. The thermometer read twenty-four below.

We continued to cut and haul firewood, play endless games of Scrabble, work on a Christmas jigsaw puzzle, and watch a lunar eclipse—the first visible one since 1996. A boreal owl called from a spruce near the dock, but we couldn't spot it. We listened, then walked, then looked, narrowing its possible location. The call reminded Charly of a woodcock, a rapid series of six to ten hollow *hoo* notes. Even after we narrowed the field to four trees we couldn't see the owl. Charly shined a flashlight and scanned it up and down and around the trees, but the owl remained heard and not seen. In the back of our journal we kept a list of the birds we'd seen: spruce grouse, willow ptarmigan, northern hawk owl, black-backed woodpecker, gray jay, common raven, black-capped chickadee, pine grosbeak, and common redpoll. There is a longer list, about four times the length of ours, of birds we could potentially have seen, but never did.

And then there was always the trapper radio. Charly continued his conversations with Kasba Lake Harold, asking him questions about breakup—the time in spring or summer when the ice turns to water. Our plan was to haul our gear and canoe to Kasba Lake by snowmobile, return to Wollaston to ditch the snowmobile, snowshoe back to Kasba Lake, await breakup, then paddle the Kazan River north, working our way to the Back River and the Arctic Ocean. It was a logistical mind-bender. The rivers break free of ice before the lakes, and some of the lakes we were considering traveling on didn't thaw until July, if at all. For instance Dubwant Lake is famous for having ice into August. If frozen lakes slowed us down, we could face the start of winter at the other end. Charly had been told that the weather near the Arctic Ocean starts to get really windy and stormy in early September. In other words, our start date, end date, and everything in between depended on weather, weather, and weather—all of which fascinated Charly and held little interest for me. Just tell me when we're leaving, honey.

Harold had told Charly that people snowmobile on Kasba into late May, ice starts breaking up in early June, and the lake is free of ice in July. Harold said to watch the snowfall closely. The deeper the snow, the more likely that snow would stay on the land longer. The land usually loses its snow by late May. He described a period when it's impossible to travel. John referred to this period as a time when the snow is "losing its water," and the lakes flood on top of the ice. After a few days the snow sets up and there's a period of good snow travel. The water drains into the lakes and the surface is once again ice. Charly discussed, analyzed, and pored over maps regularly, attempting to arrive at a plan for the upcoming season, tossing ideas around most nights. We were definitely on the path less traveled, maybe never traveled.

A few days later we began to truly practice for our snowshoe trek. After the full moon we loaded our sleds, strapped on our snowshoes, and headed out for a few days of winter camping. It felt like the start of spring. The sun now rose earlier—about nine—and closer to the east, moved higher in the sky, and set later—nearly six. It gave enough heat to warm my cheeks. We each pulled sleds that we had built from a roll of thick black plastic. The wind had packed the snow on Wollaston Lake into a swirling landscape of drifts and layers, creating crazy patterns and textures.

We rounded the point to the tall cliffs of Trout Narrows in the late afternoon and set up camp among the wind-scoured snowy cliffs. That night we watched amazing ripping northern lights. "The best I've ever seen," Charly said, lying in the snow. Green, pink, and lavender shimmied across the sky like a curtain swirling itself into a circle. At the center, psychedelic colors exploded like fireworks for nearly fifteen minutes.

We woke to the trill of a red squirrel—a sure sign of spring—and a thick layer of fog. The gray wet mask lifted by lunchtime to reveal hoarfrost on the land and a pink glow in the sky. It was the kind of day that made us believe we could walk ten miles on snowshoes pulling a toboggan—our goal for the spring trek. The sun began to set, our shadows a quarter-mile long. The glow turned Heike's tongue an unnatural red. Running to and fro all day long, her path twisting and turning, she had covered more miles by far than we had. I wished for her four legs. The last few hours we walked beneath the clear starry skies, watching Orion's Belt, the Big Dipper, the Seven Sisters, and the North Star. I felt completely content watching a faint display of greenish northern lights dancing overhead.

25

Trail of the Caribou

F inally cold enough for you to go camping?" Capitalist Jim asked
with a grin. Charly and I stood inside Welcome Bay Store, wearing
fur hats and four layers of clothing. Valentine's Day and it was
thirty degrees below zero. Jim had called to tell us that two months after
we had requested a snowmobile, it was finally ready. We wanted to take
it camping farther north. According to chatter on the trapper radio, the
caribou herds were at Charcoal Lake, about eighty miles north of
Wollaston. Jim told us to take both machines—the loaner and our new-
to-us one—and agreed to watch Heike while we were gone.

Charly took the lead on our new-used Arctic Cat Lynx, pulling a
loaded sled behind. I followed on the loaner Bravo sans sled. We stopped
at the Ministry of Natural Resources office to look at maps. As we walked
out of the building, four dark-haired girls gathered around, pointing to
my "white" hair and blue eyes.

"Are you John Elander's kids?" they asked.

Charly and I looked at one another and laughed out loud, thinking
of John's response to that one. He was no more than a decade older than
us.

"Yeah," we replied, smiling.

The four of them and another friend then jumped onto Charly's sled. "Pull us, pull us! We'll jump off, we promise." Charly pulled them in a circle. Kids began piling out of houses until there were nearly ten trying to ride on our loaded sled. Finally, Charly lured them off for a moment, then hit the gas, trying to go faster than they could jump back on. I followed behind, laughing, dodging kids rolling on the road.

Snowmobile trails left town in several directions, and there were no road signs for visitors. We carried a compass, a map, and some local advice on finding "the road." Charcoal Lake was on the Cochrane River system that drains from the northeast corner of Wollaston Lake and makes a snake-like turn east then south, crossing the Manitoba border and eventually emptying into Reindeer Lake. The Cochrane was familiar territory for Charly. Both of his previous expeditions had started there, but Charly had never navigated this region in winter. We knew the trail to the Cochrane was heavily used by the caribou hunters, but outside Wollaston Post all the trails looked heavily used. Charly chose one that veered to the right. A while later a man on a snowmobile passed us heading toward Wollaston Post. Charly waved for him to stop so he could check directions.

"Is this the way to the Cochrane?" Charly asked.

"No, Lac Brochet."

The man pointed us in the right direction. Twenty minutes later, with the dim light fading further, Charly motioned for us to camp.

"Are you cold?" Charly asked, as we turned off our machines.

"Really cold," I said, my teeth beyond chattering. My fingers didn't work, and I had lost sensation in my toes. My mind dulled and I couldn't think beyond *I'm really cold.*

"Start shoveling snow until you warm up."

I shoveled down about two feet, and feeling returned to the tips of my fingers. I packed a twelve-foot circle with my snowshoes for a sleeping platform, and my toes started to tingle. Then I dug out a section for a stove area, and my body flooded with a burst of heat. Charly unloaded the tent and stove and set it up while I collected wood and chopped and sawed enough for the night. We didn't need a lot, just enough for cooking dinner, heating the tent until bedtime, and cooking breakfast. I set up our sleeping bags and organized the tent. Charly cooked chili and made hot chocolate.

"No more northern trips," I said, sitting near the fire. "I want to go somewhere warm and soak in the sun. Mexico. Cuba. Just south."

"I suppose it could be worse. You could want to move to Chicago or L.A."

Both snowmobiles started smoothly the next morning, always a welcome surprise. I was nervous about traveling so far with snowmobiles. Unlike the native people, who could perform complex repairs out on the land, neither of us understood motors. In fact, we were totally incapable of much more than changing a spark plug. We packed up and continued north on Wollaston Lake, following the tracks of the caribou hunters.

As we reached the north end of Wollaston Lake the trail turned down a bay, left the lake, and followed a glacial valley with a series of small lakes connected by creeks and wetlands. This route avoided all the current and rapids on the Cochrane and proved to be a straighter shot to Charcoal Lake. Snowmobile trails followed lakes and rivers through the bush the way a canoe might, but swerved ashore at the slightest hint of current. Current eats away at the ice or keeps it from forming, creating dangerously weak ice or pockets of slush that can sink or trap a snow-machine. On land, the trails followed esker ridges and long linear valleys carved by glaciers.

Caribou tracks, wolf tracks, fox tracks, caribou carcasses, and imprints of raven wings in the snow indicated that we were on the correct trail. Charly was a regular snowmobile biologist, catching the signs at thirty miles an hour. I focused on watching his machine and the trail, not noticing anything until he pointed it out.

Charcoal Lake looked like a movie scene in which the protagonist arrives after the battle. Piles of caribou hides were scattered about on Charcoal Lake, and ravens flew overhead. No hunters or hunted remained.

We stopped at a small rustic fly-in fishing camp John had told us about. Caribou hides, legs, and heads lay in a heap at the dock, and a caribou hindquarter hung on the porch. The cabin served as a camp for transient caribou hunters and was filled with their leftovers. We didn't stay long. Instead, we searched for a camping spot and settled on a cozy wind-protected opening on an island. We went through our usual winter camping routine: shovel, tromp, dig, set up, saw, chop, and cook.

The next day, after a breakfast of oatmeal, we explored Charcoal Lake by snowmachine. In the first hour Charly spotted caribou, the "gray shepherds of the tundra" as poet John Haines called them. One Dene family might eat up to eighty of these gray shepherds each year, we had been told. Two caribou trudged through the snow, the second following directly in the first one's tracks to conserve energy. North American caribou are divided into three groups—woodland, Peary, and barren-ground—with more than thirty recognized Arctic herds. These two caribou trudging through the snow belonged to the Kaminuriak herd of the barren-ground group. They stopped to look at us, paused, and then continued on.

"You can see why they're so easy to kill," I said.

I followed Charly as we headed to Caribou Rapids. I alternated between looking at the back of Charly's puffy green down jacket and looking ahead toward the rapids. There mist rose as open water that was thirty-three degrees slammed up against air that was thirty below. So when my snowmobile hit slush while I was looking at open water, my mind said I was going down.

My heart started pounding and adrenaline pushed sweat through every pore on my body. Once I realized something solid existed beneath the slush, my fear of drowning turned to fear of freezing or of trapping the snowmobile in the slush. If the snowmobile became stuck we would have to cut trees to make a deck for setting the snowmobile track on, then let the slush freeze overnight beneath the snowmobile.

In the end, John Elander's advice saved us. I pushed on the gas, giving the machine all the power it had. Charly did the same, and we pulled onto solid ice between the slush and the rapids. Charly got off his machine, wild from the ride through the slush. "Ohmygodohmygodohmygod," he muttered, pacing back and forth.

I was cold with fear. "I hate breaking new trails. I hate open water," I said through chattering teeth. Charly pulled out the thermos filled with hot cocoa and poured us both a cup. I was shaking from cold, fear, and adrenaline.

The hot cocoa worked its way through our bodies. Charly pointed up to a gyrfalcon flying overhead. "Kings of the arctic," he whispered. I had never seen one before. Year-round residents of the arctic, they are the largest of the falcons. Gyrfalcons look a lot like peregrine falcons, only bigger and lacking the dark helmets. This one was in its dark phase, chocolate brown and white.

Slush and gyrfalcons remain forever mingled in my mind. We sat on the seat of the Lynx, looking at the sky for a few moments, the rest of the tension and adrenaline slipping away.

"Turn back?" Charly asked.

"Turn back."

On our return to camp Charly spied a red fox walking across the ice. We turned off our machines to watch, and it headed directly for us. The low-angle sun highlighted its amber coat, black legs and paws, and fluffy tail. Moving slowly, Charly took out the camera and set up for a shot. The fox moved closer to us, then even closer. I began to think it might be rabid, but it had learned to associate snowmobiles and humans with caribou scraps, and if we were stopped, a carcass shouldn't be far behind.

It came within fifty feet of us, sniffing the air and squinting its eyes. It paced back and forth then sat down, sniffed some more, and at last headed into the woods. After a winter with nary a gray jay for company, a close encounter with a red fox was downright awe-inspiring. And wasn't this the way of the north? These moments of exquisite beauty sidled right up to moments of terror and near death.

Back at camp we snowshoed around the island looking at caribou tracks everywhere. We saw ravens and foxes cleaning a caribou carcass.

Charly untangled the antenna to the trapper radio. We planned to take the radio on our spring journey, so we wanted to test it on the trail. Charly cut two long spruce poles, found the east-west direction on his compass, then hung the antenna. He ducked inside the tent, where I was baking brownies in the BakePacker. It was twenty-five below zero outside. The orange radio and batteries warmed near the fire, and in a few minutes we called LaRonge.

"XLB51, this is VEE864. Do you read me?" Charly said into the microphone.

"Loud and clear," said the operator.

We cheered. "Let's call Mom and Dad," I said.

Mom and Dad were home and teased me about my latest letter, filled with food and liquor requests for their trip north in March.

Next we called Mike and Phyllis.

"Your article got a full page spread in the *Daily Press*. It looks great," Mike told us. "Looks like Julie gained fifty pounds with all the clothes she's wearing. Over."

Charly turned to look at me and laugh.

I rolled my eyes.

Next Kasba Lake Harold.

"Kasba Lake Harold are you out there?" Charly tried.

"Hello, Charly, see any caribou at Charcoal? Over."

He had been listening.

"Only two so far. Over."

Harold said that we could store our supplies at the fishing lodge where he stayed and hang out there while awaiting ice out.

"Points North is hauling and working up at Ennadai Lake starting in mid-February, probably into mid-March, so you might be able to throw your supplies onto one of their loads. Over."

Later, as we sipped hot chocolate, Charly commented, "Funny, it seems you're much more interested in the radio than the new titanium stove."

"The radio is fun, you have to admit."

"We'll see how much fun you think it is when we get our next bill."

The temperature warmed to zero or above the next day, and we had an easy morning of packing. Packing camp was so much easier in winter. No canoe and Duluth packs, no wind or waves; just a hard-packed trail and a sled. The ride back to Wollaston Lake was smooth and pleasant with the weather so much milder. We saw nearly a dozen ptarmigan. They appeared like crazed snowflakes, contrasting with the backdrop of the dark spruce forest as they fluttered away. They were nearly invisible in the snow, but when one flew, the black triangle on its tail gave it away. The ptarmigan were fleeting joy as we roared past so quickly on the snowmobile, scaring them up in small bunches.

We didn't see anyone for the entire trip back to Wollaston Post—just snow, ice, and spruce trees for eighty miles. It appeared that no one had traveled that route since we had passed through a few days before. We reached town by midafternoon with plenty of time to run errands.

At the post office I ran into an elderly Dene man—all smiles and no teeth. "You were at Charcoal Lake," he said.

"We were. How did you know?" I asked.

"I heard you on the radio," he smiled.

"Ahh, the radio," I nodded.

"Did you see any caribou?" he asked as the postal woman handed him his mail.

"Only two," I replied.

"They probably moved to the side lakes."

I returned the Bravo to Jim, and Charly and I reunited back at John's house. John boiled tortellini for the three of us and told us about a trapper named Solomon who would be able to tell us more about the route to Kasba Lake. John pointed us in the general direction to Solomon's house. We rode together on the Lynx for a bit then stopped and asked a man, "Where does Solomon live?"

"Over there," he said, pointing with his chin, "Look for the blue pickup buried in the snow."

We drove up and down two streets, observing all kinds of trucks buried in the snow. Kids played outside. Charly asked one group, "Where does Solomon live?"

"Solomon who?" they asked

We didn't know.

We drove to the laundromat and snowmobile repair shop to ask them for further directions. One man marked a map in the grease of the floor. "He's got a blue-and-white truck," another man offered.

We found someone along the way who pointed to an actual house, where Charly knocked on the door while I sat on the snowmobile. We'd been told that in Wollaston only white people knock on doors. John said even after twenty years there he couldn't break himself of the habit. A Dene woman in her twenties answered the door.

"Hi. My name is Charly Ray. My wife and I are staying out at Estevan Island. We paddled here from the United States. People tell us there's a Solomon who traps up toward Kasba and that we should talk to him. Does he live here?" Charly asked.

She stared silently for a few moments then said, "Where are you staying?"

"Estevan Island."

She didn't seem eager to get Solomon, but then a man poked his head out of the door. He and the woman exchanged words in Dene then went inside, closing the door and leaving Charly standing alone. He turned to me and shrugged his shoulders. Finally the man, apparently Solomon, emerged alone.

"What do you want?"

Charly repeated his earlier introduction. I gave a small wave when he looked my way.

"Meet me at the Confectionery."

"Okay."

We drove across the bay to the site of our first dinner at Wollaston. Charly ordered a piece of cherry pie and a grapefruit soda. I ordered tea. Charly rolled out the map of the region, and he and two other men gathered around our table. In my experience, maps are like magnets and northern men are paperclips. Solomon spread the map across the table, smoothing it repeatedly.

"Here," he said, pushing his finger across forty miles of wilderness, showing without hesitation his trapline route to Kasba Lake from Phelps Lake. Charly tried to follow with a pen, marking the portages. I was simply an observer. This was male territory.

"Like this," Solomon said, again sliding his forefinger across the map.

It took moments for Charly to trace the route with the pen, asking questions as he moved his pen. "Follow the esker here?"

"Yes."

"Out of the bay?"

"Yes."

"This looks like a circuitous route to me. What about coming by Numin Lake?" Charly asked, pointing to some possible routes out of Kingston Lake he'd marked on the map.

"Yeah, that would be straighter, faster," Solomon agreed. "I was just up there. There's a trail to Kohn Lake. J.B. is trapping up there. He stays at Cochrane River."

The three men told us how they'd broken a trail from Wollaston to Kasba, some two hundred miles, in one day then made it back in twelve hours.

"I'd be lucky to make it back in three days," Charly joked.

"When are you coming back?" Solomon asked, assuming we would paddle back to Wollaston.

Charly took out our trip brochure and showed them our route to Baker Lake then to Taoloyak. All three laughed and shook their heads.

"You go halfway around the world!" said the big man across the table.

As we lay in bed that night, Charly read aloud the letter from his dad that we had just picked up.

Dear Charly and Julie,

Canceled my usual trip to Florida because of the cough I got and a long inventory on my procrastination report. Am still left with a residual cough. The doc gave me another round of pills to relieve the bronchial irritation. They help but I still haven't been able to finish off the irritation. The colon business seems about stable, not better, not worse. Had a CAT scan two weeks ago and the good news is that there is no indication of any spread of the cancer. I'm still hopeful that the therapies I am now on will result in improvement.

Have been working on two loans to inner-city churches for the Centennial Loan Fund. Am of course still on the Samaritan Institute Board writing grants and sitting on the finance committee. Also on the finance committee of the Win Cong Church. More recently got talked into serving for two years on the Winnetka Caucus Committee. Almost talked myself into being treasurer of it then I found wisdom and backed off. Decided I had enough on my plate. I do intend (again) to put the house on the market late spring or early next summer.

Am still spending a fair amount of time playing with my investment portfolio. Of course it is great fun when the market is generally tending upward. I don't mess with any Internet or dotcom type stocks because I don't understand them. I suppose this is all gibberish to you. In any event I am still living by the motto that it is taking me longer and longer to do less and less. A perfect program for retirement.

Love to you both, Dad

Charly got up the next morning and typed a return letter.

Dear Dad –

It's just after 7 a.m., pitch dark outside. I'm typing by kerosene lamp. Just finished Terry Tempest William's Refuge, *a beautiful book about dealing with the loss of her mother to cancer. She sets it against the backdrop of losing her favorite bird refuge during the same period as Great Salt Lake rises to all-time highs. Obviously it brought back lots of memories for me. Very cathartic. I have resisted reading it or any "cancer" book, I think, because I like to deal with things on my own. But this was a wonderful read and experience. I'd recommend it highly. . . . Another great northern lights display last night. I always think of you and your comment that you hadn't seen the lights like these since you were a kid. I've come to greatly appreciate the moonless night sky with the brilliant stars and the regular northern lights. I figured I would be pining for the moonlight but not so. . . .*

Love, Charly

The month of February continued. Although we had mobility, we were often cabin-bound by the dark and cold. The sun still didn't rise until almost nine, and some days the temperatures dropped to as low as seventy below with windchill. One morning I started Bernd Heinrich's *Mind of the Raven* and found a new activity: observing ravens. Heinrich admired the big corvids and made me appreciate them as well. I had watched them in town stealing food from the dogs and leading a pack of them on a chase. The ravens were huge and black and vocal. Heinrich had reports of ravens hanging from their feet, sliding in snow, flying upside down, rolling in midflight, tugging at wolves' tails, and defending their nests with rocks. I set out chunks of our mixed dried fruit hoping to lure ravens to the cabin.

Heinrich devised an intelligence test for ravens from a copy of *Ranger Rick* magazine. An article described the clever things that birds can do, like pulling up food suspended by a string. Heinrich theorized that if a raven could figure out how to pull up food—a ten-step process—without a lengthy trial-and-error period, it might indicate intelligence. Well, the ravens aced the test. He also spent time figuring out how ravens and wolves work together. At Yellowstone National Park, Heinrich observed that ravens arrived at all wolf kills, but avoided carcasses where wolves were absent. Ravens need wolves for at least two reasons: to kill the prey and to open the carcass. Wolves also need ravens. Ravens have been reported to alert wolves to potential food sources and to danger.

Heike ate most of the dried fruit, but ravens did fly overhead. Charly had noted one that made a daily patrol over the cabin and toward the point each day. I called out to it one day, and just as Heinrich had described in his book, the raven paused, called back, and dipped a bit as if to tip a hat.

In late February, as Charly's birthday cake was cooling on the kitchen table, Capitalist Jim motored into the yard with Martina, the young school teacher I had met at Welcome Bay Store during the supplies-are-in frenzy. Looking like circus clowns, they arrived on her Indy Lite, a small snowmachine made for one. Jim's machine, they told us, had broken down at Big Narrows, so he abandoned it and hopped on with Martina.

Martina was twenty-six and smart. She laughed easily. She had grown up in Toronto, earned a degree in geological engineering, then decided she wanted to teach. Her Croatian grandparents had moved to Canada, had children, and moved back to Croatia. Martina had moved to Wollaston three winters ago to work for Capitalist Jim at Welcome Bay Store. She had met him through a mutual friend. She started teaching fourth grade after two years and now hoped to get her teaching credentials.

Away from the store and the telephone, Jim turned out to have a great sense of humor, and I could suddenly envision how he and John had once been friends. He had planned to come the day before but couldn't because of thick fog. That story prompted him to tell a funny one about the time he lost his way driving the barge that travels twenty-eight miles between the road and Wollaston Post. He had started the trip as a passenger, but the captain of the barge, who was nearing retirement, had some sort of heart condition that required that he take medication. Those meds caused him to pass out. So, on a very foggy day with Jim on board as a passenger, the boat captain took his meds and promptly passed out. Jim took control. The navigational instruments were not working, so he started going in circles hoping to get his bearings. He lost his bearings completely and ended up at a place called Blue Island.

"That's where I started both of my expeditions," Charly interjected.

After a short discussion about Blue Island and Charly's two expeditions out of Wollaston, Jim continued. He sat in the fog on the barge with the passed out captain and waited for the fog to clear. And waited. The captain awoke; said, "What the hell?"; popped more pills; and passed out again. Meanwhile in Wollaston Post, people noticed that the barge was missing and sent a plane to look. The captain awoke, saw a plane flying overhead, and shouted, "A plane! Shoot the flare gun." He jumped up, ran to the deck, and shot the gun, missing the plane by only twenty feet.

We all doubled over laughing, wiping our tears. And the stories continued.

Jim told us about the time his dog of seventeen years disappeared. He looked for her for twenty-four hours without any luck. He wanted to find her body just to have closure. I thought about Knock-Knock and nodded. We still had no idea what had happened to her. Jim hung a sign offering a one-hundred-dollar reward for anyone who brought her in dead or alive. For months, he said, kids dragged in dead dogs.

Martina and Jim stayed for a bowl of chili and chocolate cake before heading home. Jim took our snowmobile so he could pull his machine home. Martina said she would return our machine early the next day with John.

John and Martina drove in at eleven the next morning, the earliest we'd ever had anyone visit. We hadn't seen John for a while, since he had been away when we were in town. After a hearty handshake and greetings John announced, "Now for door prizes!" From the bag we had given him as a door prize at our New Year's Eve party, he produced prizes of his own: a box of crackers and a big bag of dried tortellini, a favorite I had eaten at his house. He immediately inspected the work Charly had done on the toboggan he'd lent us and approved it all—a standing board, lines, and tin on the bottom.

We sat around the kitchen table eating spaghetti and garlic bread, sharing more stories. Martina brought books for me, and I gave her a stack that I'd already read. She shared school stories, including one about spring dry-meat farts from the protein-rich diet of dried caribou. "Most of the time it's not too bad, but some days you just gotta say, 'Okay, who wants to open the window?'"

John told us about a road grader that went through the ice up on Black Lake. The grader operator was widening the road to keep it from drifting in. He hadn't checked the ice, and the machine went through with him in it. "People are pushing the season all over in the north," he said. In Wollaston a road grader had hit a crack and almost gone through. In Hay River in the Northwest Territories, a semi hauling ten thousand gallons of fuel fell through the ice. The driver lived, but they had to dynamite the river to open it enough to haul the truck and fuel out.

After a round of coffee and cheesecake, John and Martina bundled up and rode away.

26

Winter Carnival

I was in a trance. Well, not a trance really, but the drums, the chanting, the smoke, the repetitive hand claps, the bodies bowing as if in prayer—it all had me pleasantly disoriented. I was in the old band hall at Wollaston, thousands of miles from home, for Winter Carnival. We were watching eight men play a traditional Dene hand game. I looked over at Charly, who'd been sniffling and coughing, trying to beat the flu, and even he was transfixed. The hand games had overcome the virus, overcome the darkness and cold of winter, overcome the lethargy of cabin fever. And yet I had absolutely no idea what was going on. I tried to guess which hand held the chit, and always, *always*, I was wrong. "I've been watching this game for twenty years and still haven't figured it out," John said, leaning over so we could hear him over the noise.

The man sitting in the middle of the circle of men revealed the chit in his left hand. He smiled. The Dene men all smiled and nodded. One of the men moved the peg on something that looked like a cribbage board, but not really; maybe an Alice-in-Wonderland cribbage board—oversized, distorted, and off kilter. Two four-man teams faced one another. They knelt, buttocks resting on their calves and ankles. The guessing team played three drums made of caribou hide. The hiding team held jackets and blankets in their laps and swayed and bobbed to the rhythm of the drums. Bowing down, the hiders reached under their blankets and jackets for the chit, concealing their hands and movements. They pounded the floor once, twice, sat up quickly, and crossed their arms with their fists clenched, one hiding the chit. No one smiled.

The man from the guessing team who wasn't drumming guessed who had the chit. He slapped his hands once, twice, and then signaled with complicated hand gestures. The drumming stopped. Eight fists opened. Not a word was spoken the entire time. Ah, that guy, in *that* hand. A round of laughter, knowing smiles, and rapid chatter in Dene. I laughed, not because I got the joke but because it felt good to laugh and, hell, everyone else was laughing. I looked over at Charly. He laughed and wiped his nose. John smiled and nodded as if to say *I told you it's complicated.*

Winter Carnival was by far the most eagerly anticipated event of winter. It was to Wollaston what the film festival is to Cannes. People had been telling us about Carnival since we paddled into town seven months ago. After the question of whether we would purchase a snowmobile, the question we'd heard most frequently since we had arrived was whether we would attend Carnival. Winter Carnival ran all through the winter season, rotating from one Dene village to another on a not-too-specific schedule. I don't know who decided which town would host which weekend or when it was decided. I never saw a flyer or a brochure. Charly had gone to the band office—kind of a city hall for the reserve—and asked for a schedule a few weeks before. They looked at him as if he had asked where the spider monkeys lived. People just knew where to go, when, and what would be happening. Entire towns drove their snowmobiles hundreds of miles for a weekend of games, dancing, and socializing.

Wollaston Post hosted Carnival the first weekend of March. Charly and I didn't plan to miss a minute. We had packed food, clothes, our wall tent, and gear into the sled and set out early to catch the first sled dog races. Heike had run behind. We had snowmobiled for about eight miles and were just coming onto the ice road, a few miles from town, when we heard a pop. Before we could mentally process the noise and what it meant, we lost all power. We'd blown a piston. If this were a movie, the soundtrack would shift to the hollow hiss of wind in the open. The camera would then pan ever so slowly to the miles of snowdrifts behind, around, and in front of us. We stood on four feet of ice. It was twenty-some degrees and there was not a manmade thing in sight, except for our broken snowmachine, a sled full of gear, and the ice road.

The people of Wollaston looked forward to winter for, among other reasons, a chance to drive out of town, across the frozen lake, and onto a gravel road where another eight hours of driving got them to the next town. With great anticipation, the road crew measured the thickness of the ice until it was solid enough—nineteen inches. Road graders then set out constructing a 28-mile-long, 150-foot-wide road. When the ice thickened to twenty-nine inches, they opened the road to the public.

I did not worry about our predicament. I felt irritated, or rather disappointed, that we would miss the sled dog race—the first promise of easy entertainment in months. But worried, no. I never really counted on our snowmobile, and had certainly come to expect delays. Charly fussed with the lines on the sled. I sat down on the foam seat of the snowmobile, secure in the knowledge that someone would come along. And sure enough someone did. I could see a tan-colored truck a few miles away. While I would have not been surprised to have John pull up at that moment, Doug, who managed the food co-op in town, drove the tan truck. He was hauling a load of potato chip bags and hot dogs to sell at Carnival. All three of us walked around the snowmachine, assessing the situation.

"I could give you a tow," Doug finally offered, and so he and Charly hooked the machine to the back of the truck with a chain. Doug did not offer to give Heike a ride. He didn't even look at her pitiful face or floppy ears as he told us to get in the front. I watched for Heike in the side-view mirror, the snowmachine and sled zig-zagging along behind the truck. Charly watched me watch Heike and gave me a sympathetic what-can-I-do look. Once we lost sight of her, I asked to get out of the truck. Doug didn't question my motive, just stopped the truck and let me out.

"I'll walk in and meet you," I told Charly.

I waited until the little black dot in the distance turned into Heike, and the two of us walked the last two miles into town. What did I think about? Winter, solitude, attitude. I craved social interaction and wildly looked forward to the weekend. Around the last bend I saw snowmobiles, lots of them. A square of ice just outside of town looked like a used-snowmobile lot. Yellow ones, green ones, and red ones. Big ones, small ones, and really small ones. Children rode child-size machines, called Kitty Cats, four or five to a machine. One boy pulled his older brother on a snowboard behind the snowmobile like a water skier behind a boat. From this snowmobile lot emerged seven teams of sled dogs heading for the snowy horizon. And then they were gone. With dogs racing into the abyss, the snowmobiles took off in all directions, only to return when the dogs did. The purse for the sled dog races was significant—about twenty-five thousand dollars for the weekend of races—so it attracted mushers from outside the region. Only one local musher raced his dogs. I walked among the motorized revelry and the dog trucks toward John's house to find Charly.

"So what's the word on the snowmachine?" I asked.

"It'll be a Wollaston ordeal," he responded.

"Meaning . . .?"

"We dropped it off at Jim's, but he wasn't around," he said.

"Did you see the sled dog race?" I asked.

"I saw them getting ready," he said, starting to assemble our tent that we had used as a sauna all winter. John was in Stony Rapids for an inquest regarding the road-grader operator he had told us about who went through the ice and died. We weren't sure why John was involved with the inquest, but he seemed integral to all official matters involving the North. John had granted us permission to set up camp in his yard—in the exact same location we had camped our first night in town. The canvas tent looked like a Mongolian yurt—a round creamy canvas body with a conical-shaped roof. The wall was three feet high then sloped upward, reaching eight feet at the peak. We staked out the edges by jabbing sticks deep into the snow. Snowshoes stood outside the door, and a silver pipe carried away smoke from our stove. Even though John lived in town, his property was a secluded spot surrounded by spruce on one side, outbuildings on another, a hill on the third, and his house on the fourth. Conveniently, John's weathered outhouse, complete with magazines, was located only yards away. Heike leaned her head against the center pole, next to our bed.

It was only twenty degrees, but that felt so warm that I changed out of my mukluks and into hiking boots for the weekend. Charly felt like he was fighting off the flu, so he lay down to sleep. I went inside John's house, boiled red potatoes for lunch, and clicked through the television stations until I found *Northern Exposure*. It was an episode about cabin fever during the lowest light of winter.

The next morning I stood outside our tent, sipping a mug of tea. Charly fiddled with the stove. I noticed smoke rising from John's house, above the satellite dish and power lines.

"John's back," I said, finishing my tea and dumping the dregs onto the snow, and stood to head over to the house.

Inside, John fussed with his woodstove. Creosote leaked from the pipe. He and Charly discussed it like they always did. What were the causes? The solutions? But then he remembered something and led us outside to look at his latest treasure—a yellow Ski-Doo called an Elan. "It's a classic," he said. I'd seen my dad driving the same snowmobile, a gun strapped to his back, in home movies from Alaska dated 1969.

We told him about our broken piston. "Take my Bear Cat; I'll drive the Elan," he said, and we headed out to see more of the sled dog racing.

Charly started the Bear Cat and turned it around while I tied Heike to a post. I hopped on the back and we followed John toward the races. Crazed dogs of all shapes, sizes, and colors wearing red, green, purple, and blue harnesses were hooked by their rears and necks to a gangline. Mostly men and a few women ran up and down the lines, refereeing fights and straightening tangles. The dogs looked like a mixture of husky and greyhound. Long lean bodies, a wild assortment of colors—gray and white, tan and black, gold and cream—all ready to run like hell. One well-known racer handled the dogs with his daughter. He drove a red truck with an intricate painting of an Indian man riding a dog, a raven overhead, and spruce trees casting a shadow onto an icy lake. It was done in the Pacific Northwest Native style of art. The race started with little warning and all the whines, howls, barks, growls, and yips turned into a deafening silence. And they were gone. The daughter returned to the cab of the red truck to sit and wait for her father.

"Let's cruise to the top of the hill to see what we can see," John suggested.

We passed three kids aboard a lime-green Z120—a miniature snowmobile. The front two—a boy and girl—were dressed in black caps, winter coats, and snow boots. The girl in back wore tennis shoes and no hat. She urged the girl driving to speed up, but they could move no faster than a walking adult. And sure enough a fourth kid, a boy, jumped on the back bumper, riding along in a standing position. Charly stopped to take a photo. We caught up with John across the bay, followed him up the side of the well-worn hill, past the community center, and up to the radio tower. We turned off the machines and looked for the teams out on the lake. Nothing but ice, snow, spruce trees, and a truck and a few snowmobiles traveling down the ice road. "There's guys from Tadoule Lake coming in today for Carnival," John said.

"Where's Tadoule Lake?" I asked.

"Way the hell over by Churchill," Charly laughed.

"About 170 air miles from Wollaston," John said

"About two hundred trail miles," Charly added. "Or more."

"How long does that take by snowmobile?" I asked.

"From Wollaston to Lac Brochet takes you four or five hours, but people can make it on their big machines a lot quicker. But it takes longer if you're hauling gas. Then you spend the night in Lac Brochet. Then the next day you take off and it takes six or seven hours on the road again to get over to Tadoule Lake. You follow the main trail to the Seal River then follow it down," John said.

"I've looked at it on the map," Charly said. "Tadoule Lake's on the Wolverine River."

"Yeah, but you follow the Seal River to get there. You look at your map and you can see where you go out of Lac Broche up to Maria or Marie Lake and then keep going into Nickel Lake or something, and you follow along across the Seal River all the way to Bain Lake. Then instead of continuing on the Seal River, you get to one of the eskers there just twenty miles north of Tadoule Lake and you head south from there. I can almost see the trail in my head."

"How often have you been there?" I asked.

"I don't know. I've been there, what? Three times by airplane and three times by snowmobile."

"Are the guys from Tadoule coming by snowmobile or air?" Charly asked.

"Snowmobile," John answered.

The route to Tadoule Lake, the one that John described as if he were driving a car from Madison to Chicago, goes through thousands of square miles of wilderness. There are no roads, no marked trails, no signs, no tourist information booths, and no gas stations. To John, the esker—a long winding trail of stratified sand and gravel left over from the glaciers—was like an off-ramp on the interstate. But I knew differently. I could barely make the trip from Wollaston to our cabin without getting lost. It all looked the same: snow, ice, trees, lakes every which way I looked.

John led us to the new band hall to get information about the snowshoe race and tea boil competition. This newer building served as a community center. It had bathrooms, a concession stand, and a band stage, and it could accommodate more than two hundred people. Volunteers were sweeping up a mountain of potato chip bags, bingo pull tabs, and soda cans from the previous night's dance. John walked us along the wall, pointing to framed photos of elders living and gone—some great faces, weathered and wizened, in black and white.

Jim had invited us over for Doug's birthday dinner. We walked into an empty house, and we had even arrived an hour late knowing about the McKay brothers' unique time zone. The smell of turkey led us to the oven. There was a turkey roasting but nothing else. I surveyed the refrigerator for salad items, then tossed a Greek salad and boiled potatoes. Doug walked in and we talked briefly about the hand games. "It used to have more spiritual significance," he told us, never taking off his coat or hat. "But now it's about gambling." He then walked out the door without explanation, leaving us alone again.

John poked his head in thinking maybe he would join the dinner party and saw the two of us cooking. "No thanks," he said, shaking his head and backing out the door. I was impressed that he made it as far as the door. I had never seen him and Jim in the same room.

We ate alone.

Doug's teenage son, Jason, walked in the door and took off his coat, mittens, and hat. "Sorry I have such a lame family," he said, piling food onto a plate. I could hear the stud in his pierced tongue click against his fork as he ate, like nails on a chalkboard to me. He then handed over *Horse Whisperer*, a new movie from the store. We popped it into the VCR and were watching the closing credits when Doug arrived again. Jason lit half the candles on a cake he had brought over from the store and yelled out "Happy Birthday, Doug" in the sarcastic, insincere way so natural to teenagers. He then tossed the candles, pushing them to the bottom of the trash. "So Jim won't see them and bitch about wasting candles," he said.

Jim showed up at ten just as we were leaving.

"Come back in an hour or so. Rick should be here," Jim said, never mentioning that he had invited us to dinner and not shown up.

"We're going to the dance, then we'll be back," I said.

"The Welcome Bay Store dinner party—we provide the food, you cook it, and maybe we'll join you," Charly joked as we walked toward the snowmobile.

When we came back, the rye whiskey was flowing. Jim sat with Rick at the table with a bottle of Coke and liquor he had released from under lock and key. Rick was a fishing guide who had chosen to spend his winters watching Wollaston Lake Lodge—a fishing camp that catered to wealthy Americans (or anyone willing to pay the 1999 rate of eight hundred dollars a day for fantastic fishing. Rick rolled a cigarette and told us about clients, fishing, and northern life. He and Jim both were superb storytellers, each inspiring the other to tell another tale. With the added motivation of Charly and me as a fresh audience, they told stories at rapid-fire speed.

Jason and Doug returned and joined us at the table.

"There's a group of people from Tadoule Lake," Doug announced.

"That's what John said," Charly replied. "So what's the story with them?"

"The government brought the Tadoule Lake people in off the land and relocated them at Churchill in 1956. They were Dene and living among the Inuit and Cree. Everyone shit on them. They lived at the edges of town," Doug said.

"Until someone got a whiff of sovereignty and asked if they might be allowed to go home," Charly interrupted.

"Right. The government had to concede they didn't have to stay in Churchill and flew them all back," Doug said. "It's a great honor to have them here for Carnival."

"And maybe a sign of their cultural survival?" Charly asked rhetorically.

I am embarrassed to report that the evening disintegrated into a card game of "Asshole." If there were any rules, I don't remember them. The point was that for each round someone was appointed "asshole." And for that round, everyone referred to said person as an asshole and could order that person around. So the most sophisticated dialogue during this game was "Hey, asshole, get me a drink of water." Doug didn't drink, but played along and remained good humored even when he assumed the role of asshole, much to the delight of his son.

Jason declared the night a total success, saying that it was the most fun he'd ever had with his dad and Uncle Jim. Charly got ripping drunk for the first time since I'd known him. With each drink, his vocabulary blossomed. He used words like arbitrary and capricious. The guys around the table couldn't pronounce the words, so they used the word Confucius. Light crept through the windows and Charly walked outside to see the northern lights. He returned to report that it was actually morning. I walked to the living room and lay down on a sleeping bag, and soon everyone followed. Just knowing it was morning had broken the spell, and we all fell into a group slumber.

"People are already splitting town because Carnival is too boring," John told us the next day. "Nothing to do except play bingo."

"What about the tea boil and snowshoe races?" I asked.

"Cancelled," he said.

"Cancelled? I brought my snowshoes."

"Everyone wants to play bingo," John said.

It was an unusually mild day, and the snow had begun to melt. "I'm beginning to worry we're going to lose our snow early," Charly said to John in the form of a question.

"I've never seen it so mild during Carnival. But don't worry. There will be plenty of winter left," he assured us.

To celebrate our fixed snowmachine, Charly and I entered the poker rally, a combination of cards and snowmobiling. The purpose was to drive from spot to spot collecting playing cards in hopes of a winning poker hand. We paid fifty dollars to enter the rally. The three top prizes were snowmobiles worth twenty thousand dollars, and only two hundred people had entered. We did the math and figured our odds were good—we could always sell the prize. We were handed a blurry copy of a topo map showing hundreds of square miles of untracked country with some dashed lines and X marks. We blazed off into a bright clear day, our hearing deafened by the roar of our machine, fresh air filled with exhaust as we pounded our way across the wind-packed drifts yelling, "POKER RALLY!"

Three stations were set up on islands a few miles out in the lake, and two were in town. The poker stations were wall tents staffed by volunteers. We could spot the poker rally sites by the ascending smoke curl. Each wall tent had been outfitted with a woodstove and balsam-bough floor. At the first island, poles were assembled in a tipi formation but without any canvas or furs covering them. A wall tent erected near the poles, with spruce and snow as a backdrop, held the cards. I pulled a card from a barrel and a guy wrote down my pick. We sledded away. At the second island, Martina and another teacher guarded the station. Martina stood and the other teacher sat on her snowmachine and wrote down my next pick. I had drawn a ten and a four.

On our way to the third station, someone passed us on the loudest, rustiest, most junked-out snowmachine I'd ever seen in motion. He smiled and waved as he clunked along. It reminded me of a cartoon in which chunks of metal blow off a vehicle as it speeds along. A few hundred yards later, he stopped, lifted the hood of his machine, dove inside with a pair of pliers, returned to the seat, and started it again. We passed him, waved and smiled, and looked back to make sure he followed. I hoped he would win the new snowmobile. We ended up drawing a pair of fours. A full house won. I was glad to hear it went to a local person.

The hand games continued throughout the weekend, drawing us back time and again. The darkened room, the drums, the chants, and the intrigue were too much to resist. Charly and I never took pictures because it didn't seem right. For those hours in the dimly lit room we just wanted to be part of something real, and we were. A few men and women, and sometimes children, stood around with us watching. One team lost, often after hours and hours of playing, then stood, and another team took their place. We started to recognize players and styles of play. One team seemed to always be there. The whole scene—the smiles, the peg board, the cigarette smoke—would come clearly to mind even years later, moving a half beat off in my memory as if part of a home movie.

As John promised, winter did return. A cold front blew in and dropped the temperature thirty degrees. We watched as the people from Tadoule Lake, fully bundled, drove out of town on less-than-new snowmobiles, a two-day journey before them. One rider sat atop the toboggan pulled by a snowmobile, wrapped in layers and layers of clothing and maybe even a sleeping bag. Still he smiled and waved as they drove away. We left shortly after, taking down our tent, loading our sled, and driving the ice road out of town. Heike followed behind.

27

Spring Break

L ost. In the dark, alone, at twenty below. On a lake that sprawled across 662,000 acres, with so many islands that it was impossible to distinguish them from the shoreline. And only one town in this entire space. Away from town, there was no one—except for us when we were at our cabin. I had no idea how to get to town. I rode my snowmachine in circles, following snowmobile trail after snowmobile trail. I behaved like an idiot. Everything looked the same—lake ice mixed with islands of spruce and jack pine. If I could just get back to the powerline, I would have a landmark I understood.

Charly and I had decided to start hauling our canoe-trip gear to town, and I had volunteered to take the first load. Alone. It would be an adventure and a chance to use the telephone and interact with people. Without Charly. So I had done just that. I'd hauled supplies that would be flown aboard the *Empress of Black Lake* to Ennadai Lake, where we would connect with them after our snowshoe trek. I had also hauled a few boxes that could be sent home with Mom and Dad when they came to visit in two weeks. I had kissed Charly goodbye and told him I would be home for dinner, then revved the engine and drove off on the Arctic Cat Lynx. All by myself!

I'd stopped at John's to unload the sled, then gone to the laundromat, where I washed the six items that we weren't wearing and used the pay phone to call Dawn and Link. Speaking without the awkwardness of the "overs" was heaven.

When I'd left town I followed a set of snowmobile tracks, wrongly assuming that all of us snowmobilers were headed in the same direction. I needed to cross to the powerline then follow the right side of the island to the next powerline crossing. I knew the route well. Or at least I thought I did. But now nothing looked familiar. I drove on for twenty or more minutes before I started thinking seriously about gasoline and how lost I could get. After all that time of trees and ice and nothing familiar, I finally turned and drove back in what I hope was the direction I'd come for twenty minutes. At last, I found the powerline. *I got it now*, I thought, relieved, and set off again. Still nothing felt right, but I so desperately did not want to screw this up that I kept going and going. I circled, turned back, and returned. How complicated could this be? I sweated beneath my coat, thinking about a long night out on the ice. I imagined running out of gas, freezing to death, never being found.

Charly had become lost one night on a mission from our cabin with Doug, looking for hot dogs that had fallen off the snowmobile. Charly said they both got disoriented and started circling and turning on themselves. The trees and snow and ice blended into one long confusing blur. Finally they saw lights and a dock, and Charly thought, *Shit, we're really lost*. Then he realized he was back at our cabin.

John and some friends had been turned around on the lake trusting a GPS unit. Eventually they rolled up in sleeping bags, and as John looked at the sky, he laughed to see the north star where the GPS unit had indicated south.

Completely panicked now, I somehow managed to get back to the powerline and follow it to town. I knocked on John's door at nine-thirty. He started to laugh and tease. He had no idea I had been out on the lake, but thought I hadn't left town yet—and then he looked at my face.

"What's wrong?" he asked.

"I'm cold," I replied, my teeth starting to chatter. "I've been wandering around on my snowmachine for four hours."

"Oh, let's warm you," he said, heating water for tea and stoking the stove.

I had assumed in all that time that a search party would have been sent, that at least Charly would have called John looking for me. But, alas, no one seemed to notice my absence. John called Charly and told him I was okay.

"Honey will be with me tonight," John said, giggling, amused at this turn of events. He remembered that Charly had called me Honey the first day we paddled into town, and he had never forgotten it.

I fell asleep in a sleeping bag on John's floor and dreamed of following endless snowmobile tracks. The next day I set out after breakfast and couldn't believe I had been lost. It all made sense in the daylight, and I was home by lunch.

Two days later, Charly hauled in our food to go to Ennadai Lake. Ninety days worth. Charly called Points North from John's house to talk logistics and got the news that the *Empress of Black Lake*, the DC-3 plane Doug had hugged so passionately, had crashed on the ice runway at Ennadai. The crew of two died in the crash. John knew both the pilots and took the news hard, as did many others. A report completed a year later attributed the crash to the aircraft's center of gravity and unsecured lumber that may have shifted. Leaks in the heater system that allowed carbon monoxide into the cockpit may have adversely affected the pilot's performance. The plane would have hauled our gear, so now that plan was on hold until Ennadai Lake Lodge figured out how it would proceed with construction and we could send along our supplies with their building materials.

The last people we had seen from the "outside" were my parents back in September, six months before. Now they were returning with my brother, Link, bringing food and booze and laughter. They would take away all of our nonessential supplies to lighten our load. I was wild with anticipation. I cleaned the cabin. Charly scrubbed the floor. I inventoried the food, jotting out a four-day menu. Charly packed trails for skiing and snowshoeing. I dug out the horseshoe pits, which were buried deep under the snow. Charly filled the bird feeders. I felted three pairs of slippers. Charly drove to town to make copies of a letter we had written for the seventy-five people that we corresponded with. Mom would mail the letters when she was back in Wisconsin.

March 2000

Dear Correspondents,

Well, just as we are learning the ways of Wollaston and the dinner invitations have started to trickle in, we're heading further north. The weather is our timekeeper and the promise of spring dictates that we leave now or lose our snow. We plan to depart on snowshoes, pulling toboggans, the first of April and travel 300 miles to a fishing camp on Ennadai Lake, where we will rendezvous with our canoe and summer supplies. Ennadai stays frozen into July, but the Kazan River—our ride to Baker Lake—will break free of ice by May.

Julie and Charly

We sorted and boxed items for Mom and Dad to take back—favorite books, skis, extra clothing, and Christmas presents. Charly made plans to rent additional snowmobiles from Jim for their visit. Mom called from LaRonge to tell us that they were in the final stretch. Over. A few hours later Charly and I hooked our sled to the Lynx and drove to town. It was cloudy, windy, and cold.

John Elander, as always, got right into the spirit. He and Charly painted "Welcome Buckles" in fluorescent orange on a long strip of canvas. As they painted the final letters, I looked out at the bay and spotted a red van on the ice road more than a mile away.

"They're here!" I shouted, pulling on my winter outdoor gear.

"Take this flag," John said, handing me a Canadian flag mounted to a stick.

Charly started the snowmobile and I hopped on the back, flying the Canadian flag. We motored across the bay and jumped onto the city dock—the very same place we had landed so long ago when we first arrived in town, the place where Doug had greeted us and sent us to the Confectionery. Here we unrolled the banner, holding it high so my family could see it as the van drove toward town. John joined us on his Ski-Doo to take photos and to say hello. Mom, Dad, and Link hopped out of their minivan—an upgrade from the last trip—laughing and full of hugs. The back window was broken, knocked out by a rock on the road from LaRonge.

"It got a bit nippy," Mom joked.

John turned for home and the family followed us to Welcome Bay Store. As promised, Jim had found two working snowmobiles to rent. We loaded two toboggans with luggage and boxes of supplies. Mom took control of the Bravo snowmachine, a "No Fear" sticker on the front. Link was assigned the biggest machine and a toboggan, with Dad on the back. Charly drove our machine and I rode on the toboggan. We paraded through town, Charly waving the Canadian flag, laughing all the way. As we drove the twelve miles to Estevan Island, Link zigged and zagged, attempting to throw Dad off the toboggan.

We did all the things we'd looked forward to: skied, ate, played games, fished, and talked. But the most memorable part was my brother snowmobiling. Link loves fast travel. In the first home video footage we have of him, he's two years old and racing down an incline on a trike. He moved on to bicycles, never content to just ride along at a normal speed. Before he was seven he had splattered himself against the shed at the bottom of the hill more than once while racing his bicycle down our driveway. He'd be flattened for a moment like the Wile E. Coyote cartoon character, and then he'd hop back on and try again.

Charly reached Ennadai Lake Lodge on the trapper radio, and the caretaker said we could still send our gear on an available flight, and he reiterated that we could stay with them while we waited for ice-out.

Charly and I high-fived one another over the good news. Since the radio reception was so good, Charly called Rick at Wollaston Lake Lodge to set up an afternoon of ice fishing for himself, Dad, and Link.

The next day I pulled together a picnic, and we headed to Inner Estevan on snowmobiles. Charly dug out a bonfire pit and started a fire. Mom, Dad, and I watched Link bomb around on his snowmachine, racing up steep inclines, getting stuck and unstuck. Link owned a motorcycle before he had a license. He appreciates speed and has no fear. Motors divided Link and me. It was a world I didn't understand and one he never bothered to explain. Wollaston provided a bridge of sorts. After a winter in Wollaston, I'd gained an appreciation for people who knew how to ride snowmobiles—really knew how to ride, even when the trails weren't groomed, and when they didn't lead to a tavern. Link understood and could respond to the machine, the snow conditions, and the terrain. As we picnicked at Inner Estevan, Link circled and stopped some distance away. I pointed to a good spot for jumping, and he raced off and went for it over and over. During one jump he bounced off his machine but never let go of the handlebars—like a rodeo cowboy.

The next day, the guys set out to fish. Mom and I talked like we had never talked before—nonstop for five hours. She told me about work, family, and friends. I told her about our new life—just insignificant small details, which I wouldn't shared on the trapper radio or by letter, but that made me feel great to share with someone. The winter had been such a foreign one with so many emotions. Charly had taken the brunt of all the extremes. In my mother I had a great listener whom I trusted. At the time, I thought it might be the last conversation of substance I would have with a woman for six months, and I took full advantage of our day together.

The men eventually returned, hauling a few fish. We cooked them up and then sat around a bonfire toasting marshmallows for s'mores. John snowmobiled out with Martina, and I ran inside to hand out a bag of door prizes—banana chips (never did learn to like those), batteries (we had a surplus), and peanuts (ditto). I didn't even try to get rid of the dried dates Charly and I had grown to despise; instead I fed them to the ravens. John had brought door prizes of his own—Air Athabaska hats for our American guests.

On the last morning Dad and I went for an early morning ski. A fresh coat of powder over our tracks from the day before made it the best skiing of the winter. It was about twenty degrees. Link, Mom, and Charly followed—Mom and Link on snowmobiles, Charly on skis. The snowmobile allowed Mom to be as mobile as any of us and let Link be as free as he could be. Link was blown away by the space, the powder, and the lack of development and people.

"You two should stay here every winter and I'll come visit," he laughed.

Mom agreed. "This has been the best outdoor time I've had in years."

I'd asked Link once why we weren't closer. We had been close in earlier years in a younger brother–older sister kind of way. But as adults we'd never found a way to connect. "We just don't have that much in common," he had responded. I had to agree. Yet here at Wollaston, he had come to my world and given me a glimpse of his.

For the last breakfast with my family, Charly fried fish we'd caught during an afternoon of ice fishing. We loaded the sleds and drove back to town. We stuffed their van full of our extra gear. Link sat in the backseat next to boxes. John drove over for the send-off. The three of us watched the van until it was out of sight, then got back to the work of making arrangements for the next leg of our journey.

Link, Heike, and me

28

Going Home

Our last day here fills us with sadness. How ridiculous to leave all this. Where will we ever find a better place?

– Elliot Merrick, *True North*

The call Charly had dreaded all winter came the night after Mom, Dad, and Link departed. At six o'clock the orange box called out, "VEE864 this is XLB51." I assumed it would be Mom calling to check in. It was Herb. He was in the hospital. Charly stood facing the window, his back to me, his shoulders slumped, as Herb told him about his leaky heart valve. Herb sounded awful—a weak, scratchy voice and lingering cough, a strange conversation made stranger by the technology.

"Kati wanted me to call and tell you—I'm in the hospital. Over."

"I love you, Dad. Over."

"I love you too. Over."

Herb offered brief details between coughs, then Charly's sister, Kati, got on the phone.

"I'll call you tomorrow at ten from a land line. Over." Charly told her.

There wasn't much else to say.

"I gotta go home," he said, turning toward me.

"Home? You don't even know what's going on."

"I know Dad is in the hospital."

Charly left for town the next morning. I stayed home, baked bread and cookies, paced, brooded, read. I sulked. I missed Charly and wondered what was taking him so long. He called me at six. Kids had stolen our snowmobile outside the Welcome Bay Store—for "just a joyride"— but he'd tracked them down and taken it back. He'd washed clothes at Martina's, and in two days he was flying to Chicago. He and John had found a round-trip flight from Saskatoon to Minneapolis, then on to Chicago for nine days, then back to Saskatoon. "He said he was glad I was coming. Over," Charly told me.

"It must be bad then. Over." To admit needing his children or any help at all was not typical of Herb. This was a guy who had undergone angioplasty surgery and never told anyone.

I had a hard time coming to grips with the thought of Charly flying home without me. It had been nearly a year since we departed from the Sioux River Beach.

Mom and Dad called later and said they made it home in three days and two nights—but not without the drama of mud and failing roads on the trip to LaRonge. "Thick mud was the best we could hope for. Over." she said. I filled her in on the latest news about Herb as best I could.

The next day the reality of Charly leaving really hit, and I nearly lost my mind. I wanted to head back out on the trail. I *needed* to head back out on the trail. The entire winter had been focused on preparing to push on. To give it up, or even delay it, seemed impossible to bear. Just the thought of sitting for a few more weeks drove me to despair. I slept and cried and hated myself for being so self-absorbed. Charly began to talk about alternative plans—maybe skipping the spring leg, paddling the Kazan another year.

"How can you give it up so easily?" I asked after he returned to pack for Chicago.

"Because I worked the entire summer that my mother was dying of cancer to earn money for a paddling trip. This is my chance to make up for that," he responded. We both leaned on the kitchen counter and stared straight ahead at the place where we had stuffed rags between logs for insulation.

"I just don't see how you can be so casual," I said, turning toward Charly, touching his hand.

"I almost feel relief. We've known about his cancer for more than a year, and now I can finally do something to help him."

I sympathized, but I couldn't rally. I couldn't talk myself out of my mood. As much as I analyzed how irrational I was being, it didn't matter. I wanted to get back out on the trail. We went skiing but didn't talk. It was a crappy cloudy gray day. We began to store a few of Felix and

Linda's belongings. If Charly decided to stay longer than nine days in Chicago, I would have to close the cabin for the year. Charly sorted through his things trying to decide what to take. He didn't have any appropriate boots to wear to Chicago. It was either mukluks or steel-toed, insulated rubber boots. He decided on the rubber boots. We played Scrabble. I read most of *Impossible Vacation*, by Spalding Gray and barely laughed. Finally I gave up and went to bed.

I awoke the next morning feeling more like myself, like the insanity had slipped away in the night. "Hey, I love you. This is about you and your dad. Not about our trip," I whispered into Charly's ear.

"Thanks, Honey. I didn't know what to do yesterday," he said, rolling over and pulling me into a hug.

We hauled more tubs of supplies to town, either for sending ahead to our postal points or for storing. I called Mom and gave her an update. Then I called Kati, who reported a grim scenario. It was his heart, colon, and lungs—and all were of concern to the doctors deciding how to proceed with his care.

"I'll head to Chicago once I have a better idea of what we're going to do," I told Kati.

"Dad is being Dad. He doesn't want to have surgery until his estate is in order," she said. "But he's weakening."

I drove Charly to the tiny Wollaston airport. We hugged for a long time, like we both understood this was the end of something big. Charly boarded the plane. I stood wiping away the silent tears that slipped down my cheeks before they could freeze. Once his plane had flown out of sight, I climbed onto the snowmobile and drove back to Estevan Island, without getting lost.

After months of dreaming and joking about getting to "the outside," I had no desire to go back. In the book *Water and Sky*, Marypat Zitzer was reluctant to paddle into Baker Lake because it marked the end of her and her husband's trip. I understood her feelings now. I didn't want long hot showers or restaurants or even movie theaters. I stared at the sunset and felt awe at the light and the space and the snow. Sunset didn't come until eight-thirty. Mom called as I walked inside and was surprised it was still light out. "It's pitch black here."

The next day I organized food boxes to ship to Baker Lake. I made plans to haul them into town. I hauled and cut wood. By then it was forty degrees. I walked our trail and decided it was still okay for skiing, so I went for an afternoon ski.

Later I loaded boxes onto the sled and headed for town. I found John at his office, two pilots crowded around the computer with him.

"Did you see us?" he asked.

"Flying over this morning?"

"We went to Points North for lunch," he grinned.

"Must be nice."

I unloaded and taped the boxes. John looked over the snowmobile like a doting father to make sure everything was in order.

Charly called me at the cabin the next morning.

"I think you should come home. Over," he said.

"Not good? Over," I replied.

"We had a family meeting this morning with the doctor, and his prognosis is not good. Over."

"Wish I was there. Over,"

"I'll make reservations for you. When can you be ready? Over."

"I need a few days at least. Over."

"How about Tuesday? Over."

I had four days to clear out. I dug into the final mess. Every item needed to be scrutinized. If the item was for the trip, it remained. If it had sentimental value, I packed it for Chicago. If it was expendable, I set it aside to be given away or left behind. I pulled all the rags-turned-insulation from the walls, took down the door to the porch and returned it to the addition, tore down cardboard from the windows. It was so warm that I let the fire die and opened the door.

Heike paced and whined and looked off at the horizon. I speculated that she missed Charly and sensed change was coming. I cleaned until dark, then lit a bonfire of cardboard and miscellany. I sorted the last of the food. The next day I took a load to town. John and I readjusted the canoe to get it out of the snow. I called Charly from John's house. Herb's condition was now officially terminal, he told me.

"It's in his lungs. The doctors say he has six months to a year to live," Charly said in his softest voice.

It was not at all what I expected to hear. I really wanted to be near Charly, to touch and hug him.

"What's next?" I asked.

"Dad's coming home for a few days, then back to the hospital for a colostomy."

"What about the trip? What do you want to do?" I asked.

"I gotta be here."

"I know."

"Can you get everything together up there?"

"Yeah. I need time, but yeah, I can do it."

"You should leave everything stored at Wollaston, in case we decide we can finish the trip. Or we can drive up and get it later."

"How's your dad doing?"

"You know Dad. When the doctor told us he had six months to live, Dad just said, 'Well, I've lived a good life.'"

"It's kind of peaceful, and it's kind of frustrating," I said.

"I know."

I needed time alone after I hung up, some time to process the information. The trip was off. Herb was going to die. But John was there and practically manic to talk about alternative plans.

"You could paddle the Seal River. Doug and I would start out with you then fly back from Lac Brochet," he said, pacing.

"We'll see."

John and I returned to his office to scrutinize boxes, munching on almonds and emu sticks while we worked. My brother-in-law raised emus back then, and Mom and Dad had brought his gift of slim emu sausages. Martina stopped by as we were sorting boxes of supplies.

"I need to get out of town," she said.

"Come back here at seven and go with me," I told her.

Martina and I roared away from Wollaston together. We sat at the kitchen table at Estevan Island drinking wine and cognac with coffee until one thirty in the morning. I put Martina to work the next morning sawing cookstove wood, enough to refill the wooden boxes for Felix and Linda. I packed and repacked, trying to figure out what should go where. Martina settled in on the deck to read Alice Munro's short stories. I joined her, and we talked until she left in the late afternoon.

I sat alone that evening, my last evening on Estevan Island, alone with thoughts of Herb, Kati, Charly, and our fading trip.

After a few hours of sleep I rolled over and looked at the clock. Not even five thirty and already reddish light crept into the living room. My mind clicked off a mental to-do list, but my body didn't move. I wanted to savor my last moments on the island. Heike stood, circled, and flopped back down. In spite of all those gray November days when I had fantasized about fleeing Estevan Island, now I didn't want to leave—not alone, not under these circumstances. Charly should have been here. We should have left together, heading for Gjoa Haven.

My eyes scanned the room so familiar to me—blue vinyl chair, yellow foot stool, dart board, the jack pine log walls, woodstove, stack of *Reader's Digests*, row of Western books, bulletin board of photos, red vinyl chair, writing table, and back to the blue vinyl chair. The sun appeared over the trees around seven and I sat up. My plane didn't leave for eleven hours, but so many things could go wrong—like the snowmobile running out of gas. I figured I had at least two hours of errands to do in town. I needed to store our supplies, check on the canoe, return the dog, mail our trapper radio, and return the snowmobile. I stuffed my sleeping bag away, turned off the propane for the last time, cached any remaining valuables, mopped the floor, and rearranged the room to look exactly as we had found it when we first sat with Linda and Felix and shared stories for two days during "snarkly" weather.

After loading boxes, skis, and the axe into the sled, I walked to the top of the hill and stared at the view I knew so well—sprawling islands on a sparkling white lake. Leafless birch trees, dark spruce, balsam, and pine. Charly and I had celebrated our first anniversary from this vantage point, then watched the seasons change from green to gold to white. I whispered a choked goodbye to the lake and the trees and the cabin, then walked back down to start the snowmobile. I drove at a leisurely pace to save on gas and to let Heike keep up, turning off the snowmachine at the halfway point to lie back on the seat, soak up the sun, and watch the blue sky. I thought about Charly and Herb and about all the people who had helped us that winter. I thought about how I didn't want to leave Heike behind.

"You ready, Heike?" I asked as she caught up with me, panting from the exertion. "Because I'm not." I patted her head and let her rest a few moments then started the machine. I steered the snowmobile into John's yard. He stood in the kitchen butchering caribou on a cutting board. Pieces of meat still in need of cleaning sat in a blue tub next to him. His hands bloody, he turned and said we shouldn't store our stuff at the airport, where he worked. Kids would likely hear about the food and gear and break in. "I've already got permission for you to keep your stuff in James's basement," he said, cutting fat away from meat. So much for a simple two hours of errands. Now I had to move everything across town, including seven heavy plastic tubs filled with six months' worth of food. I snowmobiled to Welcome Bay Store to buy gas and leave Heike. I tied her up next to Jim's house and left a bowl of water nearby. She watched me with her trusting brown eyes.

I crossed the bay to the airport and borrowed a truck from one of the men at SaskAir to haul the tubs. I wore my wool pants, wool shirt, anorak, insulated rubber boots, beaver hat, and dog-fur mittens. I was hot, but there was no time to change, and I needed to keep my layers on for running the snowmachine. I loaded 750 pounds of supplies into the truck, drove across town, and carried the tubs into James's house, through the carpeted take-off-your-boots living room, and down a flight of stairs to the basement—load after load. The roads were muddy and icy, and I got stuck in James's driveway trying to depart. I revved the truck forward then rocked it backward, but the tires only spun. Troy, who lived next door, was just arriving home from work and helped push me free. I was drowning in my own perspiration and anxiety.

I raced to the co-op store, mailed the trapper radio, and dropped off the snowmobile. I walked out back to check on Heike and felt satisfied with her location—nice and cozy. I hoped Jim would return soon because Doug wasn't much of a dog person. Martina appeared on her little Bravo like a guardian angel and offered me a ride to the airport. It seemed the entire town of Wollaston Post had converged on the little airport to say goodbye to the six people leaving on the plane. Kids circled the adults, including me. A few quick hugs goodbye and, still sweaty from the exertion of hauling tubs, I stuffed myself into the small plane. A woman boarded, carrying her sweaty sick child who coughed and vomited for the entire trip.

As soon as the plane took off, I forgot the stress of the day. From my front seat window, I saw a tapestry of green and white spread below me. Wollaston Lake was so huge! The plane passed over Estevan Island, allowing me a last look from the air. I stared at the green-and-white expanse passing beneath the plane, without roads, towns, or lights for an amazing hour.

We passengers switched to a larger plane at LaRonge, flew thirty minutes to Prince Albert, then boarded an even larger plane that flew to Saskatoon. Passengers departed at each of the stops, and only the woman with the sick child and I remained at Saskatoon. I should have felt some excitement at being back out in the world again, but I didn't. I felt restless and ill at ease and desperate to get back to Charly. The airports and layovers were little more than a nuisance. In the lobby of the Saskatoon airport, a throng of people returning from the Caribbean engulfed me. What seemed like hundreds of vacationers walked into the airport all at once, wearing shorts and sandals, the women and girls flinging their Bo Derek braids. They smelled of coconut oil, warmth, and the ocean. They were light and airy. They laughed and smiled and waved enthusiastically. I clung to my filthy Duluth packs, fidgeting in my wool pants and rubber boots, and hoped to get out of there quickly. If this was Sesame Street, I was the thing that didn't belong.

A woman with perfectly manicured red nails behind the counter only confirmed my feelings. She looked at me and at the heavy packs I plopped down on the scale. If this had been post-9/11, security would have been called. "Any gas or explosives?" she asked.

"No," I answered.

"Where have you been?"

"In northern Saskatchewan. We were on a long canoe trip," I responded.

She paused, assessing that comment. After all, it was still winter. She tapped her fingers on the counter and turned to her coworker behind the counter, but didn't say anything.

"Can I ask you to come back here and lift these," she said, giving me a look I'm sure she reserved for rotten meat and soiled diapers. I picked up the packs, flagged as heavy cargo, with little effort. She feigned busyness with something else so she wouldn't have to wish me well. Then I went to board my plane for home.

Four hours later, like a time traveler, I exited the past and entered the future. At O'Hare airport, sleek smartly dressed men and women clip-clopped past me in suits and polished shoes. These fast-moving creatures talked into cordless telephones—a transformation since we'd been gone—and typed on thin compact computers. I had changed out of my long underwear and put on my "good" pair of jeans, but I still felt like a slob, exposed under the bright fluorescent lights. I regretted every one of the thirty pounds I had gained over winter. Sweat cascaded down my back and collected at the waistband of my brown Gap jeans. Walking in slow motion due to the weight of my boots, I carried a blaze-orange ammo box, Charly's birch bow—one of his winter projects—wrapped in cardboard, and my faded green canvas pack. I didn't know if he cared about the birch bow; I just couldn't bring myself to burn it or leave it behind. Plus I wanted to take a piece of something, a memento, back to him—proof that we had paddled seventeen hundred miles and stayed for the winter on a remote island.

I spotted a man who resembled my husband, but this man was scrubbed clean. He wore tan slacks, a striped red-and-white dress shirt, and ultra-white tennis shoes. Tennis shoes! This man had shaved and had been in a barber's chair. He smelled of soap and the city. We stood looking at one another as people pushed past us. I felt like a relic from his past. Tentatively, timidly, we hugged. Charly had only been gone two weeks, but he smelled months away.

"I'm so happy to see you," he whispered in my ear. "I spotted you about a mile away."

"I brought your bow back," I said.

"I see that."

I laughed while wiping away a tear. I realized in that moment that even though the trip was originally Charly's dream, I had adopted it as my own. I felt as disappointed as Charly did, if not more, about coming back—years' worth of our work and dreams slipping away like a paddle lost in the rapids.

As we headed to the car I told Charly about the plane trip and the woman at the Saskatoon airport who wouldn't touch my packs. We spoke about doctors and hospitals and family dynamics, but we didn't talk about the end of the trip or Herb's prognosis—that would come later. We were dealing with so many emotions all at once, who knew where to begin. Disappointment, regret, guilt, relief, sadness, fear, anger—feelings about the trip and Herb's cancer that would rise and fall like the tides over the next year.

Charly turned off the interstate into the manicured suburbs of northern Chicago. Spring had triumphed here already. Trees budded, flowers exploded, and grass grew green. "I want to have you to myself for a few moments longer," Charly said, driving past his childhood home—the place that would be our home for the next five months. I nodded, unable to speak for fear of crying again. We drove to the beach and instinctively looked skyward, but saw only the dull orange fuzz of urban light pollution.

"I feel lost without the sky," Charly said, his arms around me. "I've lost half the world."

"Orion's Belt is all I ask for," I said.

We searched the sky for anything other than the airplanes lined up for landing at O'Hare. If we could find just one constellation, one star, we would find our footing in this foreign territory. We leaned against one another and kept looking.

Herb and Charly at the beginning of The Trip

29

Epilogue

September 2000

Herb died in August, as the doctors had predicted, six months after we returned. He died in the night by himself in a hospital room. One month later, Charly drove three days north and rode the barge to Wollaston Post, intending to collect our supplies and Heike, the dog. The blue tubs were still in James's basement. However, Heike, it turned out, had been eaten by wolves. We didn't take journal notes during that period, and Charly doesn't remember much about the trip except that the waves were huge and coming up and over the barge. The same week that Charly returned to Wollaston Post for our supplies, I went even farther north with my parents, Link, and family friends. We drove to The Pas, then took the train to see the polar bears of Churchill, Manitoba. It was a trip my family had planned so they could meet us at the end of our trip. We did, indeed, see a polar bear.

March 2001

We planned to continue The Trip the following spring. Charly continued talking with John and all our contacts up north, making plans and working out logistics. But then I made good on the decision we had made on Lake Winnipeg and got pregnant. And while I believe pregnant women belong in the wilderness, hormones did the talking and I wanted to stay home, to nest. In the end, the pregnancy didn't stick, but it was too late to restart The Trip. We dug back into our north woods life, preparing a garden, taking jobs.

December 21, 2001

I'd been through another round of pregnancy and unpregnancy, listened to the radio coverage of planes flying into the Twin Towers, and grown blue—really blue. I was turning thirty-seven and feeling the ticking of time.

Charly talked me into a day of dogsledding with John and Mary Thiel, the friends who had given us Knock-Knock, even though there was little snow. Knock-Knock was gone, but they had given us another husky named Smokey. She never loved me like Knock-Knock did, but she was full of spirit. After a bruising afternoon of sledding with John, Mary, and their toddler, Emma, over rocks, branches, and dirt, Charly took my hand and led me into our friends' pole barn, like there might be thirty-seven ice candles inside.

"Happy Birthday!" he shouted, pointing to a plywood box with holes.

A plywood box did not have the impact of ice luminaries.

"What is it?" I asked.

"A dog box."

"For what?" I asked.

"Dogs."

"Huh?" I didn't get it.

"We're going to go pick them up tomorrow on the way to your parents' place," Charly said. "I talked to a guy who has six for us to look at. I figure we'll get three."

"So this is why you've spent so much time over here," I said. "I thought you were just looking at maps."

"Well, some of that too," he smiled, looking over at John, Mary, and Emma.

The next day I chose five dogs for my own: Shaggy, Nick, Zinia, Glitter, and Blizzard. With Smokey, we now had a six-dog team. Not even a week into having dogs, Charly not so subtly started talking about a winter expedition—beginning at Wollaston, of course.

April 2002

We had picked up three more dogs, and now we drove into Pilger, Saskatchewan, to say hello to Linda and Felix. Felix had organized an event at the local library—our slideshow of The Trip. When it was finished, Felix asked if we could give dogsled rides through a field for the kids of Pilger. Charly and I glanced at one another. We had no idea how the dogs would do. They were young—barely two years old—a team of teenagers charged with leading us into the frozen wilderness, much like Charly and his gang in their youth. "Sure, we can give rides," Charly correctly responded.

Two days later, we stood in John Elander's kitchen at Wollaston Lake, grinning like Goofy. I was no longer blue. Dogs had knocked the sadness far away. We didn't know anything about dogsledding. Neither did our team. But there we were.

Two-toothed William Hansen was there, and so was Capitalist Jim—the only time I'd ever seen Jim and John in the same room. Our return had brought them together if only for a brief moment—my Disney fantasy realized. Our nine sled dogs were loaded in the truck sitting on the ice outside, ready for three weeks of sledding and camping.

"You got a lead dog?" William asked. "A good lead dog will never lose the trail."

William had run dogs until the snowmobile arrived in the North in the late 1960s.

"We don't know if we have a good lead dog," Charly responded. "We don't even know if we have a lead dog at all."

April in Wollaston was everything we expected—a blur of snow, sunshine, and cold; of ravens, ptarmigan, and wolf tracks; of caribou, ice fishing, swapping stories with John Elander, and meeting caribou hunters. The temperatures hovered at twenty-plus below when we arrived, and John told us how the weather had warmed for our arrival. Charly and I spent three weeks working with the dogs, figuring out conditions, and working our way north—details for another book. When we were done, we both felt satisfied, like a two-year-old itch had been scratched.

April 2005

On April fourth, one of the first warm days of the year, the snow melted and the wetland in front of our house filled with meltwater. Charly returned home from his job as the manager of the Living Forest Cooperative.

"Let's go for a paddle," he said, looking out at the wetland.

"You're kidding," I replied.

"No. I've always wanted to paddle in our front yard."

"You're on your own," I said.

I watched him portage *Le Strubel* to the end of the driveway and then paddle solo to the middle of the wetland. He and the canoe looked beautiful. The late sunlight cast a pinkish hue, making him and the boat look like something from a magazine cover. I reached down and picked up Caroline.

"See Daddy out there?" I asked.

She watched, unsure of what she was supposed to be looking for.

"Daddy," she whispered.

I dressed her in her boots, hat, and coat, and we walked slowly to the end of the driveway. Charly paddled over.

I set Caroline in the canoe, in the stern, between Charly's knees.

"Hey, Little C., we're on the water," he told Caroline. We explored the wetland, our family of three. Caroline loved the water. She splashed and played and squealed, "Whee!" when we hit a small bump. She was our biggest adventure of all.

One of the first nights with Caroline, she had cried and cried. We walked her and hummed to her, rocked her and rubbed her back. We tried everything we had read about soothing babies. Finally I suggested taking her to the Sioux River Beach, one mile down the road—the same beach where we had started our journey six years before. We sat in the sand and reasoned that even if she didn't stop crying, it was a darn nice spot to sit and listen to our beautiful daughter wail. I don't know what did it, whether it was the lapping of the waves or the cries of the gulls or the sound of our voices made softer by so much space, but she stopped crying and fell asleep.

Charly and I talked often about taking Caroline to Wollaston someday when she could handle the drive. We'd already taken her to the Boundary Waters for a week. Many things had changed in the last five years at Wollaston. Sasktel no longer used the trapper shortwave radios. They had distributed satellite phones instead. Felix and Linda were trying to sell their cabin on Estevan Island. Jim's Welcome Bay Store had burned down. John had a plane and a girlfriend in LaRonge. He had dropped by on his motorcycle one weekend in July, on his way to an airplane show a few hours south of us. At last we had a chance to show him around our area. He e-mailed and called now and again with snow and ice reports.

March 2013

It is evening and I am at the computer making the final chapter revisions to this book. Charly e-mails John Elander to ask him a question about the winter road. John responds that he is in Mexico for the winter, not thinking at all about Wollaston Lake. We're making plans to drive up this summer for a week-long canoe trip with Caroline and our son, Jackson, to see him. We hope to see Linda and Felix as well. They've been waiting a long time for this book.

I look over at a haiku Charly wrote for me on Valentine's Day last month.

> *Red Canoe Haiku*
>
> *Old red canoe hangs,*
> *From beams holding up our house,*
> *Love and boats still floating.*

Whenever Charly or I start to skid off track, we have The Trip to return to, a solid touchstone for our marriage. We still paddle every summer, now with our children, who love it maybe more than we do. "Just give 'er" has become a family slogan.

Jackson, age six, crawled onto Charly's knee one day and out of the blue asked, "Can we go to Wollaston Lake this summer?" Charly's proudest moment. In his mind, we've never really talked about Wollaston Lake with the kids, but The Trip permeates our entire life. It's in our DNA.

Caroline, nine, wants to know if I am going to read her a chapter tonight. She is a wonderful editor. This book has become a family affair. I hit print and tell her yes. She and Jackson crowd next to me in bed, ready to hear about the gray months of November, when Mom cried because Dad said it was laundry day. Charly stands at the door and we all laugh until our bellies hurt, and then I continue until they are ready for sleep.

Acknowledgments

Many people have encouraged and helped me along the way. Saul Landau at the Institute for Policy Studies (IPS) provided the sagest advice I've ever heard on becoming a writer: "Quit talking about it and just sit your butt down and write." The group of young writers at IPS—Sarah, Ona, Dawn, Ted, Jeremy, Heather, Kristen, and others—believed the written word mattered and made me believe it as well.

I wish to acknowledge my mentors at Antioch University Los Angeles—David Ulin, Brenda Miller, Sharman Apt Russell, and Hope Edelman—and my Antioch cohorts who helped get me started; and my publisher, Johnna Hyde at Raven Productions, who helped me finish. A big thanks to all my friends who have encouraged me over the years— Gina, Big Jim, Dawn, Andy, Ted, Ann, Gail, Mike, Phyllis, Liz, Danielle, Peter, Ralph, my Bunko crew, and all the rest of you. In particular, my friend Jill designed the cover and maps and was with me every step of the way. She and her husband, Mark, read and commented on the entire manuscript. My fellow reporter gal pals, Claire and Danielle, did the same in the last stages. Stacy and Alan read the manuscript while house-sitting one weekend and suggested I send it to Raven Productions. Bob volunteered his talents to shoot the book cover one early winter morning. Mary and Ted provided loads of nourishment, camaraderie, and offers to watch the children during the final stages.

I would like to thank all the Canadians who helped us along the way. John Elander, Doug McKay, and Felix and Linda Fischer have remained great friends and have helped keep me honest. Lynda Holland, a canoeist and historian for the Wollaston region, read my manuscript for factual errors. Any remaining errors are my own.

I would like to thank my extended family and in particular acknowledge my grandmother, who, unfortunately, died before this was published. She eagerly read every rough chapter, always gave positive feedback, and then asked for more. She also taught me to make great pies. My parents infused me with the spirit to head out into the wilderness and the confidence to write about it. My daughter, Caroline, was a great napper when I wrote the first draft and a darn good editor when I revised. My son, Jackson, always makes me laugh. And most of all I would like to thank my husband, a tireless editor, enthusiastic cheerleader, and endless source of ideas and information. He helped when I asked and backed off when I didn't, letting me tell our story.

Julie Buckles is a writer who lives one mile from the white sand beaches of Lake Superior in northern Wisconsin with her husband, Charly Ray, their two children, and a recreational kennel of Siberian huskies. She is a regular contributor to *Lake Superior Magazine* and Wisconsin Public Radio's *Wisconsin Life* and teaches journalism and film at Northland College in Ashland, Wisconsin. To read more about her visit JulieBuckles.com.

Raven Productions Inc. is an independent publisher in Ely, Minnesota, whose mission is to encourage children and grown-ups to explore, enjoy, and protect the natural world and share experiences with one another through storytelling, writing, and art. They have an award-winning selection of children's picture books as well as outdoor titles for grown-ups. To learn more visit RavenWords.com

Snapshots

Laundry day at Estevan Island

Charly cooks on Lake Winnipeg

The calm before the storm on Lake Superior

Heading into Lake of the Woods. The solar-powered radio with a picture wire antenna extension could sometimes pick up CBC broadcasts.

Duff day on the Winnipeg River

Winnipeg River rapids

Lake Winnipeg's western shore—fine limestone beaches

Cedar Lake—jagged limestone beaches

Gib's mobile summer residence in The Pas

Pulling the canoe up the Sturgeon-weir

Savoring the Frog Portage

Calm morning on the Churchill River

Berries and mushrooms on the Reindeer River

Wild blueberry crepes on Reindeer Lake

End of a storm on Reindeer Lake

The Muskeg Portage

Aerial view of the Fischer cabin on Estevan Island

Linda creating wood carvings

Felix and the biggest fish I ever caught

The Fischers' garden that we inherited for the fall

A spruce grouse on Estevan Island

The last paddle to town

Hauling wood

William Hansen

J.B.

Hoarfrost on our point

Getting water through thin ice

Winter camping trek

Getting water through thick ice

Snowshoe trail

Early sunset

The fox

Our winter carnival camp at John Elander's

Northern lights over the cabin

Spring break snowball fight

The family at Otter Lake on the Churchill River north of LaRonge
August 2013